Worldview: Advanced Human Thought

By Ralph Wing

ISBN 978-0-9801487-1-8

Printed in the United States of America

Visit www.booksurge.com to order additional copies.

This book is dedicated to my wife. Without her love and support this book would not have been possible.

Despite all efforts to make this book error free and accurate, due to the fact that this book has been written, edited and self-published by the author, there will be errors and omissions. You cannot proofread your own work. I have tried to add references and citations for sources used. Since the work has occurred over a period of twenty years some citations and references may not have received the credit they deserve. If you find any factual errors, omissions, or missing citations and references please let me know. When submitting corrections please include the page number and paragraph where the error or lack of citation occurred. The corrections, citations, and reference information will be added to the second edition. Please forward all requests to the address below:

Worldview
36 Four Seasons Center Suite 267
Chesterfield, MO 63017

Table of Contents

Introduction

What is advanced human thought? Advanced human thought is about understanding the origins of the universe and humans. Understanding how life and the human species evolved. Understanding how humans evolved to form small groups eventually leading to civilization. Understanding how civilization evolved and the major accomplishments of the human species, Ultimately, it is about understanding how to live a long, prosperous, happy, and virtuous life, how to be satisfied with yourself and your abilities, and how to use the human brain for optimal existence.

These words are written to assist individuals in obtaining a better life, improve the human condition, and to serve as a foundation for the pursuit of knowledge. Many of the subject areas will be controversial and will no doubt be read with considerable scorn and anguish. The subject matter will more than likely drive certain special interest groups crazy. Some will say that it is a simplistic view of the world. Others will claim that it is biased and rather than offer contrary proofs or arguments based on evidence or facts will resort to labeling and name-calling. The information presented is unbiased and based on observation and available evidence alone. Unfortunately, many people with their own agendas try to make things more complex than they are and refuse to accept evidence and facts. The author's only agenda is to help make peoples lives better and improve the existence of humankind. Some believe that emotion, faith, and intuition are superior to reason. These people are often referred to as irrationalists. For these people there is little hope. For those with an open mind who are willing to learn and use the tools of logic and reason, have the inner strength to face their fears and doubts, and have the will to succeed, this is a starting point on a journey of knowledge and understanding.

As has been said many times, the truth sometimes hurts, and reality isn't always pretty, but in the long run, people are much better off facing up to the facts, no matter how dreadful they may be. Rather than moping and complaining, and hiding from the truth, it is time to get to work to improve the human condition. You will not find sugarcoated information or sympathy in this book. It is blunt and honest. If it is going to affect your life it has to be. Although certain sections may seem harsh, or to some even cruel, it really is meant to reduce your stress, improve your health and well being, and make your life more fulfilling. Nothing in life is easy. From birth on it is a struggle to survive and succeed. A little luck now and then certainly helps, but most of life's accomplishments are obtained through self-discipline, perseverance, and hard work.

At first the contents may seem overwhelming. I have tried to consolidate the vast amount of knowledge that exists into the areas that you need to understand in order to develop a worldview. It is very difficult to succeed in life if you don't understand how things work. Many people live their whole lives not understanding the basic functioning of the world. Although not all the subjects of interest could possibly be covered in one book, it is hoped that the information presented will fuel your quest for additional knowledge. For more detailed information on the topics presented there is a list of references and suggested readings at the end of the book. For additional information you can also enter keywords and phrases into an Internet search engine. There are so many wonderful things to learn. Knowledge is a lifetime pursuit. In this modern era, no one can possibly know everything about every subject, or even know everything about his or her own field of study or specialty.

There are topics in this book that some people will consider controversial and will disagree with right away. These sections include the origins of matter and life, the sections on religion and atheism, and the sections on capitalism and socialism. Even if you don't agree with any of the information presented you should still read these sections so you at least understand the arguments. It is hoped that by reading and applying the information in this book you will overcome your only real weakness, a lack of faith in yourself; my sincere wishes for your health, happiness, and a long and prosperous life.

Developing a Worldview and a Life Plan

A worldview is a comprehensive philosophy or conception of the world and of human life. It can also be referred to as a philosophy of life. The word philosophy itself is from Greek words *philos* meaning "loving" and *logos* meaning "thought". In practice, philosophy is studying and thinking about the most basic questions that human beings can ponder. These questions include: What is the true nature of the universe? What is human nature? What are a human being's ethical and moral responsibilities? What are the origins of matter? What are the qualities of truth, goodness, and beauty? What is the meaning of human life? Is there a physical force known as evil? Is there life after death? In the distant past these questions were answered in terms of mythology and superstition. Today they are answered by religion and science.

As recently as the early 19th century, natural philosophy was the study of the physical sciences and mathematics. The study of ethics was referred to as moral philosophy. Today, students of philosophy are still interested in the nature of the universe, the foundations of knowledge, the correct use of logic and reason, the standards of justice, and the qualities of beauty. These problems are the subject matter of the five branches of philosophy - metaphysics, epistemology, logic, ethics, and aesthetics. A brief description of each branch of philosophy is given below. As an example of a related philosophy, the objectivist view of each branch of philosophy is also provided.

Metaphysics' is concerned with the principles, structures, and meanings that underlie all observable reality. Metaphysics, epistemology, and aesthetics are speculative approaches to philosophy. Their conclusions cannot currently be verified. It is speculation on the nature of being and existence and of the cause, substance, and purpose of everything. Metaphysics asks questions such as: Is there a first cause, or God, that has created everything and put it in motion? Is there a separate reality apart from that of humans? The objectivists view is that reality, the external world, exists independent of man's consciousness, and independent of any observer's knowledge, beliefs, feelings, desires or fears. This means that the task of man's consciousness is to perceive reality, not create it or invent it. Objectivism rejects any belief in the supernatural and any claims that individuals or groups create their own reality.

Epistemology means "theory of knowledge." It is derived from the Greek *episteme*, meaning "knowledge," and *logos*, which has several meanings, including "theory." Whereas metaphysics is concerned with the underlying nature of reality, epistemology deals with the possibilities and limits of human knowledge. Knowledge may be regarded as having two parts. First there is perception, what one sees, hears, touches, tastes, and

5

smells. Then there is the way these perceptions are organized by the mind to form ideas or concepts. The problem of epistemology is based on how philosophers have understood the relationship of the mind to the rest of reality. The objectivists view is that man's reason is fully competent to know the facts of reality. Reason is man's only means of acquiring knowledge. Objectivism rejects mysticism (any acceptance of faith or feeling as a means of knowledge), and it rejects strict skepticism (the claim that certainty of knowledge is impossible or there exists universal doubt).

Ethics is the branch of philosophy concerned with human behavior, morality, and responsibilities of people to each other and to society. Because ethics plays such a large part in the way people live, it has always been a subject of great interest. Some philosophers have asserted that there are definite, knowable standards for human behavior. Others (the relativists) deny this and say that decisions should be based mostly on the situation in which one finds oneself, varying with individuals and their environments, and that ethical decisions are related to specific circumstances. The objectivists view is that reason is man's only proper judge of values and his only proper guide to action. Man must work for his rational self-interest, with the achievement of his own happiness as the moral purpose of his life. Objectivism rejects the claim that morality consists in living for others or for society. A system that sacrifices the self to society is a system of slavery.

Aesthetics is the branch of philosophy that deals with the nature of beauty, the arts, and taste (or appreciation) with a view toward establishing the meaning and validity of critical judgments concerning works of art, and the principles underlying or justifying such judgments. The term is derived from the Greek word meaning "sense perception." The basic questions for aesthetics are: How do humans judge what is beautiful? Is it a reasoned assessment, or is it merely an emotional preference? Do aesthetic judgments have any relationship to moral or scientific judgments? Aesthetics seeks to lay foundations for criticism in the arts, or it tries to show that such foundations are impossible. The objectivists view is that art is a selective re-creation of reality according to an artist's metaphysical value judgments. The purpose of art is to concretize the artist's fundamental view of existence.

There are many philosophies to choose from. To be truly content and happy with your life you need to decide for yourself which philosophy to follow. Are you a realist or an idealist? Realists see objects as objects of sense perception, which have an existence independent of the act of perception or existing independently from human minds. All objects are wholly mind-independent. Idealists believe that all objects depend for their existence on the mind. All objects are at least partly mind-dependent. Are you a Materialist? Materialists believe that all existence is resolvable into matter and that matter is the ultimate reality. Are you a Positivist? Positivism is based on experience and empirical knowledge of natural phenomena in which metaphysics and theology are regarded as inadequate and imperfect systems of knowledge. Are you a Deist? Deism was developed by freethinkers who maintain a belief in God while at the same time making it compatible with the rationalism of the enlightenment. Deists believe that the development of science is compatible with a belief in God as first cause, creator and source of universal and immutable laws but reject supernatural revelation. Are you a Theist? Theism is the belief that God created the universe and actively intervenes in its operation through miracles. Theists also believe in revelation.

Why is it important to have a worldview? Once you have defined your worldview and understand how the universe and world function you are free to pursue other interests without worrying that you might have missed something, or you don't understand your place in the universe, or that you are missing some piece of knowledge that will make your life more complete. Establishing a worldview provides peace of mind and confidence. This frees the mind so that your energy can be directed to the pursuit of happiness and allows you to focus on the things that are really important in your life.

6

The purpose of this book is to help you understand how the world works; provide a platform for further knowledge and understanding, and to assist you in developing a worldview and a life plan. The fundamentals of developing a worldview are as follows:

1. Determine your belief system - Are you satisfied that your belief in a particular religion is warranted and will make your life better or do you feel more comfortable being agnostic or atheist?

2. Determine your political economic system - Do you agree with the facts of history that socialism is a failed system and that capitalism is the only system that works, or do you believe that a communist utopia is still possible?

3. Determine your lifestyle system - Do you want to have a plan for life or drift aimlessly through life? Do you want to have a long, healthy, happy, and prosperous life or do you admit defeat and settle for a life of misery and want? Lifestyle choices are always up to the individual.

4. Determine your philosophy of life - What in general is your philosophy or outlook on life? Are you an optimist (a tendency to look on the more favorable side of events and to expect the most favorable outcome) or a pessimist (the tendency to emphasize only bad or undesirable outcomes)? Are you going to be a strict hedonist (pleasure and happiness are the highest good) or are you going to follow a balanced path like Aristotle's golden mean, the middle way, as a guide to excellence? For example, a mix of Stoicism (repression of emotions, and indifference to pleasure and pain) and Epicureanism (pleasure and peace of mind achieved through reason is the highest good).

5. Document and implement your life-plan. Once you have your answers you can get started by putting your belief system, your political-economic system, your lifestyle system, and your philosophy of life in writing. Writing forces you to think and assists in creating order out of your thoughts, and if you don't write things down, you have a tendency to forget them over time. Once your worldview has been established you are ready to implement a time management system and identify and document your life goals.

Once you have completed these steps, you will be ready to face any challenge with confidence. Hopefully, by the time you have finished this book, you will have the answers to your questions and a foundation from which to build on.

The Origins of Matter and Life

"Perfection; the capacity to change, to adapt to the
environment, not the capacity to remain what one is."
Charles Darwin

The following material is a supplement to the Cosmological / Evolutionary time line below. It is meant to be a summation of the current state of knowledge on the origin and development of the universe, galaxies, stars, planets, atmospheres, life, and humans. The information provided is in an extremely condensed form, with as many of the complex technical details omitted as possible, while still attempting to maintain continuity and the basic ideas of these processes. The amount of detailed information available on these topics would fill hundreds of books, and covers a broad spectrum of scientific disciplines.

Cosmology and the Evolutionary Universe

The grounds once held exclusively by the theologians are now giving way to science. For the first time in human history experimental science is at the point of answering all the questions about the origins of the universe and man. Cosmology is the scientific study of the origin, evolution, and nature of the universe. The field of cosmology today is a very specialized and complex area of study. It encompasses the fields of astronomy, astrophysics, physics (including particle physics, relativistic physics, and quantum physics), chemistry, and mathematics. Because of the complexities of these fields, some of the best minds in the world have devoted their lives to the pursuit of knowledge about our universe. The understanding of the origin and fate of the universe really is the final frontier.

The currently accepted view of the origin of the universe is that it began from an infinitely dense primordial atom sometimes referred to as a singularity or a quantum vacuum fluctuation. At a time some 13 to 15 billion years ago this primordial state exploded in what is referred to as the big bang. From this rapid expansion the four fundamental forces and space-time formed, and the universe as we now know it began. After the big bang the universe went through a period of rapid expansion known as inflation and continues to expand today. Calculations show the earth to be moving at a velocity of about 300 kilometers per second towards the Virgo constellation. Additionally, the solar system and our galaxy are moving at 600 kilometers per second or .2 percent of the speed of light. The more distant objects are moving faster as the expansion continues.

The four fundamental forces, which are thought to have been a single unified force at the very early stage of the expansion, are the weak force, the strong force, electromagnetic force and gravitational force. The weak force is responsible for radioactive decay and neutrino interactions. It has a very short range and, as its name indicates, it is very weak. The strong force is very strong, but very short-ranged. It acts only over distances of 10^{-13} centimeters and is responsible for holding the nuclei of atoms together. It is basically attractive, but can be effectively repulsive in some circumstances. The electromagnetic force causes electric and magnetic effects such as the repulsion between like electrical charges or the interaction of bar magnets. It is long-ranged, but much weaker than the strong force. It can be attractive or repulsive, and acts only between pieces of matter carrying electrical charge. The gravitational force is weak, but very long ranged. Furthermore, it is always attractive, and acts between any two pieces of matter in the Universe.

The big bang model of the universe has successfully met the two major tests against observations. The first theoretical prediction of the model is the relative abundance of hydrogen and helium. The observed abundances of these two elements in the universe are, as predicted, 75% hydrogen and 24% helium. The additional elements of oxygen and carbon, and the heavy elements, make up only trace amounts of the total mass of the universe.

The big bang model also predicted that the temperature of the universe has cooled with the expansion and that space should be filled with blackbody radiation. The Cosmic Background Explorer, a satellite launched in 1989, has also verified this prediction with a high degree of accuracy. This radiation is now known as the cosmic background radiation. The current temperature of the universe in all directions is 2.7 degrees Kelvin. Zero degrees Kelvin, is equal to -273.15 degrees Celsius, or -459.67 degrees Fahrenheit. The observed cosmic background radiation also seems to confirm the hypothesis of large-scale isotropy (equal physical attributes along all axes) and homogeneity (unvarying and essentially alike) of the universe. Recent data from the NASA Wilkinson Microwave Anisotropy Probe (WMAP) has confirmed the inflation theory, has put the age of the universe at 13.7 billion years old, and has shown the composition of the universe to be 4 percent ordinary matter, 23 percent to be cold dark matter, and 73 percent unaccounted for, or according to some theorists consisting of so-called dark energy. This new information is providing the basis for a standard model for the evolution of the universe just as experimental data has led to a standard model of particle physics.

The Evolution of Galaxies

The evolution of galaxies began in the early stages of big bang expansion. Shortly after the decoupling (separation) of radiation and matter, it is believed that small primeval density inhomogeneities (fluctuations) occurred which contributed to the conglomeration of gas and dust that are now the raw materials of galaxies, galactic clusters, and superclusters. Two of the most promising theories explaining these inhomogeneities are the inflation-produced curvature fluctuation and the cosmic-string produced isocurvature fluctuation theories. See suggested readings for additional information on these topics.

By the time matter was dominating the evolution of a transparent, dark, and cooling universe, it was already grouped into clumps that because of the constant force of gravity, did not thin out as rapidly as the rest of the universe. This coupled with the so called dark matter, which apparently makes up the additional mass required for galactic evolution, is the basis of galaxy formation.

Galaxies follow an evolutionary progression from featureless ellipticals (E0, E3, E7 representing progressively flatter ellipticals) to more complex spirals and barred spirals. The two spiral groups each have three subcategories - a, b, and c - representing a sequence toward smaller nuclear regions and more open arms. SO type galaxies act as a bridge between the ellipticals (shaped like an ellipse) and the spirals. Flatter than an E7, the most elongated elliptical, SO's lack spiral structure. Spiral galaxies account for more than half of the observed galaxies, while only about 15% are elliptical galaxies.

The Milky Way galaxy - the galaxy where the earth resides - is a typical rotating spiral galaxy. The earth and its solar system represent only a very small portion of our galaxy. Characteristics of the Milky Way galaxy include the following:

Age: 13 - 15 billion years
Number of stars: 100 billion
Linear diameter of disk: 100,000 light years
Thickness of disk at Sun: 700 billion light years
Diameter of central bulge: 25,000 light years
Distance of Sun from galactic center: 27,000 light years
Orbital velocity of Sun around center: 135 miles per second
Time for the Sun to complete one orbit: 230 million years

The speed of light in a vacuum is roughly 3×10^8 meters per second or 186,000 miles per second. A light year is the distance that light travels in a vacuum in 1 year, which is 5.88 trillion miles or 9.46 trillion kilometers.

The Evolution of Stars

Stars have a definite life cycle. They are born, they burn hydrogen, they exhaust their hydrogen supply, and then they die. The form they take after they burn all of their hydrogen depends upon their initial mass. All stars begin as protostars, which are concentrations of luminous gas, found within larger and more diffuse clouds of dust and gas (nebula). Collapsing inward under its own gravity, a protostar becomes denser and hotter until hydrogen-fusion reactions ignite. This is known as the main sequence of a star (from the Hertzsprung-Russell diagram). Many stars, like our sun, remain on the main sequence for billions of years. After the star exhausts its fuel it goes through a variety of different stages, depending on its mass, and becomes one of the following:

- Black dwarf - The hypothetical remnant of a dwarf star that has completely consumed its nuclear fuel
- Brown dwarf - a dim body of less than 0.1 solar mass with insufficient self-gravity to fuse hydrogen to helium
- White dwarf - a star which has a stellar mass but planetary dimensions, Sirius B was one of the first white dwarf stars to be discovered
- Red dwarf - a dim, long-lived, low mass, M-class star
- Red giant - an aging, low mass star that has greatly expanded and cooled after consuming most of its core hydrogen
- Super giant - an old, high mass star greatly expanded from its original size. Expanding to 300 times the size of the sun, after all fusion options have expired, it will either supernova or become a black hole
- Black hole – First hypothesized by Laplace in 1799, and named by John Archibald Wheeler, black holes were predicted by the general theory of relativity as a consequence of the distortion of the gravitational field around a massive body. Black holes are extremely warped areas of space-time caused by high-density objects. The gravitational force related to these objects is so great that even radiation, including light, cannot escape from it. The proposed varieties of black holes include mini black holes, which are low mass objects that were formed at the beginning of the universe, stellar black holes, which form from the cores of old massive collapsed stars, and super massive black holes that reside in the center of galaxies, equivalent to millions of solar masses (at least 107 solar masses). These super massive black holes are thought to

be the energy source of Seyfert galaxies and high-energy quasars (distant bright energetic objects). Evidence of a black hole exists in the binary star system Cygnus X-1. This star is a strong x-ray source, with a high temperature spectrum and millisecond flickering, all of which represent predicted parameters of black holes. There is also evidence for the presence of super massive black holes in two galaxies – the Milky Way and the nearby Seyfert II galaxy NGC 4258.

When looking for stars that contain planetary solar systems astronomers look for stars that have gravitationally induced aberrations in their orbits. This gravitational aberration would indicate another massive object is within close proximity to the star. This type of aberration was first observed in the Sirius star system. Other possible planetary systems are those of Lalande 21185 (8.2 light years distance), Epsilon Eridani (10.8 light years), 61 Cygni (11 light years), and DB+42 degrees 4305 (16.9 light years). There are thought to be hundreds of other planetary systems in the universe. If planetary solar systems were to be confirmed, there would be an even higher probability that life forms exist beyond our tiny corner of the universe.

The Evolution of the Solar System and Earth

The formation of earth and the solar system began approximately 4.6 billion years ago. This formation began in a rotating, contracting gaseous molecular cloud of dust, or a solar nebula, whose shape and internal movements were determined by both gravitational and rotational forces. When the core of this cloud became dense enough, gravity became the dominant force. Matter continued to fall inward for about 1 million years. With time the cloud flattened out into a disc and material within the cloud drifted towards the center, eventually accreting (an increase by accumulated matter) into a proto-sun. Internal heat created by the collapse of matter and the increased density of the gases raised the temperature to the point at which thermonuclear reactions began. The cooler more distant portions of the nebula contained the raw material of a planetary system.

The current theory of planetary formation is known as the planetesimal theory. In this theory, tiny dust grains existed in the disk, which consisted of carbon, silicates, and metals, as well as ice particles made up of water, carbon dioxide, methane, and ammonia that had condensed as the solar nebula continued to cool. These particles then coalesced into rocky or icy aggregations, growing in size from millimeter, through meter, to kilometer sized particles, and taking the form of what we now call asteroids and comets or planetesimals. These planetesimals were the building blocks of the planets.

Because planetesimals aggregated at different distances from the sun's heat and light, the composition of the planets varies according to their distance. The four planets that are most earth like occur at the inner portion of the solar system: Mercury, Venus, Earth and Mars. Each of these planets is a solid sphere with a metallic core. In the past they all had active volcanoes, earthquakes, and craters from meteor strikes.

The four outer planets Jupiter, Saturn, Uranus, and Neptune contain 99 percent of the material in the solar system excluding the sun. All are gaseous spheroids of hydrogen and helium with some methane-ammonia, and water. In fact, if Jupiter would have had more mass, it too could have formed into a star like our sun. A planetary system, which contains two stars, is known as a binary star system.

The earliest phase of atmospheric formation included a short-lived period with an atmosphere of hydrogen, which came from the original planet-forming nebula. This hydrogen was lost due to a lack of gravitational attraction. The earth's early atmosphere began forming by a process known as outgassing. Most of these gases were supplied by volcanic eruptions. As a result the atmosphere changed from a hydrogen-rich methane-ammonia atmosphere, to a methane-nitrogen-water mixture, to a hydrogen-poor carbon monoxide-nitrogen-water based mixture.

Earth's early atmosphere consisted of water vapor, hydrogen, hydrogen chloride, carbon monoxide, carbon dioxide, and nitrogen. The atmosphere was further modified by the release of heat and molecules during cratering, continued outgassing from volcanoes, chemical reactions between the molecules of the air and those of rocks, atmospheric circulation via evaporation and condensation, and radiation from the sun.

Carbon dioxide dominated the earth's atmosphere until 2 billion years ago when the earliest photosynthetic aerobic bacteria began producing oxygen. Today the lower atmosphere, as a percent by weight, consists of about 76% nitrogen, 23% oxygen, 1.23% argon, and .05% carbon dioxide with the remaining gases all below .05 percent or occurring only in trace amounts.

The Evolution of Life and Man

There are many creation myths. The Haida Indians believe that humans came out of a clamshell discovered by the Raven. The Hopi believe that man enters the earth from a small hole in the floor of the Grand Canyon that supposedly is the entrance to the underworld. Then there is the Judeo-Christian myth that God created first a man from clay, then a woman from one of his rib bones. These origin fables are all ancient myths. But even today many people still believe that divine creation is the way man really came into existence. In actuality, Homo sapiens, as a species, developed through millions of years of evolution. Modern humans (Homo sapiens or "wise man") arose in Africa around 100,000 years ago, then made a second great outward migration, which lead to the eventual peopling of the world that we have today. About 35,000 years ago scattered hunter-gatherer groups in Europe and Asia underwent a cultural revolution and for the first time began to create symbols of themselves, of the animals around them, and of the passage of time.

Recent studies led by Dr. Spencer Wells of the Wellcome Trust Centre for Human Genetics and his colleagues, including Li Jin of Fudan University in Shanghai indicate that all modern humans are descendents of people who lived in Africa some 60,000 years ago. The scientists examined the Y-chromosomes of more than 12,000 people from across Africa and Asia. They tested the samples for a set of three markers associated with a mutation of the male Y-chromosome known to have originated in Africa an estimated 44,000 years ago. The results indicate that modern humans of African origin completely replaced earlier populations in East Asia. The study not only explains how humans populated the earth, it also shows why racism is not only socially divisive but also scientifically incorrect. We are all part of the same family, as Dr. Wells puts it "we are all Africans under the skin."

Life is the property of plants, animals and organisms, which make it possible for them to take in nutrients, metabolize or take energy from these nutrients, grow and through natural selection adapt themselves to the environment, and reproduce in an attempt to perpetuate their species. It is these qualities, which distinguish living matter from dead organisms or inorganic matter.

The evolution of life begins with the evolution of a planetary system that has the proper ingredients for life. These ingredients include the basic chemical elements such as carbon, hydrogen, nitrogen and helium, molecular components such as amino acids, sugars, phosphates, and organic bases for nucleic acids, lipids for membranes, and the proper temperature gradients to allow for the necessary chemical reactions to take place.

Life on earth began approximately 3.8 billion years ago or roughly 800 million years after the formation of the earth. The origin of life did not occur in 6 days as the Bible says. It took billions of years of evolution before humans and other complex life forms appeared. The evidence to support the current theories of the origin of life are the fossil record, experimental data on the chemical synthesis of the building blocks of life, and recent discoveries from the Human Genome Project. The fossil record is covered in detail in the cosmological / evolutionary time line and will not be covered in this section other than a brief mention of dating techniques that are currently being used. This sections main purpose is to give a summary of the current knowledge of the origins of life and on the evolution of life since its inception.

The two competing scientific theories of the origin of life are the replicator first and the metabolism first theories. Both theories must start from molecules formed by non-biological chemical processes. In the replicator first model, compounds join together in a chain forming a molecule capable of reproducing itself. Through evolutionary processes cellular structure and metabolism follows. In the metabolism first theory, cellular structure and metabolism appear first followed by the development of information storing polymers (a chemical reaction in which two or more molecules combine to form larger molecules that contain repeating structural units).

As was discussed earlier, the earth's atmosphere originally contained a much different mixture of molecules than it does today. Energy sources were provided by solar radiation, corona discharge, thunderstorms, meteor impacts, radiation from radioactive decay, and cosmic rays. In experiments designed to simulate the conditions of this primitive atmosphere, amino acids have been produced. Amino acids are a group of nitrogenous organic compounds that serve as the units of structure of proteins and are essential to human metabolism. The twenty amino acids that occur naturally are the building blocks of proteins. Humans can synthesize a dozen amino acids, but eight must be ingested in the diet.

Proteins are large molecules that are found universally in the cells of living organisms. They contain carbon, hydrogen, oxygen and nitrogen, and almost invariably contain sulfur and sometimes phosphorous. The proteins are referred to as polypeptides and are large chains of amino acid residues. There are hundreds of proteins, which are very diverse in their properties and functions. Proteins are found in everything from fibers such as hair and tendons, to blood plasma, and hemoglobin. All enzymes, the essential catalysts of biological systems, are proteins. In humans, proteins account for 50% of the body's dry weight.

The most famous of the chemical evolution experiments is the Miller-Urey simulation done at the University of Chicago. This experiment involved spark discharges in a flask filled with methane (CH_4), ammonia (NH_3), water vapor (H_2O) and hydrogen (H_2). The experiment produced 20 compounds, four (glycine, alanine, glutamic acid, and aspartic acid) of which are amino acids that are commonly found in proteins. Variations of the experiment have produced additional naturally occurring amino acids including leucine, isoleucine, serine, threonine, asparagine, lysin, phenylalanine and tyrosine. From these amino acids, proteins can be produced by polymerization into polypeptides. This production of proteins is half of what is needed for the beginning of life. The other half is the ability to reproduce. For reproduction to occur nucleic acids are needed.

A cell's instructions are contained in its genome, which is the sum total of all the DNA molecules in the cell. DNA (deoxyribonucleic acid) molecules are long sequences of four different subunits called nucleotides. The sequence of nucleotides contains genetic information. Specific segments of DNA called genes contain the information the cell uses to make proteins. Proteins make up much of an organisms structure and are the molecules that govern the chemical reactions with cells. Most proteins are too small to be seen even with an electron microscope and each cell contains thousands of different proteins.

Inside the nucleus of the cell, DNA combines with proteins to form a fibrous complex called chromatin. Chromatin consists of long thin threads. Prior to cell division, the chromatin aggregates to form discrete, visible structures called chromosomes. A chromosome is a DNA molecule containing genetic information. When a cell divides all of its chromosomes must be replicated, and each of the two resulting copies must find its way into one of the two new cells.

14

For most of the life of the cell, chromosomes are too elongated and tenuous to be seen under a microscope. Before a cell gets ready to divide by mitosis, each chromosome is duplicated (during S phase of the cell cycle). Mitosis is the process of replicating DNA, and dividing it into two equal parts to generate two identical "daughter" cells from one "mother" cell. As mitosis begins, the duplicated chromosomes condense into short structures which can be stained and easily observed under the light microscope. These duplicated chromosomes are called dyads.

The complete set of chromosomes in the cells of an organism is its karyotype. It is most often studied when the cell is at metaphase of mitosis and all the chromosomes are present as dyads. In humans, each cell normally contains 23 pairs of chromosomes, for a total of 46. Twenty-two of these pairs, called autosomes, look the same in both males and females. The 23rd pair, the sex chromosomes, differs between males and females. Females have two copies of the X chromosome, while males have one X and one Y chromosome.

Depending upon the type of sugar from which they are made, there are two kinds of nucleic acid - ribonucleic acid (RNA), and deoxyribonucleic acid (DNA). RNA is a molecule that consists of a long chain of nucleotide units. Each nucleotide consists of a nitrogenous base, a ribose sugar, and a phosphate. RNA is very similar to DNA, but differs in a few important structural details: in the cell, RNA is usually single-stranded, while DNA is usually double-stranded; RNA nucleotides contain ribose while DNA contains deoxyribose (a type of ribose that lacks one oxygen atom); and RNA has the base uracil rather than thymine that is present in DNA. There are four main types of RNA:

Messenger RNA or mRNA: carries the genetic information out of the nucleus for protein synthesis.
Transfer RNA or tRNA: decodes the information.
Ribosomal RNA or rRNA: constitutes 50% of a ribosome, which is a molecular assembly involved in protein synthesis.
Catalytic RNAs: involved in many reactions in the cytoplasm of the cell.

DNA consists of systematically linked chemical units, which form a double helix structure. These units are the nucleotides, which contain a phosphate, a sugar, and a section called a base. There are four bases adenine (A), guanine (G), cytosine (C), and thymine (T). In the DNA molecule, adenine always bonds to thymine, and guanine always binds to cytosine (complementary base-pairing), which make up the base pairs. As a result of this binding the sequence of nucleotides along each strand is a chemical mirror image of its mate.

The genetic information of the DNA molecule resides in the base pair sequences. As the duplex molecule (double helix) replicates, it forms two almost identical daughters. These daughters are never exactly identical because of the errors that can occur during replication. When the chromosomes replicate during cell division the molecule's two strands separate and new bases are added on by pairing, so that two new molecules are formed identical to the original one.

Once RNA and DNA molecules had evolved, the ability to reproduce became a reality. Due to the complexity of molecular biology, the details of the reproductive processes will not be covered in this section. The complexity of the DNA molecule is ample for any function demanded of it. Even with only 4 letters (A, G, C, T) the number of potential DNA sequences is very large for even the smallest DNA molecule. Many bacterial genes contain some 1500 base pairs. The number of potential genes of this size is 4^{1500} a value much larger than the number of different genes that could have existed in all the chromosomes present since the origin of life. Since the total number of species of plants and animals that have ever existed on earth can be numbered in the low millions (2-3 million species) the allotment of a different DNA molecule to each does not make a dent in the total number of DNA molecules possible.

Once the proteins and nucleic acids were formed, a structure for containment was necessary. This structure was the protocell, which was the precursor of the modern cell. Spheroidal to globular organic microstructures in organic residues of Miller-Urey experiments, and proteinoid microspheres have been produced from thermally synthesized peptides under almost dry conditions. These microspheres can have layered membranes and are strikingly similar in size and morphology (the form and structure of an organism) to prokaryotes such as bacteria and blue-green algae. Some are able to divide asexually (do not involve the union of individuals or gametes), but no nucleic acids are involved. Significantly, this shows a tendency for abiotically produced materials to order themselves into complex structures. Random processes, although active, are subordinate to kinetically favored pathways.

Prokaryotes are the least complex form of organisms, having a simple cell structure and lacking a nucleus. Prokaryotic cell structure consists of DNA and other biochemicals enclosed in a membrane. The prokaryotes include some forms of bacteria and blue-green algae. The prokaryotes have been divided into two domains, the Bacteria and the Archaea. Archaea are among the earliest forms of life and are believed to have developed separately from bacteria from a common ancestor. Archaea inhabit some of the most extreme environments on the planet. They have been found living in temperatures of over 100 degrees centigrade (212° F) as well as under the frozen surface of an Antarctic lake with a surface that is permanently frozen.

Eukaryotes are organisms which have their chromosomes contained within a nucleus, and are distinguished from the simpler prokaryotes by other cellular structures such as organelles and certain differences in biochemical functions. The eukaryotes include higher plants and animals, protozoa, fungi, and algae other than blue-green algae.

With the advent of cellular structure and the molecular structures for reproduction, the long road of evolution towards organisms of higher complexity could begin. The earliest organisms were heterotrophic (capable of utilizing only organic materials as a source of food), unable to build their own complex organic molecules and were thereby dependent on obtaining them from their surroundings. Autotrophy is the ability to construct organic compounds from simple substances such as water and carbon dioxide. The first living things were small micrometer-sized, spheroidal, heterotrophic, bacteria-like organisms, which survived by fermenting organic molecules out of pools of organic compounds.

The next major step in microbial evolution was the appearance of the first photosynthetic autotrophs such as the blue-green algae (a highly evolved prokaryote), which released oxygen, an important stage in the evolution of the earth's atmosphere. Once oxygen became abundant in the atmosphere the more complex multicellular plants and organisms could develop. From this point to the present, thousands of different life forms have evolved and become extinct according to the laws of evolution.

Although humans are complex organisms and contain a large number of cells, (up to 5 x 10^{12}) all these cells arise initially from a single cell. Cells obey the laws of chemistry. All living organisms have a similar chemical makeup, which is based on a small number of organic compounds. These organic compounds consist of the following:

- 20 amino acids
- 20 vitamins
- 4 lipids
- 4 nucleic acid bases, adenine, thymine, cytosine, and guanine, each of which is attached to a sugar deoxyribose to form the deoxyribose nucleic acid (DNA)

The concept of evolution is not new. The Roman philosopher Lucretius (99-55 B.C.) spoke of races of living things having died out and being unable to breed and continue breeding. Aristotle (382-322 B.C.) mentions it when he says, "there is observed in plants a continuous scale of ascent toward the animal." Both Thomas Aquinas and John Locke saw the world of living organisms as a graduated scale ascending from less to more perfect forms of life.

Charles Darwin (1809-1882) formalized the ideas of Aristotle and others in his revolutionary work *The Origin of Species*. Darwin attempts to establish that new species do originate in the course of time, and describes the mechanisms of the emergence, variation, and extinction of species. Offspring differ slightly from their parents and each other (descent with modification), making some fitter than others in the struggle for existence (survival of the fittest), and that these small generational changes accumulate, mutating one species into others.

Species refers to a group of organisms, which can all potentially interbreed, one with another, to produce fertile offspring. The group is genetically isolated from other groups, and this genetic isolation allows distinctive features, characteristic of the species, to develop. Diverse species cannot interbreed. Members of the species always generate organisms, which can be classified as belonging to the same species, however much they vary among themselves within the group. Organisms of different species cannot mate productively, or if they are crossbred, like the horse and the ass, they produce a sterile hybrid like the mule. Species are not fixed but change with time.

Evolution is the development of an organism toward perfect or complete adaptation to environmental conditions to which it has been exposed with the passage of time. Evolution is based on the two fundamental concepts of variation and natural selection.

Variation means that the individual members of a species vary slightly among themselves. Those individuals with certain characteristics, which give them an advantage, in gaining food or escaping predators for example, will have an enhanced chance of survival. These variations are caused by gene recombination and mutations, which are discussed further below. As for natural selection, when environmental conditions change, natural selection assures that certain characteristics in a randomly varying population are favored. Genetic variations make some individuals better fitted than others to survive and to reproduce in a given environment, and so the inheritable traits of the better-adapted organisms were more often represented in succeeding generations. This is nature's way of causing the survival of the fittest.

Natural selection is the process in nature by which individuals (of a species) best fitted for the conditions in which they are placed to survive, propagate and spread, while the less fitted die out and disappear. Darwin identified four conditions that must be met for natural selection to operate. First, there must be a surplus of organisms: more offspring must be born than can possibly survive in the long run. Second, there must be variation between individuals in a species. This is true for both sexual and asexual species. Third, there must be differential survival and reproduction. Some traits must give their carriers an edge. Fourth, some of the traits that prove helpful in promoting differential survival and reproduction must be inheritable. As a result, the proportion of individuals in succeeding generations with these traits will increase, so the species will evolve.

Natural selection has been observed at the molecular level. All DNA sequences in the genome, and thus all genes, are constantly subject to mutation. Mutations are caused by errors made during DNA replication and recombination, by chemical DNA damaging agents and radiation, by the chemical instability of certain groups within DNA, and even by errors made by DNA repair mechanisms themselves. Many of theses mutations represent single-base substitutions (transitions and transversions). Other mutations arise from insertions of deletions of a few base pairs. Base pairs consist of two bases, a purine and a pyrimidine, which pair together in the genetic code of DNA and RNA; cytosine pairs with guanine in both DNA and RNA; and adenine pairs with thymine in DNA and with uracil in RNA. Some mutations represent gross changes in the DNA, resulting from large deletions and insertions, from inversion, or from translocations.

If the gene product is defective in any serious way, the organism producing it will be immediately subjected to a selective disadvantage; it will either die prematurely or produce fewer progeny than its unmutated siblings. Thus, natural selection does not preserve the DNA sequence of the gene per se but rather its functional product. Gene sequences change through time. New genes may be assembled from fragments of pre-existing genes. Once a gene has been duplicated, one copy is sufficient for survival of the organism, while the other gene copy is free to change. These changes will generally be useless or even harmful, and the extra gene copy will probably be lost. However, occasionally one of the gene copies will mutate in an advantageous way, and natural selection will preserve both the new gene and the old. Mutations are constantly changing gene selections, while natural selection keeps pace by preserving functional gene products.

Genes are normally copied exactly during chromosome duplication. Rarely however, do changes or mutations occur in genes that give rise to altered forms, most, but not all, of which function less well than the wild-type (normal) alleles. An allele is an alternative form of a gene that occupies a particular location on a chromosome. This process is necessarily rare; otherwise, many genes would be changed during every cell cycle, and offspring would not ordinarily resemble their parents. There is, instead, a strong advantage in there being a small but finite mutation rate; it provides a constant source of new variability, which is necessary to allow plants and animals to adapt to a constantly changing physical and biological environment.

The evidence for evolution is overwhelming. There are well over one hundred studies that have demonstrated natural selection in action. Evolution in action can be seen in the peppered moth, found in the British Isles. The original silvery form is well camouflaged on lichen-covered tree trunks, but where air pollution has killed the lichen and blackened the tree trunks with soot; a black variety of the peppered moth has become increasingly common and in some places almost replaced the original form. Other insect species have now been found to have black varieties in areas with large amounts of air pollution. This phenomenon is known as industrial melanism. The finches of the Galapagos have altered beak shapes and sizes that have changed as a result of species competition (character displacement), and climate and food resource variations. Due to the exponential growth of populations of bacteria, hundreds of generations can be observed during a human lifetime. Many strains of bacteria have mutated and become more virulent and resistant to various antibiotics.

Additional evidence comes from the E. coli long-term evolution experiment (LTEE), an ongoing study in experimental evolution led by Richard Lenski that has been tracking genetic changes in 12 initially nearly identical populations of asexual Escherichia coli bacteria since February 15, 1988. As of 2008, the E. coli populations have been under study for over 40,000 generations, and are thought to have undergone enough spontaneous mutations that every possible single point mutation in the E. coli genome should have occurred multiple times. Lenski and his collaborators reported on a particularly important adaptation that occurred in one of the twelve populations: the bacteria evolved the ability to utilize citrate as a source of energy. Normally, E. coli cannot transport citrate from outside the cell to the cell interior (where it could be incorporated into the citric acid cycle); the lack of citrate transport is considered a defining characteristic of the species.

As mentioned earlier, part of the evidence for evolution is derived from the fossil record. These fossils have been dated and again prove that the ideas contained in Genesis and other religious notions about the formation of earth and the evolution of man are nothing more than ancient myths. The following dating methods are the most commonly used:

- Paleomagnetism - This method utilizes the two main components of the earth's magnetic field (direction and intensity) for dating purposes. At present this method of dating can only be applied to fired clay materials dating back 2000 years or so.

- Potassium / argon dating - This method measures the half-life, or the time taken for a given amount of elemental radioactivity to decay to half its initial value. The half-life of potassium is 1.3 billion years. Because of this long half-life this method has been used to date earth's oldest rocks, lunar rocks and other extra-terrestrial materials.
- Radiocarbon dating - This method utilizes the half-life measurement of carbon, which is approximately 5,730 years, to date carbon based materials.

Due to recent propaganda from the Creationists it is worth mentioning some facts surrounding the renewal of anti-science. Creationism got its start back in 1925 at the famous Scopes trial in Tennessee. Schoolteacher John Scopes was brought into court on charges that he had violated state law by teaching evolution in the classroom. Clarence Darrow, arguing against Jennings Bryan, demonstrated how illogical it was to take the Bible literally.

Today the Creationist's movement has developed what it refers to as "scientific" Creationism. Most of the support for this renewed effort against science comes from the San Diego based Institute for Creation Research. This organization is an offshoot of the Baptist oriented Christian Heritage College. What these people are attempting to do, with some success, is to repackage the Bible to make it look like science. Members of this group's proclaimed goal is "the realignment of science based on theistic creation concepts" and a "commitment to the full belief in the Biblical record of creation and early history." They have already influenced textbook publishers by forcing them into the position of mentioning Creationism as an alternative to evolution and downplaying the description of evolution as a fact.

The Creationists are now using the term "intelligent design" to promote their biblical view of reality. Proponents of intelligent design claim that certain features of the universe and of living things are best explained by an intelligent designer (God), rather than an undirected process such as natural selection.

All evidence is against the Creationists view of the origin and fate of man and the universe. To deny evolution is to deny scientific fact and reality. Every one of their contentions is false. All one has to do is look at the current state of scientific knowledge to see this. Rather than repeating information that is contained in the sections on cosmology and evolution, which shows the Creationists views to be invalid, a few of their fundamental errors will be pointed out.

The Creationists claim that stars remain unchanged. This is blatantly false. Star formation can take 10 million years, so direct observation is difficult, but the formation of stars is being observed in the Orion Nebula. Additional observational evidence comes from the Infrared Astronomy Satellite (IRAS) launched in 1983. When the Large Magellanic Cloud, the nearest galaxy to our own Milky Way galaxy was scanned, a step-by-step textbook example of star formation was directly observed.

Not only is star formation being observed, the death of a star, or supernova, has been directly observed and verified using multiple techniques and observations. In February 1987 the supernova SN1987A was observed in the Large Magellanic Cloud at all wavelengths and the predicted neutrinos from the supernova were detected. Galaxies are also undergoing constant change. Not only are they moving at tremendous speeds, planetary systems are forming within galaxies, and galaxies are merging to form new galaxies. Hubble telescope studies of 81 galaxies in the galaxy cluster MS1054-03 found that 13 are remnants of recent collisions or pairs of colliding galaxies. The colliding "parent" galaxies lose their shape and smoother galaxies are formed. The whole merging process can take less than a billion years.

As for the Creationists view that no new life forms are appearing, again this is false. Man can now create new microorganisms using genetic variation and recombinant DNA techniques. Prior to 1980, life forms were considered a part of nature and were not patentable. Diamond v. Chakrabarty changed this with the 5 to 4 U.S. Supreme Court decision that genetically engineered (modified) bacteria were patentable because they did not occur naturally in nature. In this case, Chakrabarty had modified a bacterium to create an oil-dissolving bioengineered microbe. This is just one example of the ridiculous idea that something supernatural has to exist to create life.

The fact that there are gaps in the fossil record does not discount the fact that evolution is true. Just because a gap exists does not mean that a progressively ascending series is invalid. New finds are occurring continuously that fill these gaps. These discoveries will continue until the majority of the gaps have been filled. For instance in 1980 UCLA paleobiologist J. William Schopf identified bacterial cells that produced the fossils that demonstrate life existed on earth 3.5 billion years ago. These fossils were not positively identified before this discovery.

Scientists today recognize that evolution begins with a change in the DNA molecule. The process of evolution is a fact; it does occur. Biologists have observed and measured its progress at the level of the gene. There is a large amount of fossil evidence, which in many cases, is so complete that it cannot be rationally explained by any non-evolutionary argument. Recent studies of meteorites recovered in Antarctica have shown non-biological amino acids and other organic compounds of extraterrestrial origin. These finds reaffirm earlier evidence and indicate that pre-biotic reactions, which produce the organic compounds necessary for life to begin, occur throughout the solar system, not just on the planet Earth.

The evolution of man from lower life forms doesn't seem so far-fetched when you consider the fact that the chimpanzee, the gorilla, and humans, are genetically so similar that you can hardly tell them apart. These three species share 99 percent of their DNA. The remaining 1 percent is what makes humans human. This means that the three species split off from a common ancestor as recently as 5 - 6 million years ago. This has been determined by gene sequencing and again is a fact, whether a particular fossil exists or not.

New information from the Human Genome Project shows that humans have fewer genes than might have been expected for a relatively complex organism. Flies (Drosophila) have 13,000 genes and nematode worms (C. Elegans) have 18,000. From analysis of the human genome, there only seem to be 25,000 - 30,000 genes. It turns out that humans have many of the same protein families as flies and worms, although we have more in each family. Remarkably, 223 genes found in humans are more similar to bacterial genes than to anything seen in yeast, worms, flies, or plants.

Today, there are approximately 2 - 3 million different types of plant and animal life on earth. New life forms are continuously forming and being discovered. Even with this vast variety of life, the fossil record suggests that about 99 percent of all life forms that have ever existed on earth are now extinct.

Who would have believed that when the geocentric myth was shattered and replaced by the heliocentric system in 1543 with the publication of Copernicus's *On the Revolutions of the Heavenly Spheres*, that a mere 425 years later humans would be walking on the moon. You can just imagine how far man's evolution will progress in another 425 years. When you think about it, the concept of evolution doesn't seem that far-fetched after all.

In closing this section it seems appropriate to give an example of what happens when people choose not to believe scientific evidence and are blind to fact and reality. This example comes from the Soviet Union, where free thought was stifled for years. Trofim Lysenko (1898-1976) was a Russian biologist who refused to believe the reality of Mendelian genetics (modern genetics) and Darwinian natural selection. He chose instead to believe in the unproven and unsubstantiated idea of the inheritance of acquired characters or Lamarckism. With the promise of quick results in breeding animal stocks and grain crops he gained the favor of Joseph Stalin. Lysenko's Mendelian and Darwinian critics were silenced, and those who refused to accept his ideas were removed from positions of authority, and sent to prison camps. Ironically, among those who died in the prison camps was Nikolai Vavilov, perhaps the only man who could have produced the increased productivity desired by Stalin. The Soviets never recovered from this and their equally unrealistic and invalid idea of collective agriculture.

The data supplied in the following evolutionary universe time line is not currently complete. There are some gaps in the knowledge of these events, and there is some disagreement within the scientific community on the exact dates and numbers provided. Still, this is the most accurate version of the origin of the universe and man, supported by the latest scientific research and evidence. The time scale begins at 10 to 15 billion years ago when the big bang occurred and ends 10,000 years ago when modern man begins to assert himself on the planet. The timeline begins at 10^{-43} seconds after the big bang and ends 10,000 years ago at the end of the last ice age.

- 10 to 15 Billion Years Ago at $t = 10^{-43}$ seconds after the big bang - From an extremely dense primordial atom an intense explosion occurs and expansion of the known universe begins. This explosion is referred to as the big bang. The four forces of nature were combined in one primeval force. Once expansion begins, gravity becomes a separate force. Particles of matter and antimatter appear and disappear in annihilating collisions that produce more particles.

- $t = 10^{-35}$ seconds - Inflation Era begins. A new theoretical view put forth by Alan Guth states that vacuum energy dominates the energy density of the universe for a time during an exponential (de Sitter) phase of expansion. During this phase the universe is rapidly inflated to an enormous size. This theory calls for a "flat" universe. Hopes for the theory include the production of acceptably small density perturbations (small changes) that would account for the large-scale structure of the universe, and the distribution of galaxies.

- $t = 10^{-33}$ seconds - The Electro-weak Era begins. The temperature is 10^{32} degrees Kelvin and the density is 10^{94} gms/cm^3. This is a period of intense heat, chaos and rapid expansion. Where Higgs bosons (a massive boson or particle capable of transforming the electro-weak force into distinct electromagnetic and weak forces) appeared and completed the separation of the four fundamental forces.

- $t = 10^{-23}$ seconds - The expansion enters into the Hadron Era. The temperature is 10^{22} degrees Kelvin and the density is 10^{14} gms/cm^3. Heavy particles and primordial black holes are produced, some heavy particles are annihilated as matter and antimatter interactions occur.

- $t = 10^{-6}$ seconds - The universe has cooled down to about 10^{13} degrees Kelvin. The quark (elementary particle) soup of the early universe condensed into baryons and mesons, the baryons being clusters of three quarks and the mesons being quark-anti-quark pairs. Gluons are bosons, or a force-carrying particle, that carries the strong force and binds quarks together in a state known as quark confinement.

- $t = 10^{-4}$ seconds - The expansion enters the Lepton Era. Leptons are a class of elementary particle such as the electron or neutrino. Annihilation of particles continues and fireball radiation is produced. Neutrinos decouple and begin to expand freely rather than being maintained in a thermal equilibrium with the other constituents of the universe.

- $t = 10$ seconds - The temperature is 10^{10} degrees Kelvin and the density is 10^3 gms/cm^3. The decoupling of matter and radiation makes the universe transparent to electromagnetic radiation. The universe becomes dominated by radiation and nuclei appear.

- $t = 10$ seconds to 1 minute - The Neutrino Era begins. Neutrinos and antineutrinos, which evolved during the Electroweak Era, stopped interacting with other particles. Neutrinos, which still exist today, are chargeless particles with a high probability of having a small mass, and pass through the earth and humans virtually undetectable at the speed of light.

- t = 1 - 4 minutes - The Nucleosynthesis Era begins. The temperature is 10^9 degrees Kelvin and the density is 10^{-20} gms/cm^3. Nuclear reactions begin and deuterium, helium-3, helium-4 and lithium are synthesized. Protons and neutrons combine creating a deuteron, which is the nucleus of a variety of hydrogen known as deuterium or hydrogen-2. When a free proton encounters a deuteron it binds with it to form a helium-3 nucleus. The first atomic nuclei begin to form with the generation of helium in a ratio of about one helium nucleus to three hydrogen nuclei or protons. The ratio of 75% hydrogen and 25% helium is about the same relative abundance of these two elements that are observed today.

- t = 500,000 to 1 million years - The Matter Era begins. Hot clouds of hydrogen and helium have formed. There are no other elements that exist in significant quantities. At a temperature of a few thousand degrees Kelvin, the universe has cooled enough for these denser pockets of gas to clump together. Some of these pockets of gas are the size of dwarf galaxies. One result of atom formation was the gradual clearing of the cosmic plasma fog, as free electrons attached to nuclei, photons were no longer scattered by random encounters with electrons, and space began to become transparent.

- t = 10,000,000 years - The temperature is 2.7 degrees Kelvin and the density is 10^{-31} gms/cm^3. The average density of the universe is low enough for electrons to begin combining with nuclei to form stable atoms for the first time. Plasma of nuclei and electrons begins to condense into atoms. Photons can no longer interact with matter; they decouple and begin propagating freely (as they have ever since; they are now the 2.7 degree background radiation). Matter not radiation now dominates the universe and matter begins condensing under its own gravity into galaxies and stars. The essential constituents of the universe have now been formed and the prerequisites for galaxy, star, and planetary system formation now exist.

- t = 1 billion years - Further condensation has caused bursts of star formation within each galactic cloud.

- t = 2 billion years - Star clusters have merged to form distinct yet loosely bound protogalaxies, separated by the relatively unpopulated void. Gravity holds these irregular bodies intact. Within these protogalaxies the stars age, and the oldest and most massive stars begin to explode as supernovae. These explosions enrich the interstellar medium with gas that includes elements such as carbon and oxygen, created from the nuclear reactions within stars. Virtually all elements heavier than boron are produced by nuclear reactions inside stars. When these stars explode at the ends of their lives, the elements are ejected into space.

- t = 2 - 3 billion years - The formation of the galaxies begins. Protogalaxies collapse into a clumpy irregular shaped structure. They consist of a loose network of gaseous star clusters in random motion. Contracting further, the galaxy becomes more symmetrical. Stars supernova and die, ejecting gas enriched with heavy elements into the space between adjacent star clusters and creating new stars as shock waves condense local gases. The larger star clusters in the protogalaxy begin to gravitate toward its center, forming a bright nucleus. A dimmer halo of diffuse gas and globular star clusters surrounds the center. As the random motion of its gas and stars yields to a more organized orbital motion, the protogalaxy's spin becomes more obvious. An elliptical galaxy is born as the final collapse or halo gases and globular clusters close to the nucleus coincides with very rapid star formation effectively consuming all of the elliptical's free gas. The resulting galaxy is brightest at its core, dimming gradually as you approach the almost imperceptible edge. As the elliptical galaxy evolves further towards a spiral galaxy, diffuse gas clouds about the nucleus collide and merge in a process that ultimately creates the central disk of the spiral galaxy. The upward and downward movements of the whirling patches of gas cancel out, and the clouds retain only their orbital motion around the nucleus. Star formation proceeds slowly, and gas clouds gradually precipitate out of the halo into an orbit along the equatorial plane of the galaxy. A partial disk develops, forming from the nucleus outward, as a faint spiral structure begins to appear. As the gas clears out of the halo, globular star clusters become visible. A fully formed spiral galaxy takes shape as stars form in the disk and diffuse gas finishes its precipitation. Globular clusters remaining from the protogalaxy hover around the disk and the central bulge in a vast sphere.

- t = 10 billion years - The formation of the solar system and the earth begins, forming out of a cloud of dust and gas in the outer area of the Milky Way galaxy.

- 4.5 billion years ago - The Hadean Eon begins. In this period the formation of the earth's crust begins. The term Hadean is used to designate geological time from the origin of earth to the oldest terrestrial rocks at 3.8 billion years. Discoveries were made in Greenland, Labrador, and Zimbabwe, which included banded iron formations and carbon but no fossils.

- 4 billion years - In this period the earth is saturated with volcanic activity. Expelled gases from these volcanic eruptions contribute to a thick atmosphere of carbon dioxide, nitrogen, carbon monoxide, and traces of ammonia, methane and hydrogen sulfide. Meteors and comets hit the earth carrying with them many of the organic molecules necessary for life. Electrical storms, volcanism, and radioactivity from cosmic rays and the sun provided sufficient energy for life's inception.

- 3.8 billion years – The Achaean Era begins. Formation of the oceans and small organic compounds begins. During this period, and up to the formation of the first protocells, the formation of hydrocarbons, fatty acids, and proteins and amino acids occurred.

- 3.5 billion years - The emergence of simple life forms begins. The earliest living organisms were water dwelling single celled microorganisms. Feeding on carbon-rich compounds, the organisms spread in layers to form silt-filled mats. The mats in turn created fossilized forms called stromatolites. Locations of these stromatolites included the Warrawoona group (Western Australia) oldest stromalites and microfossils, and the Swaziland supergroup (southern Africa) stromatolites and microfossils.

- 3.0 billion years - Atmospheric oxygen begins to form. More and more bacteria photosynthesize, combining solar energy with carbon dioxide and hydrogen to produce energy-rich sugars. Aerobic bacteria are bacteria that utilize oxygen. Anaerobic bacteria are bacteria that live without the use of oxygen. Discoveries made in the Fortescue group (Western Australia) include stromatolites and cyanobacteria.

- 2.5 billion years - The Proterozoic Era begins. Life adapts to oxygen. Aerobic bacteria release so much oxygen that the atmosphere becomes toxic to anaerobic bacteria. Some die; others find oxygen-free habitats deep in the mud. Organisms that utilize oxygen flourish.

- 2 billion years - Large soft membraned bacteria engulf smaller ones, which then process incoming oxygen fuel for their host. No longer considered cells, the small respiration managers evolve into mitochondria, one of many such biochemical helpers, or organelles, found in both plants and animal cells. Gunflint iron formation (Canada) diverse cyanobacteria, bacteria, and stromalites appear.

- 1.5 billion years - The first signs of sex appear. Eukaryotes evolve a membrane-enclosed nucleus, where genetic material is stored, allowing eukaryotes to replace self-replication with the union of two cells. Since each contributes material to yield a third unique cell, genetic variety in living things increased dramatically. Cells without a nucleus, or prokaryotes, persist but evolve more slowly.
- 1.4 billion years - The bacterium, which is still confined to water, has transformed the Earth from a barren volcanic environment to a fertile garden. In some eukaryotes a new type of organelle called the chloroplast appears. This organelle specializes in capturing sunlight through the process of photosynthesis. By definition, cells that are equipped with chloroplasts are plant cells.
- 1.3 billion years - Eukaryotic diversification continues. The one-cell eukaryotes or protists (or "first") develop into a variety of more complicated forms. Tiny plants and animals, the protists include amoebas and some forms of algae and plankton. Many acquire lashing tails or hairs (flagella), enhancing their mobility. Discoveries include Pahrum group (California) diverse cyanobacteria, eukaryotes, Greyson shale (Montana), and algal megafossils.
- 800 million years - Discoveries include Bitter Springs formation (Australia) diverse cyanobacteria, eukaryotes and Little Dal group (Canada) algal megafossils.
- 700 million years – During this period life remains in the sea, and the first known multicellular animals appear. They range from jellyfish and segmented worms to coral-like sea pens. The newcomers give rise to a great multiplicity of species. Some species, like the jellyfish, still thrive in the seas today.
- 600 million years - Marine life continues to show variation, producing the first animals with hard outer coverage. Ediacaran metazoans, oldest skeletonized invertebrates.
- 570 million years - Oldest trilobites (Crustacea composed of three lobes or segments) discovered.
- 540 million years - The Paleozoic Era begins. The Cambrian Period, which is the first geological period in the Paleozoic Era, is marked by the appearance of the first simple marine animal and plant life, as shown by fossils found in Wales and Cumberland. Most invertebrate groups appear in the fossil record for the first time. Trilobites are numerous. During this period there were four large continents, North America, Europe, Gondwanaland (South America), and Angara (Eastern Asia). Europe and North America were moving towards each other.
- 450 million years - The Ordovician Period begins. The second period of the Paleozoic Era, characterized by the abundance of invertebrate life and, in rock strata, by deposits of limestone, lead, and zinc.
- 425 million years - The Silurian Period begins. The third period of the Paleozoic Era characterized by the appearance of the first land animals such as scorpions, and extensive coral reefs. This period is so named because its rocks were first found in an area occupied by the Welsh, assumed to be descendants of the Silures.
- 417 million years - Devonian Period begins. The fourth period of the Paleozoic Era characterized by the dominance of fish and insects and the appearance of the first amphibians. This period is so named because its rocks were first studied in Devonshire. Fish evolve to jawed forms such as the placoderms. Others crawl from the water on lobed fins, beginning the line of amphibians. Amphibians are a class that has adapted to both land and sea. Fuzzy plants begin to appear and take root at water's edge.

- 354 million years ago - The Carboniferous Period begins. The fifth period of the Paleozoic Era, characterized by the appearance of the reptiles and great coal formations. As the variation in amphibians continues, reptiles appear. The reptiles lay their eggs on land, and became the first animals to exist entirely free of the water habitat. The warm damp climate produced great lush forests as seed and pollen bearing plants anchor an evolving food chain. These forests later formed rich coal seams.
- 275 million years - The Permian Period begins. The sixth period of the Paleozoic Era characterized by increased reptile life, the formation of the Appalachian mountain ranges, and increased glaciation, especially in the Southern Hemisphere. Reptiles spread and diversify with many becoming flesh-eating predators. Some return to the sea, including the nothosaur, a predatory reptile; others evolve into the earliest mammals.
- 248 million years - The Mesozoic Era begins. All four continents had collided to form one supercontinent, known as Pangaea. Again, sea levels were low and desert conditions widespread, but in between the Devonian and the Permian there was a period of great humidity, the Carboniferous, when swamps and forests dominated the earth. The Triassic Period, the first period of the Mesozoic Era, characterized by the dominance of the reptiles, the appearance of dinosaurs and mammals and the appearance of cycadaceous trees, which are an order of plants like the palms, but having exogenous wood. The Jurassic Period, the second period of the Mesozoic Era, characterized by the dominance of dinosaurs and the appearance of flying reptiles and toothed birds. Dinosaurs diverge into many species.
- 144 million years - The Cretaceous Period begins. North America and Europe had begun to split apart, and the rift between South America and Africa followed shortly afterwards. The sea level was very high. The third period of the Mesozoic Era was characterized by the dying out of toothed birds and dinosaurs, the development of early mammals and flowering plants and the deposit of chalk beds. By the end of the Cretaceous Period the dinosaurs and the majority of plant life had become extinct. The mass extinction has been attributed to a number of different causes including dramatic climatic change caused by a large meteor collision with earth, and continental drift. Among the surviving species are crocodiles, snakes, turtles, birds, and mammals.
- 65 million years - Cenozoic Era begins. With the death of the dinosaurs, mammals proliferate in abundance and evolve into an enormous variety of species. In the Tertiary period of the Cenozoic Era up to about 1.8 million years ago, whales, rats, rodents, bats, antelope, horses and camels appear.
- 54 million years - The Eocene Periods begins. A period characterized by mammalian domination. The primates first appear. Oligocene, the third epoch of the Tertiary Period of the Cenozoic Era, is characterized by the development of the higher animals. Miocene, the fourth epoch of the Tertiary Period in the Cenozoic Era, is characterized by the development of large mountain ranges, the forests recede, and the appearance of grassy plains occurs. The Atlantic Ocean had opened up, South America was an island, as was India, which had broken away from Africa and was moving northwards. This northward movement and subsequent collision with the European continent formed the Himalayas mountain range. Australia was still locked on to Antarctica. The Pliocene is the second epoch of the Neogene period of the Cenozoic era, and is characterized by the development of modern plants and animals.
- 3.6 to 3 million years - The evolution of man begins. Australopithecus afarensis discovery by M. Bush. Possibly the best-known specimen of afarensis is AL 288-1 ("Lucy"), a 3.2 million year old partial skeleton found in 1974 at Hadar, Ethiopia.

- 3 to 2.5 million years - A. africanus: discovery by R. Broom and J.T. Robinson 1947. Site: Sterkfontein, South Africa
- 2 to 1.5 million years - A. robustus: discovery by Quarrym Fourle, 1950. Site: Swartkfans, South Africa
- 2 million years - H. Habilis: discovery by B. Ngeneo, Kenya, and Africa
- 1.8 million - The Pleistocene Period of the Cenozoic Era begins. A. Boisei: discovery by M.D. Leakey 1959. Site: Olduvai Gorge, Tanzania
- 1.5 million years - H. Erectus: discovery by B. Ngeneo, 1975. Site: Koobi Fora, Kenya
- 500,000 to 250,000 years - H. Sapiens (archaic) discovery by Greek villagers, 1960. Site: Petralona, Greece; first use of fire
- 50,000 to 40,000 years - H. Sapiens (Neanderthal): discovery by D. Peyrony and L. Captain, 1909. Site: La Ferrassle, France
- 40,000 years - The continents were almost in their present-day positions. During the Pleistocene epoch there were four major glaciations. During these the sea level was very low, so that the coastline was near the edge of the continental shelf. In between the glaciations there were very warm periods. This period was characterized by the rise and recession of the continental ice sheets and by the appearance of early modern man.
- 28,000 years - H. Sapiens (Cro-Magnon) discovery by French workmen (L. Lartet) 1868. Site: Cro-Magnon, France
- 10,000 years - The Holocene epoch of the Cenozoic Era begins. The last ice age comes to an end and the modern epoch begins. Homo sapiens master agriculture, metallurgy, tool making and other technologies, and thereby come to dominate earth's species. With the advent of modern technology man begins to explore beyond the home planet.

The Evolution of Civilization

History teaches us many lessons. Knowing how we arrived at where we are today should assist us in determining where we will be in the future. Writing a brief history of the world is extremely difficult. The details of history since the first written records of the Sumerians fill thousands of pages. The challenge is to distill this vast amount of information down to an adequate review of the major events, people, ideas and books that have had the greatest impact on human civilization. What follows is my attempt at this distillation of history.

In this evolution of civilization, we start with the Stone Age, the Bronze Age, and the Iron Age. These pre-historic periods are followed by the rise of civilization and the Sumerian, Egyptian, and Babylonian Empires. These are followed by the Persian Empire and the most influential of all empires, the Classical and Hellenistic Greek Empires. The rise and decline of the Roman Empire with its complex history and long duration are discussed next. The early Middle Ages "Dark Ages" and barbarian invasions follow the fall of the Roman Empire. Then the division of the Roman Empire, the Byzantine Empire, and the Great Schism are reviewed. This is followed by the rise of Islam and The Crusades. The late Middle Ages bring with it the Great Famine and the Black Death. Then two more empires take form, the Ottoman Empire and the Austria-Hungarian Empire. The next great age is the Renaissance, followed by the Schism of the West, the Reformation, and the Enlightenment. With the Enlightenment come the modern period and the American Revolution. The French Revolution follows the American Revolution and Napoleon builds the French Empire. One of the most important changes in the history of civilization follows when the Industrial Revolution begins. As society and science advances the Quantum Revolution begins. Then, in one of the darkest periods of human existence, the world is at war with World War I and World War II. The next major war is the Cold War, a result of the quest for world domination by the Soviet

Empire. A new age of science and technology begins with the Space Age, the Computer Age, and the Internet Age. Finally, we see the decline of the Soviet Empire and the end of the Cold War. History is all about the rise and decline of empires, and the intellectual development of the primitive human species. Since today's news is tomorrow's history, it is fitting to end this brief history of the world with the end of the one conflict that had the potential to destroy all of what civilization has accomplished since the Sumerian's built the first empire.

As seen in the origin and evolution of humans, around 40,000 B.C. Homo sapiens began to appear in Africa, Asia, and Europe. About 20,000 years later human migration to North and South America began. It wasn't until about 10,000 B.C. that one of the first settlements was formed at Jericho. Jericho is a town in the West Bank, near the Jordan River and is believed to be the oldest continuously inhabited settlement in the world. The evolutionary universe timeline utilized the geologic time scale up to the Holocene epoch of the Cenozoic Era. Modern human development is generally classified as a progression of ages, such as the Stone Age (2,000,000-3300 B.C.), the Bronze Age (3300-1200 B.C.), the Iron Age (1200-586 B.C.), and so on.

The Paleolithic or the 'Old Stone Age' was the first period of what is sometimes referred to as the three-age system. The Paleolithic period began with the introduction of the first stone tools by hominids such as Homo habilis around 2,000,000 years ago and lasted until the introduction of agriculture. One of the most important features of the Paleolithic period was the evolution of the human species from an apelike creature, or near human, to true Homo sapiens. This development was exceedingly slow and continued through the three successive divisions of the period, the Lower, Middle, and Upper Paleolithic.

Stone tools of the Paleolithic period are of the flake tradition (flake is a thin broad piece of stone detached from a larger mass for use as a tool). Bone implements, such as needles, indicate that crudely sewn furs and skins were used as body coverings. Pit houses, the first man-made shelters, were built, and sculpture and painting originated. The beginnings of communal hunting and fishing are also found during this period, as is the first conclusive evidence of belief systems centering on magic and the supernatural.

The Mesolithic or 'Middle Stone Age' was a transitional period of the Stone Age between the Paleolithic and the Neolithic periods and was characterized by hunting and fishing settlements along rivers and on lakeshores, and microliths which were a tiny blade tool formed as various geometric shapes and often set in a bone or wooden haft (handle).

It was the Neolithic 'New Stone Age' period when humans first ceased being nomadic hunter-gatherers, constantly following their food supply. Traces of the Neolithic Period have been found in Western Europe and date to around 5,000 B.C. The Neolithic Period is marked by the invention and almost universal adoption of techniques for producing food, grinding stone, and making pottery. Thus began a period where humans settled in one location and began growing food, which could be stored for lean seasons. This surplus food in turn led to a great increase in population. The new conditions made possible the accumulation of possessions, the leisure for invention and speculation, the growth of large communities and cities, and the development of more complex social organizations.

As Bertrand Russell has pointed out, "The civilized man is distinguished from the savage mainly by prudence, or, to use a slightly wider term, forethought. He is willing to endure present pains for the sake of future pleasures, even if the future pleasures are rather distant."

The Bronze Age, which dates to around 2000 B.C., followed the Neolithic Period. In this period bronze, which is a mixed metal composed of copper alloy with a certain percentage of tin, came into use as a material for tools and weapons. Because the ores required for the making of bronze and other alloys had a limited distribution, their increase in use led to the breakdown of the self-sufficiency of local Neolithic economies with a resultant growth of trade, which eventually led to the establishment of political units larger than the traditional city-state. The Bronze Age ended around 1000 B.C. when iron was first used for implements.

The Iron Age corresponds to the stage at which iron production was the most sophisticated form of metalworking. Iron's hardness, high melting point and the abundance of iron ore sources made iron more desirable and "cheaper" than bronze and contributed greatly to its adoption as the most commonly used metal. By 3000 B.C. to 2000 B.C. increasing numbers of smelted iron objects appear in Anatolia, Egypt, Mesopotamia and the Indus Valley (Pakistan and North India). The earliest systematic production and use of iron implements appears from the 14th century B.C. in the Hittite Empire.

The Jamdat Nasr period (3000–2850 B.C.) marked the culmination of the prehistoric culture of southern Mesopotamia and led up to the Early Dynastic period and the beginning of recorded history. The earliest known settlers in Mesopotamia were the Sumerians who created an irrigation culture. Mesopotamia means "the land between the rivers" the two rivers being the Tigris and Euphrates Rivers, which are in what is now known as Iraq, and was the site of the world's first civilization, Sumer. In addition to the Sumerians, Mesopotamia was occupied by a series of non-Semitic invaders from the northeastern mountains, and by West Semitic tribes from the adjacent deserts.

The city-states in early Mesopotamia were organized as temple communities headed by a priestly representative of the patron deity or deities of the city. A political assembly of citizens or elders also ruled. Later this primitive combination of democracy and theocracy gave way to rule by a governor with authority over both the religious and political establishment. This structure eventually evolved into highly centralized forms of monarchy. The Sumerian gods took on human forms and in earliest times were closely bound to natural phenomena, including fertility and the forces of nature.

The name Egypt applied in antiquity to the lands of the Nile valley. From earliest times life in Egypt was dependent on the flood of the Nile and its control through the use of irrigation systems. Egyptian history is defined using a dynastic arrangement first formulated by Manetho an Egyptian priest (c. 280 B.C.) who wrote a history in which he grouped the kings of Egypt into 30 dynasties beginning with Menes, founder of Dynasty I, and ending with the conquest of Egypt by Artaxerxes III in 343 B.C. Menes unified the rival kingdoms of Upper and Lower Egypt into a centralized state (c. 3200 B.C.) with the capital residing at Memphis. These dynastic periods are then grouped into a set of Kingdoms beginning with the Old Kingdom (c. 2615-1991 B.C.), which included Dynasties III through VII; followed by the Middle Kingdom (c. 1991-1570) and the New Kingdom (c. 1570-332 B.C.).

In Egypt, from about 3000 to 1750 B.C, a long period of political unification and stability enabled the kings of the Old Kingdom to develop and exploit natural resources, to mobilize both the manpower and the technical skill to build the pyramids, and to encourage sculptors in the production of works of superlative quality. After a period of anarchy and civil war at the end of the Sixth Dynasty the local rulers of Thebes established the so-called Middle Kingdom, restoring an age of political calm in which the arts could again flourish. In Western Asia, Babylonia was the main center and source of civilization, and her moral, though not always her military, hegemony was recognized and accepted by the surrounding countries of Anatolia, Syria, Palestine, Assyria and Elam.

Babylonia was an ancient empire of Mesopotamia. Historically the name Babylonia generally refers to the first dynasty of Babylon established by Hammurabi (c. 1750 B.C.). From the late Uruk and Jamdat Nasr periods up to the rise of Hammurabi, the most significant developments were the invention of writing in the Uruk period, the emergence of the Semites as a political factor under Sargon, and the success of the centralized bureaucracy under the Third Dynasty of Ur. In 538 B.C. the last of the Babylonian rulers surrendered to Cyrus the Great of Persia.

The next great empire to rise was the Persian Empire (c. 558-330 B.C.). The term Persian Empire refers to a series of historical empires that ruled over the Iranian plateau. The political entity, which was ruled by these kingdoms, has been known as Iran 'Land of Aryans' throughout its own-recorded history.

Generally, the earliest entity considered the Persian Empire is Persia's Achaemenid Empire (648-330 B.C.) a united Aryan-indigenous Kingdom that originated in the region known as Pars (Persis) and was formed under Cyrus the Great. The Persians built on the foundations of earlier states, borrowing the political structure of Assyria, and the arts of Babylonia and Egypt. Alexander the Great destroyed the Achaemenid Empire. After Alexander' death most of Persia fell to the Seleucids, who introduced Hellenistic culture, but were unable to maintain control. Successive states in Iran before 1935 are collectively called the Persian Empire by Western historians.

Alexander the Great (356-323 B.C.) King of Macedon, student of Aristotle, and one of the greatest military leaders of all time conquered most of the known world. Alexander first rose to power by putting down uprisings in Thrace and Illyria, and by sacking Thebes. He went on to conquer the Persian Empire, including Anatolia, Syria, Phoenicia, Gaza, Egypt, Bactria, and Mesopotamia, and extended the boundaries of his own empire as far as the Punjab in northern India. While in Egypt he founded the city of Alexandria, which become a great center of Hellenistic and Jewish culture. Alexandria had a great university, and the royal library, which was once the largest library in the world. The royal library was later destroyed on the order of Emperor Theodosius I as part of an effort to destroy pagan religions.

Alexander integrated foreigners into his army and administration, leading some scholars to credit him with a "policy of fusion." He encouraged marriage between his army and foreigners, and practiced it himself. After twelve years of constant military campaigning, Alexander died, possibly of malaria, typhoid, or viral encephalitis. His conquests ushered in centuries of Greek settlement and rule over foreign areas, a period known as the Hellenistic Age.

Traditionally, the Ancient Greek period was taken to begin with the date of the first Olympic Games in 776 B.C., but many historians now extend the term back to about 1000 B.C. The traditional date for the end of the Ancient Greek period is the death of Alexander the Great in 323 B.C. The following period is classified as Hellenistic or the integration of Greece into the Roman Republic in 146 BC.

At various times in its history Greece included all of Epirus, Macedonia, and Thrace, part of Asia Minor, and Magna Graecia. Archaeological remains show that Greece had a long prehistory, dating from the Neolithic Age (c. 4000 B.C.). By the Bronze Age (c. 2800 B.C.) important cultures had developed. The Aegean civilization had several phases, two of the most important being the Minoan civilization and the Mycenaean civilization. These cultures had disappeared by 1100 B.C. The Greek-speaking Achaeans migrated into the Peloponnesus during the 14th and 13th century B.C. The Aeolians and the Ionians apparently preceded the Dorians, who migrated into Greece before 1000 B.C. The Ionians, moving forth, possibly as refugees, possibly as conquerors, settled in the Ionian Islands and on the shores of Asia Minor, which became a part of the Greek world.

After the Dorian invasion, the peoples of Greece, under the influence of the divisive geography and the great variety of tribes, developed the city-state - small settlements that grew into minor kingdoms. Homeric Greece (named for the great epic poet Homer) was dependent on the agriculture of relatively unproductive fields but was already open to the sea. Homer (c. 800 BC) composed the *Iliad* and the *Odyssey*, the earliest literary creations. Still read today, they are the primary source from which all later European literature is derived.

This is also the period of The Seven Sages of Greece (c. 620–550 B.C.), which was the title given by Greek tradition to seven wise ancient Greek men who were philosophers, statesmen and lawgivers. Although the list varies the generally excepted standard list is as follows:

Solon of Athens - "Nothing in excess"

Chilon of Sparta - "Know thyself"

Thales of Miletus - "To bring surety brings ruin." Surety is one who has become legally liable for the debt, default, or failure in duty of another.

Bias of Priene - "Too many workers spoil the work."

Cleobulus of Lindos - "Moderation is the chief good."

Pittacus of Mitylene - "Know thine opportunity." Thine is an archaic word that means that which belongs to thee.

Periander of Corinth - "Forethought in all things."

Although the Greeks never rivaled the Phoenicians or the later Carthaginians and Romans as mariners, the sea offered them an opportunity for expansion and commerce. In the 8th, 7th, and 6th century B.C., the Greeks established colonies, many of which became separate city-states, from the Black Sea and the Bosporus (where Byzantium was founded) to Sicily, southern Italy (Magna Graecia), Mediterranean France, the northern shores of Africa, and Spain.

Because of their independence, the cities developed separately. Monarchies yielded to aristocracies, which were in turn replaced by tyrants, who usually gained power by espousing the cause of the underprivileged and by using force. Although the tyrants usually tried to establish dynasties, the hold established by their families was short-lived. Pisistratus, Hipparchus, and Hippias in Athens and the later Gelon, Dionysius the Elder, and Dionysius the Younger in Sicily were typical tyrants.

On the Greek mainland the tyrannies soon yielded to oligarchies or to democracies tempered by limited citizenship and by slaveholding; it was in Greece that the idea of political democracy came into being. Solon established a democracy in Athens. Militaristic Sparta had a unique constitutional and social development. The warring city-states had a sense of unity; all their citizens considered themselves Hellenes, and religious unity gave rise to leagues known as amphictyonies, notably the great amphictyony centered at Delphi.

The celebration of contests such as the Olympian Games also fostered unity. However, the Ionian cities in Asia Minor received little help from Greece when they revolted (499 B.C.) against Persia, which also threatened the Greek mainland, and the mainland cities were poorly united in the Persian Wars that continued until 449 B.C. Out of these successful wars, however, came the powerful surge of Greek civilization.

Athens, in particular, with the support of the Delian League as the basis of an empire, grew dramatically, and in the age of Pericles (c.495–429 B.C.) developed a culture that left its mark on the course of Western and Eastern civilization. The Delian League, or Confederacy of Delos, is the name given to a confederation of Greek states under the leadership of Athens, with its headquarters at Delos, was founded in 478 B.C. shortly after the final repulse of the expedition of the Persians under Xerxes I.

During this period drama, poetry, sculpture, architecture, mathematics, and philosophy flourished, and there was a vigorous intellectual life. The leading Greeks of the 5th and 4th century B.C. included Aeschylus, Sophocles, Euripides, Aristophanes, Phidias, Myron, Polykleitos, Heraclitus, Socrates, Plato, Aristotle, and Hippocrates. Although Athens succumbed to Sparta in the Peloponnesian War (431–404 B.C.), Athenian thought prevailed, and the culture that was to be the fountainhead of Western civilization lived on.

Plato (429-347 B.C.), student of Socrates, founder of the Academy, and with Aristotle, was one of the most influential philosophers in history. His most famous works include the *Republic*, the *Statesman*, the *Laws*, and the *Symposium*. Central to Plato's philosophy was the theory of ideas. He held that the objects seen with our eyes are, like shadows, only appearances. Behind the object is an idea. Plato also formulated the idea of the philosopher-king, where only the philosopher, who understands the harmony of all parts of the universe with the idea of the good, is capable of ruling the just state. For Plato, a philosopher is a person who loves the vision of truth.

Aristotle (384-322 B.C.), pupil of Plato, and tutor of Alexander the Great, was the first universal man. Proceeding on the conviction that unity and order prevail in the universe, he set out to inventory and describe every aspect of learning including, logic, mechanics, physics, astronomy, meteorology, botany, zoology, psychology, ethics, economics, politics, metaphysics, and literature. He produced over four hundred titles, encompassing virtually all the existing knowledge of his time. For more than a thousand years after his own time, Aristotle was the supreme authority in all-intellectual matters.

Aristotle essentially created the study of logic in a series of treatises known as the *Organon*. The *Organon* includes six treatises including the *Categories* (10 classifications of terms), *On Interpretation* (propositions, truth, modality), *Prior Analytics* (syllogistic logic), *Posterior Analytics* (scientific method and syllogism), *Topics* (rules for effective arguments and debate), and *On Sophistical Refutations* (informal fallacies).

Along with his numerous other firsts, Aristotle was the founder of ethics. His most comprehensive and complete work is the *Nicomachean Ethics*. It is believed the title is taken from the name of the philosopher's son, Nicomachus. Aristotle's aim in the study of ethics is to discover what manor of life is the most desirable and best, in order to determine man's highest good.

A summation of the impact of Aristotle on Western civilization comes from the *Encyclopedia Britannica*:

Aristotle, more than any other thinker, determined the orientation and the content of Western intellectual history. He was the author of a philosophical and scientific system that through the centuries became the support and vehicle for both medieval Christian and Islamic scholastic thought: until the end of the 17th century, Western culture was Aristotelian. And, even after the intellectual revolutions of centuries to follow, Aristotelian concepts and ideas remained embedded in Western thinking.

Hippocrates (460-377 B.C.) is known as the founder of medicine and was regarded as the greatest physician of his time. He based his medical practice on observations and on the study of the human body. He held the belief that illness had a physical and a rational explanation. He rejected the views of his time that considered illness to be caused by superstitions and by possession of evil spirits and disfavor of the gods. He urged a clear differentiation between speculation and guesses on the one hand and exact knowledge obtained from observation on the other. "To know is one thing," he stated, "merely to believe one knows is another. To know is science but merely to believe one knows is ignorance." The best known works of Hippocrates are his *Aphorisms*, which consists of precepts, observations, and summations drawn from his numerous medical treatises.

Hippocrates taught that diet and exercise are more valuable than drugs and that to prevent disease he recommended moderation in working, eating, drinking, exercising, and sleeping. Over two thousand years later, 'all in moderation' is still the best prescription for a happy and healthy life.

When Philip II of Macedon attacked the warring city-states and conquered Greece by defeating the Athenians and the Thebans in the battle of Chaeronea (338 B.C.), he paved the way for his son, Alexander the Great, who spread Greek civilization over the known Western world and across Asia to India. After Alexander's death, his empire was torn apart by his warring generals in the period from 323 to 276 B.C. Some Greek cities formed the Aetolian League to oppose Macedonian rule, but members of the Achaean League took the Macedonian side. The Greek city-states continued their rivalries, and Macedonia under the Antigonids became thoroughly Hellenized.

Incessant warfare made Greece increasingly weak, while Rome grew stronger. In 146 B.C., after the Fourth Macedonian War, the remnants of the Greek states fell definitively into the hands of Rome. Under Roman rule, the cities long retained a measure of independence and intellectual life, but had little political or economic importance. Hellenism, however, had triumphed, and Greek intellectual supremacy continued for many centuries. The Byzantine Empire was thoroughly Greek in origin. Hellenistic civilization, centered at Alexandria, Pergamum, Dura, and other cities, spread Greek influence and preserved the Greek heritage for later ages. The Greeks were the first to write narrative secular history, and the works of Herodotus, Thucydides, Xenophon, and Polybius are basic sources of events and contemporary ideas as well as classics of world literature.

The founding of Rome is attributed to Romulus around 753 B.C. on the east bank of the Tiber. During the early years of Rome, the Etruscans, who originated from Etruria, a city in the North, ruled the city. Around 509 B.C. after the expulsion of the Etruscans, the monarchy became a republic. In 390 B.C. Rome was sacked by the Gaul's, but during the 4th and 3rd centuries B.C. Rome extended its influence over Latium and Etruria, conquered the Samites, and became master of central and southern Italy.

Rome, previously a continental power, began to look seaward in the 3rd century B.C. Sicily, a granary of the ancient world, was an obvious goal, but Rome's rapid conquests could not continue there without meeting the like ambitions of Carthage (a city on the north coast of Africa), which ruled the Western Mediterranean. The Punic Wars were thus inevitable, and in this titanic struggle the fate of Carthage and the destiny of Rome were decided.

The Roman attack on the Carthaginian forces at Messana triggered the first of the Punic Wars. Over the course of the next century, these three major conflicts between Rome and Carthage would determine the course of Western civilization. The wars included a Carthaginian invasion led by Hannibal, which nearly prevented the rise of the Roman Empire. Eventual victory by Rome was a turning point, which meant that the civilization of the ancient Mediterranean would pass to the modern world via Europe instead of Africa.

Carthage was finally defeated at the battle of Zama (202 B.C.), and the Carthaginian commercial empire fell. The Roman general, Scipio Africanus Minor, destroyed the city at the end of The Third Punic War (146 B.C.). A new city was founded in 44 B.C. and under Augustus became an important center of Roman administration. Years later (439-533 A.D.), Carthage became the capital of the Vandals, a Germanic tribe, and was recaptured (533 A.D.) by Flavius Belisarius (505-565 A.D.), one of the greatest generals of the Byzantine Empire.

As a result of the Punic Wars, Rome gained dominion over Spain, Sicily, Sardinia, Corsica, and the northern shores of Africa, indisputable hegemony in the Mediterranean, and an insatiable desire for conquest. After the defeat of Carthage, the Roman republic turned its attention eastward. Philip V of Macedon was defeated after two campaigns (215–205 B.C., 200–197 B.C.), and Antiochus III of Syria was conquered at Magnesia (190 B.C.); eventually the defeat of Perseus (171–168 B.C.) made Macedonia a Roman province. Greece did not become a Roman province, but the brief opposition of the Achaean League was disposed of, and the Greeks became subject to Rome. Egypt became a vassal state to the republic in 168 B.C.

Julius Caesar (c. 102-44 B.C.) was a Roman military and political leader. He played an important part in the transformation of the Roman Republic into the Roman Empire. His conquest of Gaul extended the Roman world all the way to the Atlantic Ocean. He is widely considered to be one of the greatest military geniuses of all time, as well as a brilliant politician and one of the ancient world's strongest leaders. Caesar was considered during his lifetime to be one of the finest orators and authors of prose in Rome leaving such gems as "the die is cast" and "I came, I saw, I conquered."

In the year 46 B.C., the Greek Sosigenes convinced Julius Caesar to reform the Roman calendar to a more manageable form. At this time, Caesar changed the number of days in the months to achieve a 365-day year. In order to "catch up" with the seasons, he also added 90 days to the year 46 B.C. between November and February.

The Julian calendar consisted of cycles of three 365-day years followed by a 366-day leap year. Around 9 B.C., it was found that the priests in charge of computing the calendar had been adding leap years every three years instead of the four decreed by Caesar. As a result of this error, no more leap years were added until 8 A.D.

At Pharsala in 48 B.C., Caesar defeated Pompey, who fled to Egypt. Caesar pursued Pompey to Alexandria, but when he arrived, he learned that Ptolemy's advisor Pothinus had killed Pompey. Caesar camped his army and became involved with the Alexandrine War between Ptolemy and his sister, wife, and co-regnant queen, the Pharaoh Cleopatra VII. Caesar defeated the Ptolemaic forces and installed Cleopatra as ruler, with whom he fathered his only known biological son, Ptolemy XV Caesar, better known as "Caesarion". Caesar and Cleopatra never married.

Caesar's dictatorial powers had aroused great resentment, and he was bitterly criticized by his enemies. When a conspiracy was formed against him, however, it was made up of his friends and protégés, among them Cimber, Casca, Cassius, and Marcus Junius Brutus. On March 15 (the Ides of March), 44 B.C., he was stabbed to death in the senate house. His will left everything to his 18-year-old grandnephew Octavian (later Augustus).

The age of Caesar was a great period in Roman culture, and the cosmopolitan Roman was considered the ideal. Greek was the language of much of the empire, and Greek literature became fashionable. Even more influential was Greek thought which served to destroy Roman religion and to open the Romans to the Eastern cults, which were enormously popular for years. Cicero (106-43 B.C.), the greatest Roman orator, politician, and stoic philosopher was influential during this period.

By the time of Caesar's death (44 B.C.), the territories ruled by Rome included Spain (except part of the northwest), Gaul, Italy, part of Illyria, Macedonia, Greece, west Asia Minor, Bithynia, Pontus, Cilicia, Syria, Cyrenaica, Numidia, Egypt, and Palestine. The rule of Caesar marked an epoch, for it completed the destruction of the republic and laid the foundations of the empire. Caesar's assassination brought anarchy, out of which the Second Triumvirate emerged with the rule of Octavian (Augustus), Antony, and Lepidus.

The Battle of Actium was a naval battle of the Roman Civil War between Mark Antony and Octavian (Caesar Augustus). It was fought on September 2, 31 B.C., near the Roman colony of Actium in Greece (near the modern-day city of Preveza), on the Ionian Sea. Marcus Vipsanius Agrippa commanded Octavian's fleet; while Cleopatra, queen of Egypt, supported Antony's fleet. Octavian's forces decisively defeated Antony and Cleopatra and chased them to Egypt. Both Antony and Cleopatra committed suicide in Alexandria, and Octavian personally took control of Egypt and Alexandria. Octavian's victory led him to become the Princeps Augustus, later considered to be the first Roman Emperor. For this reason the date of the battle is often used to mark the end of the Roman Republic and the beginning of the Roman Empire.

Augustus organized a provincial government and the army, rebuilt Rome, and patronized the arts and letters. His rule began a long period of peace, called the Pax Romana. This period is generally considered to have lasted from 27 B.C., when Augustus Caesar declared an end to the great Roman civil wars of the first century, until either 180 A.D., when emperor Marcus Aurelius died or the death of his son, Commodus in 192 A.D. During this time the Roman Empire was the largest it would ever be; its boundaries included Armenia, middle Mesopotamia, the Arabian desert, the Red Sea, Nubia, the Sahara, the Moroccan mountain mass, the Atlantic Ocean, the Irish Sea, Scotland, the North Sea, the Rhine, the Danube, the Black Sea, and the Caucasus. Under Augustus, the Roman Empire became one great nation.

After the death of Augustus in 14 A.D., there was a series of emperors eventually leading to Commodus (180-192 A.D.) and the decline of the empire. The age of the Praetorian Guard (special force of bodyguards used by Roman emperors) was then at hand, when the rise and fall of emperors was determined by this elite corps of soldiers.

Emperors succeeded one another rapidly in the 3rd century. In 260 A.D. the Persians captured the emperor Valerian, and the empire fell into anarchy. The provinces suffered from increasingly bad government as well as from an outbreak of plague that killed large numbers of the population.

The division of East and West was resumed after the death of Constantine I (337 A.D.) who moved the capital to Byzantium, renamed Constantinople, and today known as Istanbul. By the Edict of Milan (313 A.D.), Constantine granted universal religious tolerance, thus placing Christianity on the same footing as the other religions. He divided the empire administratively into prefectures, dioceses, and provinces. These divisions gave the bishops greater influence by giving them shared authority in civil administration. Under the emperors, Rome had been the center of the world. After the death of Theodosius I (395 A.D.) the empire was permanently divided into Eastern (Byzantine) and Western empires and Rome rapidly lost its political importance.

Attila the Hun (406–453 A.D.) was the last and most powerful king of the Huns. He reigned over what was then Europe's largest empire, from 434 A.D. until his death. His empire stretched from Central Europe to the Black Sea and from the Danube River to the Baltic. During his rule he was among the most feared enemies of the Eastern and Western Roman Empires. He invaded the Balkans twice and encircled Constantinople in the second invasion. He marched through Gaul (later France) as far as Orleans before being turned back at Chalons; and he drove the Western emperor Valentinian III from his capital at Ravenna in 452 A.D.

In 476 A.D. the Goths (Germanic tribes), under Odoacer, deposed the last emperor of the West, Romulus Augustus. This date is commonly accepted as the end of the West Roman Empire.

The fall of the Roman Empire was more of a gradual decline then a fall, and was the result of several factors including; the size and extent of the empire, which placed a heavy burden on government and defense, a deluge of barbarians, which overwhelmed the Roman world, a general decline in morals and values and increased corruption, and economic collapse due to a shortage of currency, and an oppressive and erratic system of taxation.

The decline of Rome marked no abrupt ending of an era, for the barbarians that filled the gap left by the disappearance of the old order were quick in accepting and adapting what vital elements remained of it. The survival of the East Roman Empire, or Eastern Empire, and the creation of the Holy Roman Empire showed how much vitality was left in the imperial ideal. Italy itself, however, did not recover from the fall of Rome until the 19th century.

The Middle Ages, otherwise known as the medieval period, formed the middle period in a traditional schematic division of European history into three "ages": the classical civilization of Antiquity, the Middle Ages, and Modern Times. The Middle Ages of Western Europe are commonly dated from the end of the Western Roman Empire (5th century) to the rise of national monarchies, the start of European overseas exploration, the humanist revival, and the Protestant Reformation starting in 1517. These various changes all mark the beginning of the Early Modern period that preceded the Industrial Revolution.

As the political unity of the Roman Empire dwindled in Western Europe during and after the 3rd century, its territories were settled by succeeding waves of "barbarian" tribal confederations, some of whom rejected the classical culture of Rome, while others, like the Goths, admired it and considered themselves the heirs of Rome. Prominent among these peoples were the Huns, Avars and Magyars with the large number of Germanic and later Slavic peoples. While the Western Roman Empire went into decline, the Eastern half of the old empire still continued to function. East Romans thought of themselves as the heirs to the Roman legacy in all ways, and thought their version of Christianity was more legitimate than that of the Catholic west. Constantinople was one of the two capitals of the later empire, and was able to avoid capture by the barbarian tribes.

The Dark Ages were the early medieval period of Western European history. The term refers to the time (476–800 A.D.) when there was no Roman (or Holy Roman) emperor in the West; or, more generally, to the period between about 500 and 1000 A.D., which was marked by frequent warfare and a virtual disappearance of urban life. It is generally accepted that Petrarch invented the term "Dark Age" in the 1300s.

Between the 5th and 8th centuries new political and social systems developed across the lands of the former empire. These new systems were based on powerful regional noble families, and the newly established kingdoms of the Ostrogoths in Italy, Visigoths in Spain and Portugal, Franks and Burgundians in Gaul and Western Germany, and Saxons in England. The Christian Church, the only centralized institution to survive the fall of the Western Roman Empire intact, was the major unifying cultural influence, preserving its selection from Latin learning, maintaining the art of writing, and a centralized administration through its network of bishops.

Outside the de-urbanized remains of cities, the power of central government was greatly reduced. Consequently government authority, and responsibility for military organization, taxation, and law and order, was delegated to provincial and local lords, who supported themselves directly from the proceeds of the territories over which they held military, political and judicial power. In this were the beginnings of the feudal system. The feudal system was a system of land tenure and political structure based on the personal relationship of lord and vassal.

The High Middle Ages would see the return of centralized power, and the growth of new "national" identities, as strong rulers sought to eliminate competition (and potential threat to their rule) from powerful feudal nobles. Well-known examples of such consolidation include the Albigensian Crusade and the Wars of the Roses.

The Albigensian Crusade (1209-1229 A.D.) was a brutal 20-year military campaign initiated by the Roman Catholic Church to eliminate the religion practiced by the Cathars of Languedoc, which the Roman Catholic hierarchy considered heretical. It is historically significant for a number of reasons: the violence inflicted was extreme even by medieval standards; the church offered legally sanctioned dominion over conquered lands to northern French nobles and the King of France. Finally, the Albigensian Crusade had a role in the creation and institutionalization of the Medieval Inquisition.

The Wars of the Roses is the traditional name given to the intermittent struggle (1455–1485 A.D.) for the throne of England between the noble houses of York (whose badge was a white rose) and Lancaster (later associated with the red rose).

In the east, the Eastern Roman Empire (Byzantine Empire) maintained a form of Christianized Roman rule in the lands of Asia Minor, Greece and the Slavic territories bordering Greece, and in Sicily and southern Italy.

The Holy Roman Empire was a successor state to the empire founded in 800 by Charlemagne, who revived the title of Roman emperor in the West. The Holy Roman Empire was the designation for the political entity that originated at the coronation as emperor (962 A.D.) of the German king Otto I, and endured until the renunciation (1806 A.D.) of the imperial title by Francis II. The term itself did not come into usage until several centuries after Otto's accession.

Charlemagne was crowned emperor in Rome by the Pope on Christmas Day, 800 A.D. His rule briefly united much of modern day France, Western Germany and northern Italy. For 200 years after Charlemagne's death, Europe was in conflict, with East and West competing for power and influence in non-Christian northern Europe, and power devolving to more localized authorities.

The Byzantine Empire (527-1025 A.D.) was the successor state to the Roman Empire, also called the Eastern Empire and East Roman Empire. It was named after Byzantium, which Emperor Constantine I rebuilt (330 A.D.) as Constantinople and made the capital of the entire Roman Empire. Although not foreseen at the time, a division into Eastern and Western empires became permanent after the accession in 395 A.D. of Honorius in the West and Arcadius in the East.

The Great Schism divided Christianity into Western Catholicism and Eastern Orthodoxy. The word schism means a division or split. Though normally dated to 1054 A.D., when Pope Leo IX and Patriarch Michael I excommunicated each other, the East-West Schism was actually the result of an extended period of estrangement between the two Churches. There were two major issues that led to the Great Schism. The first were disputes over papal authority. The Pope claimed he held authority over the four Eastern patriarchs, while the four Eastern patriarchs claimed that the primacy of the Patriarch of Rome was only honorary, and thus he had authority only over Western Christians. The second was over the insertion of the filioque clause into the Nicene Creed. Filioque "and from the son" is a Latin work added to the creeds in the Western Church in the Middle Ages to state that the Holy Spirit arises from both the Father and the Son. There were other, less significant catalysts for the Schism, including variance over liturgical practices and conflicting claims of jurisdiction. The Church split along doctrinal, theological, linguistic, political, and geographic lines, and the fundamental breach has never been healed.

In 1095 A.D., Pope Urban II called together a council of bishops and clergy in Clermont in France. There, amid a crowd of thousands who had come to hear his words, he urged all those present to take up arms under the banner of the Cross and launch a holy war to recover Jerusalem (the Turks had captured Jerusalem in 1076) and the east from the 'infidel' Muslims. Enticed by the offering of eternal salvation to all those who took part in the great enterprise, many promised to carry out the Pope's command, and word of the Crusade soon spread across Europe.

The Crusades were a series of military campaigns, usually sanctioned by the Papacy that took place during the 11th through 13th centuries. Originally, they were Roman Catholic endeavors to re-capture the Holy Land from the Muslims, but some were directed against other Europeans, such as the Fourth Crusade against Constantinople, the Albigensian Crusade against the Cathars of southern France, and the Northern Crusades.

Byzantium was arguably the only stable state in Europe during the Middle Ages. Its expert military and diplomatic power ensured inadvertently that Western Europe remained safe from many of the more devastating invasions from Eastern peoples, at a time when the Western Christian kingdoms might have had difficulty containing it. Constantly under attack during its entire existence, the Byzantines shielded Western Europe from Persians, Arabs, Seljuk Turks, and for a time, the Ottomans. The collapse of the empire opened the way for the vast expansion of the Ottoman Empire to Vienna, and also enabled Ivan III of Russia, son-in-law of Constantine XI, to claim a theoretical succession to the imperial title.

The Ottomans arose from the obscure reaches of Anatolia in the west of Turkey; these Western Turks were called the Oghuz. They had come primarily as settlers during the reign of the Seljuks in Turkey (1098-1308). The Ottoman Empire was established by the tribe of Kinsik Oghuz Turks and Osman I in Western Anatolia, and was ruled by the Osmanli dynasty, the descendants of those Turks. By 1300 the Ottomans ruled a small military state in Western Anatolia, about the time the Seljuk state was falling apart. By 1400, however, the Ottomans had managed to extend their influence over much of Anatolia and even into Byzantine territory in Eastern Europe.

In 1402, the Ottomans moved their capital to Edirne, where they threatened the last great bastion of the Byzantine Empire, its capital, Constantinople. In 1453, Sultan Mehmed (1451-1481), who was called "The Conqueror," finally took this one last remnant of Byzantium and renamed it, Istanbul. From that point onwards, the capital of the Ottoman Europe would remain fixed in Istanbul and, under the patronage of the Ottoman sultans, become one of the wealthiest and most cultured cities of the early modern world.

The Ottoman Empire expanded under Sultan Selim I (1512-1520), but it was under his son, Sultan Suleyman (1520-1566), called "The Lawmaker" in Islamic history and "The Magnificent" in Europe, that the empire would reach its greatest expansion. At the height of its power in the 16th century, it included Anatolia, the Middle East, parts of North Africa, and much of southeastern Europe to the Caucasus. The Ottomans established an empire over European territory and established Islamic traditions and culture that last to the current day (the Muslims in Bosnia are the last descendants of the Ottoman presence in Europe).

The Late Middle Ages is a term used by historians to describe European history in the period of the 14th and 15th centuries (1300–1500 A.D.). The Late Middle Ages were preceded by the High Middle Ages, and followed by the Renaissance or Modern Era. The Great Famine of 1315-1317 A.D. was the first of a series of large-scale crises that struck Europe early in the 14th century, causing millions of deaths over an extended number of years and marking a clear end to an earlier period of growth and prosperity during the 11th through the 13th centuries. Starting with bad weather in the spring of 1315 A.D., universal crop failures lasted through 1316 until the summer of 1317; Europe did not fully recover until 1322. During the next few years, the European economy slowly improved, and agricultural and manufacturing production eventually reached pre-famine levels. This return to normalcy suddenly ended with The Black Death of 1347-1351.

In the early 1330s an outbreak of deadly bubonic plague occurred in China. The bubonic plague mainly affects rodents, but fleas can transmit the disease to people. Plague, is caused by bacteria called Yersinia pestis. Initial symptoms include fever, headache, and general illness, followed by the development of painful, swollen regional lymph nodes (small bean-shaped structures that occur throughout the body and produce white blood cells, and filter bacteria and other foreign particles). The disease progresses rapidly and the bacteria can invade the bloodstream, producing severe illness, called plague septicemia. Progression leads to blood infection and, finally, to lung infection. The infection of the lung is termed plague pneumonia, and it can be transmitted to others through the expulsion of droplets by coughing. The incubation period of primary pneumonic plague is 1 to 3 days and is characterized by development of an overwhelming pneumonia with high fever, cough, bloody sputum, and chills. For plague pneumonia patients, the death rate is over 50 percent.

In October of 1347, several Italian merchant ships returned from a trip to the Black Sea, one of the key links in trade with China. When the ships docked in Sicily, many of those on board were already dying of plague. Within days the disease spread to the city and the surrounding countryside.

In winter the disease seemed to disappear, but only because fleas, which were now helping to carry it from person to person, are dormant then. Each spring, the plague attacked again, killing new victims. After five years 25 million people were dead - one-third of the European population.

Medieval society never recovered from the results of the plague. So many people had died that there were serious labor shortages all over Europe. This led workers to demand higher wages, but landlords refused those demands. By the end of the 1300s peasant revolts broke out in England, France, Belgium and Italy. France and England experienced especially serious peasant uprisings including the Jacquerie (the uprising of the French peasants against the nobility in 1358 A.D.), the Peasants' Revolt (the revolt was precipitated by heavy-handed attempts to enforce the poll tax in England), and the Hundred Years' War.

It was during this same century (1454 A.D.) when Johannes Gutenberg, a German craftsman and inventor, developed a method of printing from movable type that was used without important change until the 20th century. The unique elements of his invention consisted of a mold, with which type could be cast precisely and in large quantities; a type-metal alloy; a new press derived from those used in wine making, papermaking and bookbinding; and an oil-based printing ink. Although paper and printing were first developed in China, none of these features existed in Chinese or Korean printing, or in the existing European technique of stamping letters on various surfaces, or in woodblock printing. The masterpiece of his press was the publication of the Gutenberg Bible. Its production marked the beginning of the mass production of books in the West.

In the 16th and 17th centuries, the Ottoman Empire was among the world's most powerful political entities, with the powers of Eastern Europe constantly threatened by its steady advance through the Balkans and the southern part of the Polish-Lithuanian Commonwealth. Its navy was a powerful force in the Mediterranean. On several occasions the Ottomans invaded central Europe, in its attempts to conquer the Habsburg domain, and were only repulsed by coalitions of European powers.

The Habsburg family, which can be traced to the 10th century, originally held lands in Alsace and in northwest Switzerland. Otto (c. 1111 A.D.) took the name Hapsburg from a castle near Aargau, Switzerland, when he was designated count. From Southwest-Germany the family extended its influence and holdings to the southeastern reaches of the Holy Roman Empire, roughly today's Austria (1278-1382). Within only two or three generations, the Habsburgs had managed to secure a grasp on the imperial throne that would last for centuries.

In 1867 the Hapsburg lands were reorganized as the Austro-Hungarian Monarchy. The assassination of heir apparent Francis Ferdinand precipitated World War I; the death (1916) of Francis Joseph left his grandnephew, Emperor Charles I, to witness the defeat of the Austria-Hungary Empire, which was dissolved immediately after Charles's abdication in 1918. Charles's son, Archduke Otto, succeeded him as head of the Hapsburgs. After World War I, members of the family who refused to renounce the throne were exiled from Austria; the exile was repealed in 1996.

The Battle of Vienna in 1683 was the first large-scale battle of the Habsburg-Ottoman Wars, yet with the most far-reaching consequences. The battle pitted a 30,000-man Polish relief army under Jan III Sobieski King of the Polish-Lithuanian Commonwealth, who was made Commander in Chief, and the Habsburg army of about 40,000 troops and their allies, led by Charles V, Duke of Lorraine, against the Ottoman army, commanded by Grand Vizier Merzifonlu Kara Mustafa Pasha, which numbered approximately 138,000 men, although a large number of them played no part in the battle. The siege itself began on July 14, 1683, and the decisive battle took place on September 12, when the Muslim armies were defeated at the Gates of Vienna. It was during this period that the croissant was invented, the first bagel was made, and the first coffee house opened in Vienna.

The battle marked the turning point in the 300-year struggle between the forces of the Central European kingdoms, and the Ottoman Empire. Over the sixteen years following the battle, the Habsburgs of Austria, and their allies gradually occupied and dominated southern Hungary and Transylvania, which had been largely cleared by Turkish forces.

The dissolution of the Ottoman Empire was a consequence of World War I when Allied forces, including the Arabs, eventually defeated Ottoman forces in the Middle East. At the end of the war the Ottoman government collapsed and the empire was divided among the victorious powers. Subsequent years saw the declaration of new states from the remnants of the Ottoman Empire, one of which was the Republic of Turkey.

During the period from 1378 to 1417 the second great schism (Schism of the West) divided the Roman Catholic Church. There was no question of faith or practice involved; the schism was a matter of persons and politics. The Schism of the West differed from the Eastern Schism (The Great Schism). The latter was a real revolt against the supreme authority of the Church, fomented by the ambition of the patriarchs of Constantinople, favored by the Greek emperors, supported by the Byzantine clergy and people, and lasting nine centuries. The Western Schism was only a temporary misunderstanding, even though it compelled the Church for forty years to seek its true head; it was fed by politics and passions, and was terminated by the assembling of the councils of Pisa and Constance.

There were two lines of popes. The popes of Rome were Urban VI (1378–89), Boniface IX (1389–1404), Innocent VII (1404–6), and Gregory XII (1406–1415). Those of the rival line at Avignon were Clement VII (1378–1394) and Benedict XIII (1394–1417). Schism within schism ensued. Martin V was elected, and the schism was at an end. The main effects of the schism were to delay needed reforms in the church and to give rise to the conciliar theory (pertaining to teachings of General Councils of the Roman Catholic Church of which there have been 21 in the church's history), which was revived at the Council of Basel.

The Middle Ages was also a period of great discoveries and colonization by Portugal, and the European nations England, France, Spain and the Netherlands. Christopher Columbus (1451-1506) a Genoese navigator, with the backing of the Spanish monarchs Ferdinand V and Isabella I, reached the Americas in 1492. Columbus is commonly credited as "the" European discoverer of the Americas. Historians and archeologists have discovered evidence suggesting that Vikings landed in North America in the eleventh century, 500 years before Columbus, and established settlements along the northeastern coast of the continent. The voyage of Columbus marked the beginning of the European exploration and colonization of the Americas.

The great discoveries continued when in 1513 Spanish conquistador Vasco Núñez de Balboa (c. 1475-1519), crossed the Isthmus of Panama and discovered the Pacific Ocean, and in one of the greatest feats of the period, Ferdinand Magellan became the first circumnavigator of the world, proving that the earth was indeed round. Near the end of his voyage, Magellan was killed in action during a battle in the Philippines on April 27, 1521, when warriors of Lapu-Lapu, a chieftain of Mactan, defeated Spanish sailors under Portuguese command.

The early modern period (1500-1800 A.D.) is a term used by historians to refer to the period that followed the Middle Ages and applies primarily to Western Europe and the period of colonization, and includes the period between the Middle Ages and the Industrial Revolution. The early modern period is characterized by the rise to importance of science, cumulative and increasingly rapid technological progress, secularized civic politics and capitalist economics, all monitored by the nation state. As such it represents the diminution and/or abolition of Christian theocracy, feudalism, and serfdom.

In the traditional view, the Renaissance is understood as an historical age that was preceded by the Middle Ages and followed by the Reformation. According to the usual description, the Italian Renaissance of the 15th century, spreading through the rest of Europe, represented a reconnection of the west with classical antiquity, the absorption of knowledge—particularly mathematics—from Arabic, the return of experimentalism, the focus on the importance of living well in the present (e.g. humanism), an explosion of the dissemination of knowledge brought on by printing and the creation of new techniques in art, poetry, and architecture, which led to a radical change in the style and substance of the arts and literature. The Renaissance view of this period represents Europe emerging from a long period as a backwater, and the rise of commerce and exploration. The Italian Renaissance is often labeled as the beginning of the "modern" epoch.

The term Rebirth (Rinascita), is used to indicate the flourishing of artistic and scientific activities starting in Italy in the mid 1300's, it was first used by the Italian artist Giorgio Vasari (1511-1574) in his encyclopedia of artistic biographies *Vite*, published in 1550. The term Renaissance is the French translation, used by French historian Jules Michelet, and expanded upon by Swiss historian Jacob Burckhardt (both in the 1860s). Rebirth is used in two ways. First, it means rediscovery of ancient classical texts and learning and their applications in the arts and sciences. Second, it means that the results of these intellectual activities created a revitalization of European culture in general. Thus it is possible to speak of the Renaissance in two different but meaningful ways: A rebirth of classical learning and knowledge through the rediscovery of ancient texts, and also a rebirth of European culture in general.

It was during the Renaissance that artists developed the rules of perspective. Perspective is the way objects appear to the eye based on their spatial attributes, which made paintings look three-dimensional. Additional techniques that were developed during this period were the use of oils, and shading to give objects depth and realism. Artists such as Michelangelo (1475-1564), Sandro Botticelli (1445–1510), Leonardo Da Vinci (1452-1519), and Raphael (1483–1520), transformed the production of great art.

Beginning in the latter half of the 15th century, a humanist faith in classical scholarship led to the search for ancient texts that would increase current scientific knowledge. Among the works rediscovered were the brilliant anatomist and physiologist Galen's treatise (131-201 B.C.) *On the Usefulness of the Parts of the Human Body*, and Ptolemy's (85-165 A.D.) *Almagest*. Botany, zoology, and chemistry, all advanced during the Renaissance as a result of the study of ancient texts. Scientific thinkers such as Nicolaus Copernicus, Galileo Galilei, Tycho Brahe, and Johannes Kepler made significant contributions to astronomy.

In 1543, Nicolas Copernicus (1473-1543) published *De revolutionibus orbium coelestium (Revolutions of the Heavenly Bodies)*. Because Copernicus' heliocentric theory of the planets defied 1,500 years of tradition, some historians mark the publication date of *De revolutionibus* as the beginning of the "scientific revolution." It wasn't until 1835 that his work was taken off the list of books banned by the Vatican.

Galileo Galilei (1564–1642) was an Italian physicist, astronomer, and philosopher, who made major contributions to the scientific revolution. His achievements include improvements to the telescope, a variety of astronomical observations, and effective support for Copernicanism. He has been referred to as the "father of modern astronomy", as the "father of modern physics", and as "father of science." His experimental work is widely considered complementary to the writings of Francis Bacon in establishing the modern scientific method. The work of Galileo is considered to be the first significant break from that of Aristotle. In addition, his conflict with the Roman Catholic Church is taken as a major early example of the conflict of authority and freedom of thought, particularly with science, in Western society.

With the invention of printing new ideas swept across Europe, the great thinkers and writers of the time could finally share their ideas with the general public. Two writers who stand out during this period are Machiavelli and Shakespeare. Niccolo Machiavelli (1469-1527) is generally considered the creator of modern political science. His 1513 book *The Prince* is a landmark work in the history of political power. William Shakespeare (c. 1564-1616) is the preeminent literary figure of the Western world. During England's Elizabethan period he wrote dozens of plays, many of which continue to dominate world theaters 400 years later.

This was also a period of revolution in faith, eventually leading to the division of the Christian world. The Protestant Reformation was a movement, which emerged in the 16th century as a series of attempts to reform the Roman Catholic Church in Western Europe. Martin Luther and his 95 Theses started the main front of the reformation. The reformation ended in division and the establishment of new institutions, most importantly Lutheranism, the Reformed churches, the Anabaptists, a radical branch whose name means "those who baptize again", and the Society of Jesus or the Jesuits. It also led to the Counter-Reformation within the Roman Catholic Church.

The Protestant gains in Europe and the chaotic evolution of the Counter-Reformation finally forced Pope Paul III to convene a council in Trent in order to define church doctrine once and for all. This council, called the Council of Trent, worked on these problems in three separate sessions from 1545 to 1563. The council eventually advised some far-reaching reforms in the abuses practiced by the church, such as the selling of indulgences, forcing bishops to reside in the region they presided over, and forbad the selling of church offices. In addition, the Council advised that a seminary be built in every diocese so that church doctrine could be fully and accurately represented. The rift between Catholics and Protestants would lead to the break up of large European empires into the modern nation-state system.

Seventeenth Century enlightenment thought was a continuation of the Renaissance. The two great innovations of the Enlightenment were the development of empirical thought and the mechanistic worldview. Empiricism is based on the notion that human observation is a reliable indicator of the nature of phenomena; repeated human observation can produce reasonable expectations about future natural events. In the mechanistic worldview, the universe is regarded as a machine in which all natural phenomena can be explained by physical causes. In this agnostic view, the universe functions by natural and predictable rules; although God may have created the universe, he does not interfere in its day-to-day functions.

The first major thinker of the seventeenth century to apply new methods to the human sciences was Thomas Hobbes (1588-1679) whose book *Leviathan* is one of the most revolutionary and influential works on political theory in European history. *Leviathan* presents a bleak picture of human beings in the state of nature, where life is "solitary, poor, nasty, brutish, and short." Fear of violent death is the principal motive that causes people to create a state by contracting (the social contract) to surrender their natural rights and to submit to an absolute authority of a sovereign.

René Descartes (1596-1650) is one of the most important Western philosophers of the past few centuries. Descartes, known for his famous statement, "I think, therefore I am" founded 17th century continental rationalism, later advocated by Baruch Spinoza and Gottfried Leibniz, and opposed by the empiricist school of thought, consisting of Hobbes, Locke, Hume and Berkeley. Mathematical methods were introduced into philosophy by Leibniz, Spinoza and Descartes who were all versed in mathematics as well as philosophy, with Descartes and Leibniz making significant contributions to science and mathematics. As the inventor of the Cartesian coordinate system, Descartes founded analytic geometry, the bridge between algebra and geometry crucial to the invention of the calculus and analysis. Gottfried Wilhelm Leibniz (1646–1716), known for his independent development of calculus, is often described as the last universalist, having contributed to virtually all fields of scholarly interest of his time, including law, history, theology, politics, engineering, geology, physics, and perhaps most importantly philosophy, mathematics, and logic.

Perhaps the most important philosopher, besides Descartes, of human sciences in the seventeenth century was John Locke (1632-1704). He wrote two far-reaching influential philosophical works, *An Essay Concerning Human Understanding* (1690) and *Two Treatises on Government* (1690). Locke believed that natural law dictated that all human beings were fundamentally equal. For Locke, the purpose of authority is to protect human equality and freedom; this is why social groups agree to a "social contract" that places an authority over them. When that authority ceases to care for the welfare, independence, and equality of individual humans, the social contract is broken and it is the duty of the members of society to overthrow that ruler.

Another important step in the evolution of scientific thought came with Carl Linnaeus and his *Systema Naturae* published in 1735. Known as the father of modern taxonomy (the study of the general principles of scientific classification: systematics), his binomial nomenclature for the classification of plants and animals first described in *Systema Naturae* remains unchanged and in use today.

The Baroque Period (1600-1750) and the Classical Period (1750-1825) was the pinnacle of musical genius and creativity. The great composers or these periods include Antonio Vivaldi (1678–1741) *Le quattro stagioni* (The Four Seasons), Johann Sebastian Bach (1685–1750) *The Art of the Fugue* and *The Goldberg Variations*, Domenico Scarlatti (1685–1757) Sonatas for Harpsichord, George Friedrich Handel (1685–1759) *The Messiah* and *Water Music*, Wolfgang Amadeus Mozart (1756-1791) *The Marriage of Figaro* and *Eine Kleine Nachtmusik* (a little night music), Franz Joseph Haydn (1732-1809) *The Creation* and *The Seasons* and over 100 symphonies, and Ludwig van Beethoven (1770–

1827) *Symphony No. 5., and the Moonlight* and *Pathetique* sonatas. Unequaled to this day, the Baroque and Classical periods produced the finest composers and music in the history of civilization.

The most significant event of the modern period was the American Revolution in 1776. The American Revolution was the struggle by which the Thirteen Colonies on the Atlantic seaboard of North America won independence from Great Britain and became the United States. It is also called the American War of Independence.

The British government, like other imperial powers in the 18th century, favored a policy of mercantilism. Mercantilism is an economic system, which developed during the decay of feudalism to unify and increase the power and especially the monetary wealth of a nation by a strict governmental regulation of the entire national economy. This was usually accomplished through policies designed to secure an accumulation of gold bullion, a favorable balance of trade, the development of agriculture and manufacturing, and the establishment of foreign trading monopolies. Various laws such as the Navigation Acts were intended to regulate commerce in the British interest. In June 1767, The English Parliament passed the Townsend Acts, imposing a new series of taxes on the colonists to offset the costs of administering and protecting the American colonies. The Townsend Acts were followed by the Coercive Acts which further limited the rights of the colonists. As the British became more repressive, the colonists became more rebellious.

In January 1776, Thomas Paine wrote his famous pamphlet, *Common Sense.* In three months 120,000 copies had been purchased. As Robert Downs, author of *Books that Changed the World* points out "nothing comparable to *Common Sense* in its immediate impact is to be found in the history of literature." It was a clarion call to the American colonists to fight for their independence. Paine's philosophy of government is clear when he states: "Government, even in its best state, is but a necessary evil; in its worst state an intolerable one," and in his view that the origin and rise of government was "rendered necessary by the inability of moral virtue to govern the world."

The "shot heard round the world" fired at Lexington on April 19, 1775 began the war for American Independence. On the morning of April 19, 1775, colonists and British soldiers had exchanged shots, men had been killed, and a revolution had begun. On the very day (May 10, 1775) that the Second Continental Congress met, Ethan Allen and his Green Mountain Boys, together with a force under Benedict Arnold, took Fort Ticonderoga from the British, and two days later Seth Warner captured Crown Point. Boston was under British siege. Before that siege was climaxed by the costly British victory usually called the battle of Bunker Hill (June 17, 1775) the Congress had chosen (June 15, 1775) George Washington as Commander in Chief of the Continental Armed Forces. The war officially ended eight and a half years later September 3, 1783 with the Treaty of Paris, which formally recognized the independence of the United States.

The Declaration of Independence is conventionally dated July 4, 1776. Drawn up by Thomas Jefferson, it was to be one of the great historical documents of all time. The political philosophy of the Declaration was not new; John Locke and the Continental philosophers had already expressed its ideals of individual liberty. What Jefferson did was to summarize this philosophy in "self-evident truths" and set forth a list of grievances against the King in order to justify before the world the breaking of ties between the colonies and the mother country. The beginning of the second paragraph summed up the ideals of a new nation:

We hold these truths to be self-evident, that all men are created equal, that they are endowed by their Creator with certain unalienable Rights that among these are Life, Liberty and the pursuit of Happiness. -- That to secure these rights, Governments are instituted among Men, deriving their just powers from the consent of the governed, --That whenever any Form of Government becomes destructive of these ends, it is the Right of the People to alter or to abolish it, and to institute new Government, laying its foundation on such principles and organizing its powers in such form, as to them shall seem most likely to effect their Safety and Happiness.

The 55 delegates who attended the Constitutional Convention were a distinguished body of men who represented a cross section of 18th-century American leadership. Almost all of them were well-educated men of means who were dominant in their communities and states, and many were also prominent in national affairs. Virtually every one had taken part in the Revolution; at least 29 had served in the Continental forces, most of them in positions of command.

The Honorable Jack Brooks, Chairman, Committee on the Judiciary of the House of Representatives provides a fine summation of their efforts, the United States Constitution:

The genius of the Founding Fathers is reflected in the intricate set of checks and balances the Constitution builds into our system of government. By preventing any one of the three branches from acquiring dominance over the others, these structural and procedural safeguards have preserved a fundamental, albeit not always neat, separation of powers. Moreover, although developed over two centuries ago, they continue to perform this essential function despite the dramatic societal, technological, economic, and political changes in the United States over the past two centuries. The Framers made the conscious decision of choosing constitutional generality over the overly specific civil codes of the European nations. By so doing, they wisely built in a flexibility to accommodate change (through the amendment process) so that a living instrument of government could be passed down to succeeding generations.

Just as important as the governmental structure established by Articles I through VII of the Constitution are the personal freedoms guaranteed by the Bill of Rights and the 13th, 14th, and 15th Amendments. Approved by the First Congress in 1789 and ratified by the States in 1791, the first ten amendments to the Constitution--the Bill of Rights--assure basic individual liberties essential to a free and democratic society. In the aftermath of the Civil War, the 13th, 14th, and 15th Amendments continued the mission of the Bill of Rights by abolishing slavery, by assuring citizens due process in actions taken under color of State governments, and by taking the first steps toward providing suffrage for citizens regardless of race. These Constitutional guarantees have not only stood as a bulwark against governmental abuses in this country, but they have also provided inspiration to people around the world in their quest for individual freedom and liberty.

The French Revolution (1789-1799) followed the American Revolution. French society was divided into three Estates or Orders. The First Estate consisted of the clergy and the Second Estate the nobility. At the bottom of this hierarchy was the vast Third Estate, which basically meant everybody else. This social structure was based on custom and tradition, but more important, it was also based on inequalities, which were sanctioned by the force of law. The causes of the French Revolution are many. The main reasons typically include corruption, poor financial management, and the encouragement of the Enlightenment and the American Revolution.

During this time, republicanism replaced the absolute monarchy in France, and the French sector of the Roman Catholic Church was forced to undergo radical restructuring. While France would oscillate among republic, empire, and monarchy for 75 years after the First Republic fell to a coup d'état by Napoleon Bonaparte, the revolution nonetheless spelled a definitive end to the Ancien Régime. It is widely seen as a major turning point in continental European history, from the age of absolutism to that of the citizenry as the dominant political force.

Napoleon Bonaparte (1769-1821) was a general of the French Revolution, the ruler of France as First Consul of the French Republic from 1799 to 1804, then as Emperor of the French Empire and King of Italy under the name Napoleon I from 1804 to 1814.

In 1801 Napoleon signed the Concordat with Pope Pius VII. The Concordat ended the schism between the French government and the Catholic Church, by returning lands to the clergy that were confiscated from the Church during the anti-clerical periods of the French Revolution, and by assuring the Pope that France would remain a Catholic country. Relations between France and Britain were another matter as competition between the two colonial powers escalated.

The Berlin Decree (1806) was issued in Berlin by Napoleon I in answer to the British blockade, initiating the Continental System. Claiming that the British blockade of purely commercial ports was contrary to international law, Napoleon retaliated by declaring the British Isles under blockade and forbidding any trade to or from them. The Continental System was Napoleon's plan to stop all shipping of British goods into Europe. The Continental System resulted in a British blockade of all European shipping, and ended up hurting France more than Britain. By trying to spread the Continental System into Spain, Napoleon and France had to endure the constant harassment of the disastrous Peninsular War (1808-1814). The Treaty of Tilsit in 1807 between France, Russia, and Prussia, left Napoleon master of the continent. The Treaty required Russia and Prussia to abide by the Continental System.

When Czar Alexander of Russia rejected the Continental System Napoleon made a fatal mistake, one that would be repeated by Hitler years later, and attacked Russia with the 500,000-man Grand Armée. Without a formal declaration of war, Napoleon's army crossed the Niemen River into Russia during the night of June 23, 1812, with the intention of penetrating between the two Russian armies and crush them in rapid succession, the French army moved swiftly. Czar Alexander hoped to halt military actions and avoid war, but his delegation to Napoleon was rebuffed. The Russians employed a strategy to initiate a slow retreat toward the interior. By September Napoleon reached Moscow, but by October, Napoleon and his troops were facing enormous difficulties. His army was exhausted and short of supplies and shelter, and Russian forces disrupted supply lines, logistics, and communications.

Snow began to fall on November 4, 1812, followed by bitter cold, further impeding the French retreat. Ill-provisioned, weak from hunger and poorly dressed, the French were barely able to march, much less fight. Harried on all sides by the Russian armies, Cossack irregulars and partisan militias, the French Grand Armée was reduced to a rag-tag, disorganized mob. In the last action of the Napoleonic Wars, Napoleon suffered an overwhelming defeat at Waterloo (1815) and his career was over. In 1821, the once proud Emperor of French died in exile on the island of St. Helena.

The Industrial Revolution is the term usually applied to the social and economic changes that mark the transition from a stable agricultural and commercial society to a modern industrial society relying on complex machinery rather than hand tools. It is used historically to refer primarily to the period in British history from the middle of the 18th century to the middle of the 19th century. The Industrial Revolution was the most far-reaching, influential transformation of human culture since the advent of agriculture seven thousand years ago. The consequences of this revolution would change irrevocably human labor, consumption, and family and social structure.

The Industrial Revolution began with James Watt's invention of the steam engine in 1773, the invention of the power loom by Edward Cartwright in 1785, and the invention of the cotton gin in 1793 by Ely Whitney. Historians generally agree that the Industrial Revolution originated in England, both in a series of technological and social innovations. Historians propose a number of reasons. Among the most compelling is the exponential increase in food production following the enclosure laws of the eighteenth century; Parliament passed a series of laws that permitted lands that had been held in common by tenant farmers to be enclosed into large, private farms worked by a much smaller labor force. While this drove peasants off the land, it also increased agricultural production and increased the urban population of England, since the only place displaced peasants had to go were the cities. By the end of the 18th century, the traditional system of agriculture had been replaced in most of England by a new system of larger, more efficient farms operated on rational and capitalistic principles.

Other factors contributing to the rise of industrialization include the printing press and the spread of information, the rise of Protestantism and the Protestant work ethic, advances in boat technology, and the development of the compass and the Harrison timepiece. John Harrison (1693–1776) was an English clock maker, who designed and built the world's first successful maritime clock, one whose accuracy was great enough to allow the determination of longitude over long distances leading directly to an expansion of trade and globalization.

In the early 18th century, British textile manufacturing was based on wool, which was processed by individual artisans. These individual artisans performed the spinning and weaving on their own premises and were referred to as a cottage industry. Industrialization led to the creation of the factory. The factory system was largely responsible for the rise of the modern city, as workers migrated into the cities in search of employment in the factories. For much of the 19th century, production was done in small mills, which were typically powered by water and built to serve local needs.

During the period 1733-1901 the world would see incredible advances in business, technology, and the sciences, and the printing of the most important and influential book ever written on economics, Adam Smith's *Wealth of Nations* in 1776. This period also saw the adoption of the gold standard by Great Britain, and the formation of the Bank of England. In the United States on May 10, 1869, the greatest historical event in transportation occurred at Promontory, Utah, as the Union Pacific tracks joined those of the Central Pacific Railroad, signaling the completion of the transcontinental railroad.

Before the Industrial Revolution and Adam Smith's *Wealth of Nations*, every aspect of economic life was under strict governmental control. Prices were stabilized, wages and hours were fixed, production regulated, and foreign trade, both imports and exports, were completely dominated by the state. Any suggestion of an equitable distribution of wealth was violently opposed by the ruling classes. Education was reserved for the privileged few, and political rights for the masses existed largely in theory rather than in practice.

Adam Smith's work is based on two major premises. First, every human being is motivated primarily by self-interest and second, the division of labor and the accumulation of capital make modern industry possible. Smith believed that the selfishness of the individual is conducive to society's welfare, and allowing man to better his condition can best provide for a nation's prosperity. It naturally followed that there should be a minimum of government interference with the economic order. Adam Smith agrees with Thomas Paine, that the best government is the government that governs least. The greatest happiness for the greatest number became Smith's ruling philosophy.

The Industrial Revolution continued with four technological developments that had the greatest impact on society since the development of the steam engine. The first was Thomas Edison's development of the incandescent light bulb. In 1879, using lower current electricity, a small-carbonized filament, and an improved vacuum inside a glass globe, he was able to produce a reliable, long-lasting source of light. Edison is considered one of the most prolific inventors in history, holding 1,093 U.S. patents in his name.

The second was the development of commercial electricity. On September 4, 1882, the first commercial power station, located on Pearl Street in lower Manhattan, went into operation providing electricity and light to customers in a one square mile area; the electric age had begun. Thomas Edison's Pearl Street electricity generating station introduced four key elements of a modern electric utility system. It featured reliable central generation, efficient distribution, a successful end use (the light bulb), and a competitive price. Although eventually replaced with an alternating current system proposed by Nikola Tesla, Edison's direct current system proved that such a system was feasible.

The third was the development of the automobile by Karl Friedrich Benz (1844–1929) and the development of assembly line manufacturing by Henry Ford (1863–1947). Benz was a German automobile engineer, and is generally regarded as the inventor of the petrol-powered automobile. Benz championed the new internal-combustion engines, and worked single-mindedly to create a car powered by one. He built a little three-wheeled car in 1885 and sold his first one two years later. He went into production with a four-wheeled model in 1890. His company, the Mercedes-Benz Company, is today one of the largest automobile manufacturers in the world.

Henry Ford was the founder of the Ford Motor Company. He was one of the first to apply assembly line manufacturing to the production of affordable automobiles. He not only revolutionized industrial production in the United States and Europe, but also had such influence over the 20th century economy and society that his combination of mass production, high wages, and low prices to consumers is called "Fordism."

The fourth development occurred on December 1903 when Orville and Wilbur Wright of Dayton, Ohio, flying their "Wright Flyer" at Kill Devil Hills, near Kitty Hawk, North Carolina, achieve the first powered, heavier-than-air, controlled and sustained flight with a pilot on board.

The 19th century (1800-1899) was a pivotal year in the development of modern society. Inventions during this period include, the telegraph (Morse 1837), photography (Daguerre 1838), the first postage stamp (1840), the Bessemer process of making steel (1856), telephony (Bell 1876), and the motion picture camera (Edison 1891). Scientific discoveries that would lead to the biotechnology revolution and the quantum revolution also occurred during this period. These included Gregor Mendel's treatise on heredity (1865), Robert Koch's isolation of the bacteria that causes anthrax (1877), Martinus Beijerinck discovery of the tobacco mosaic virus (1899), and J.J. Thomson's discovery of the electron (1897).

Robert Koch (1843–1910) was a German physician. He became famous for isolating the pathogenic agent of anthrax (Bacillus anthracis), tuberculosis (Mycobacterium tuberculosis), and cholera (Vibrio cholerae), and for his development of Koch's postulates. He was awarded the Nobel Prize in Physiology or Medicine for his tuberculosis findings in 1905. He is considered one of the founders of modern bacteriology and microbiology. Bacteria are single-celled spherical, spiral, or rod-shaped micro organisms lacking chlorophyll that reproduce by simple binary fission. Bacteria lack a cell nucleus and classified as prokaryotes. Bacteria are ubiquitous in every habitat on Earth, growing in soil, acidic hot springs, radioactive waste, water, and deep in the Earth's crust, as well as in organic matter and the live bodies of plants and animals. A single gram of rich, undisturbed soil may contain as many as 5,000 different species of bacteria.

A virus (from the Latin virus meaning toxin or poison) is a sub-microscopic infectious agent that is unable to grow or reproduce outside a host cell. Viruses infect all cellular life, including bacteria (bacteriophage). Since the discovery of the tobacco mosaic virus more than 5,000 types of virus have been described. Viruses are segments of RNA and DNA enclosed in a protective coat. Viruses are parasites, which have evolved to reproduce inside and survive outside the cells they infect. Viruses arose as an unavoidable consequence of rapid genetic evolution. There are over fifty different viruses that can cause human disease. Viruses are extremely small, approximately 15 - 25 nanometers in diameter. The viral genome can consist of a very small number of genes or up to hundreds of genes depending on the type of virus. Hepatitis B is the smallest known human viruses with only four genes, but it is one of the world's most deadly pathogens. Over 1 million people die each year from hepatitis B associated liver disease.

Gregor Mendel (1822-1884) was an Austrian monk who is often called the "father of genetics" for his study of the inheritance of traits in pea plants. Mendel showed that there was particular inheritance of traits according to his laws of inheritance. The significance of Mendel's work was not recognized until the turn of the 20th century and is now referred to Mendelian genetics.

J. J. Thomson (1856-1940) was experimenting with currents of electricity inside empty glass tubes. He was investigating a long-standing puzzle known as cathode rays. His experiments prompted him to make a bold proposal: these mysterious rays are streams of particles much smaller than atoms; they are in fact minuscule pieces of atoms. He called these particles "corpuscles," now known as electrons, and suggested that they might make up all of the matter in atoms. It was startling to imagine a particle residing inside the atom--most people thought that the atom was indivisible, the most fundamental unit of matter. Thompson was awarded the 1906 Nobel Prize in Physics for his work.

Other important events that occurred during this period include the American Civil War (1861-1865), the purchase of Alaska by the United States from Russia (1867), the opening of the Suez Canal (1869), the infrastructure of globalization began with the establishment of regular transatlantic ship service between Liverpool, England and New York (1816), and in 1866 the laying of the first transatlantic communications cable.

Asia was undergoing its own transformation. Events in Japan would lead to the return of the Emperor as Japan's supreme ruler. The period from 1603-1867 marks the governance of the Edo or Tokugawa Shogunate, which was officially established in 1603 by the first Edo shogun Tokugawa Ieyasu. The period ended with the Meiji Restoration, the restoration of imperial rule by the 15th and last shogun Tokugawa Yoshinobu. The Edo period is also known as the beginning of the early modern period of Japan. This period also marked the decline of the samurai warrior class and the rise of ultra-nationalism and militarism that led to the Japanese December 7, 1941 attack on Pearl Harbor.

The Constitution of the Empire of Japan, more commonly known as the Imperial or Meiji Constitution, was the fundamental law of the Empire of Japan from 1889 until 1947. Enacted as part of the Meiji Renewal, it provided for a form of constitutional monarchy based on the Prussian model, in which the Emperor of Japan was an active ruler and wielded considerable political power, but shared power with an elected diet. In 1947, following Japan's defeat and occupation at the end of the Second World War, the Meiji Constitution was replaced by a new document, called simply the 'Constitution of Japan', which replaced the imperial system with Western-style liberal democracy.

Two publications that would have a major impact on the world for years after their initial publication also appeared during this period, the publication of Karl Marx's *The Communist Manifesto* and Charles Darwin's *Origin of Species* (originally titled *On the Origin of Species by Means of Natural Selection, or the Preservation of Favored Races in the Struggle for Life*).

The Communist Manifesto was commissioned by the Communist League and written by communist theorists Karl Marx and Friedrich Engels, it laid out the League's purposes and program. The Manifesto suggested a course of action for a proletarian revolution to overthrow capitalism and, eventually, to bring about a classless society. Vladimir Lenin attempted this in Russia in the early twentieth century, but as with all utopian ideas that are contrary to human nature, Marxist-Leninist doctrine failed miserably.

Charles Darwin's (1809-1882) *Origin of Species* is one of the most important and revolutionary treatises ever published. Essentially, the two basic postulates of Darwinian Theory are natural selection (genetic variation exists within species), and sexual selection (differential reproductive success favors some varieties over others). According to this theory, individual variability means that some organisms have a slight advantage over others. The advantage will allow the organisms to compete better in the "struggle for existence" and produced more offspring, which will inherit the advantageous qualities. The process whereby favorable traits in the most "fit" animals allow it to survive and reproduce Darwin determined that as long as there was heredity, variation among offspring, and environmental change, there had to be evolution. Evolution had produced every organism on earth. By showing how an entirely new species could evolve, Darwin realized that all species had evolved.

The *Origin of Species* was extremely controversial, because the logical extension of his theory was that Homo sapiens were nothing special among species and evolved like all other organisms. It also destroyed the prevailing view that the earth as it existed in the

19th century was created by God in seven days some 6,000 years earlier. Predictably, the Church attacked Darwin vehemently as many religious believers do today. Darwin's theory of evolution has stood the test of time and is now been proven at the molecular level, but his controversial work will most likely be debated for years to come.

The quantum revolution laid the foundation for the technological revolution of the 20th century. Not since the time of Isaac Newton has the world seen such intellectual brilliance. The four main contributors to the quantum revolution were Max Planck (relationship between the energy and the frequency of radiation), Louis de Broglie (wave nature of electrons), Niels Bohr (atomic structure), and Albert Einstein (photoelectric effect). Quantum mechanics is the branch of mathematical physics treating atomic and subatomic systems and their interaction with radiation in terms of observable quantities. It is based on the observation that all forms of energy are released in discrete units or bundles called quanta.

For a classical system made up of particles, you can completely specify the state of the system by giving the position and momentum (or equivalently velocity) of every particle in the system at any particular time. In quantum mechanics the situation is a little more complicated. The systems that you study are still made of particles, and the basic procedure is in some ways similar: You measure the state of a particle at some initial time, you specify the forces acting on that particle (or equivalently, the potential energy function describing those forces), and quantum mechanics gives you a set of equations for predicting the results of measurements taken at any later time. There are two key differences between these two theories. First, the state of a particle in quantum mechanics is not just given by its position and momentum but by a mathematical construct known as a "wave function." Second, knowing the state of a particle (i.e. its wave function) does not enable you to predict the results of measurements with certainty, but rather gives you a set of probabilities for the possible outcomes of any measurement.

Quantum mechanics uses complex number wave functions (sometimes referred to as orbital's in the case of atomic electrons), and more generally, elements of a complex vector space to explain such effects. These are related to classical physics largely through probability. Probability in the context of quantum mechanics has to do with the likelihood of finding a system in a particular state at a certain time, for example, finding an electron, in a particular region around the nucleus at a particular time. Therefore, electrons cannot be pictured as localized particles in space but rather should be thought of as "clouds" of negative charge spread out over the entire orbit. These clouds represent the regions around the nucleus where the probability of "finding" an electron is the largest. This probability cloud obeys a quantum mechanical principle called Heisenberg's Uncertainty Principle, which states that there is an uncertainty in the classical position of any subatomic particle, including the electron; so instead of describing where an electron or other particle is, the entire range of possible values is used, describing a probability distribution.

Max Planck (1858-1947) is often referred to as the "father of quantum physics." Planck was able to deduce the relationship between the energy and the frequency of radiation. In a paper published in 1900, he announced his derivation of the relationship: this was based on the revolutionary idea that the energy emitted by a resonator could only take on discrete values or quanta. The energy for a resonator of frequency v is hv where h is a universal constant, now called Planck's constant. Planck's work on the quantum theory, as it came to be known, was published in the *Annalen der Physik*. His work is summarized in two books *Thermodynamik* (Thermodynamics) (1897) and *Theorie der Wärmestrahlung* (Theory of Heat Radiation) (1906).

Louis de Broglie (1892–1987) hypothesized (1924) that particles should also exhibit certain wavelike properties, a prediction that led to the development of wave mechanics, a form of quantum mechanics. The existence of these matter waves was confirmed experimentally in 1927. In 1929 the Swedish Academy of Sciences conferred on him the Nobel Prize for Physics "for his discovery of the wave nature of electrons."

Albert Einstein's (1879-1955) main contribution to quantum physics was his 1905 paper on the photoelectric effect, *On a Heuristic Viewpoint Concerning the Production and Transformation of Light*. Einstein argued that light could act as though it consists of discrete, independent particles of energy, in some ways like the particles of a gas. A few years before, Max Planck's work had contained the first suggestion of discreteness in energy, but Einstein went far beyond this. His revolutionary proposal contradicted the universally accepted theory that light consists of smoothly oscillating electromagnetic waves. But Einstein showed that light quanta (photons), as he called the particles of energy, could help to explain phenomena being studied by experimental physicists. Einstein received the 1921 Nobel Prize for Physics, for this work on the photoelectric effect. A practical application of the photoelectric effect is the solar cell, which through the use of semiconductor materials converts light energy into electrical energy.

Niels Bohr (1885-1962) was a Danish physicist who made essential contributions to understanding atomic structure and quantum mechanics. These contributions include Bohr's model of atomic structure. The theory that electrons travel in discrete orbits around the atom's nucleus, with the chemical properties of the element being largely determined by the number of electrons in each of the outer orbits, and the idea that an electron could drop from a higher-energy orbit to a lower one, emitting a photon (light quantum) of discrete energy (this became the basis for quantum theory). The principle of complementarity, which is a basic principle of quantum theory, and refers to effects such as the wave-particle duality, in which different measurements made on a system reveal it to have either particle-like or wave-like properties. Niels Bohr is usually associated with this concept; in the orthodox form, it is stated that a quantum mechanical system consisting of a boson (a particle with integer spin) or fermion (a particle with half-integer spin) can either behave as a particle or as wave, but never simultaneously as both. Bohr was awarded the Nobel Prize in Physics 1922 for his "services in the investigation of the structure of atoms and of the radiation emanating from them."

Wave-particle duality can be observed by shinning a light through two slits. The light wave travels through both slits, so that two smaller waves come out from each slit. These waves interfere, producing a series of light and dark fringes when projected onto a screen. As particles, light appears as photons. When the photons are aimed at a detector a count of the discrete number of photons can be made. If the photons are sent through the slits one at a time, each photon produces a spot on the screen. When multiple events are collected an interference pattern emerges.

Additional work by numerous physicists including Erwin Schrödinger (wave properties of matter), Paul Dirac (theory of wave mechanics), and Werner Heisenberg (uncertainty principle), and the development of quantum electrodynamics (QED) and quantum chromodynamics (QCD) has resulted in a fundamental understanding of matter now known as the Standard Model.

Quantum electrodynamics (QED) is a relativistic quantum field theory of electrodynamics that basically describes how light and matter interacts. The development of the theory was the basis of the 1965 Nobel Prize in physics, awarded to Richard Feynman, Julian Schwinger and Sin-itero Tomonaga. More specifically it deals with the interactions between electrons, positrons and photons. QED mathematically describes all phenomena involving electrically charged particles interacting by means of exchange of photons. QED makes extremely accurate predictions of quantities like the anomalous magnetic moment of the electron, and the Lamb shift of the energy levels of hydrogen.

Quantum chromodynamics (QCD) is a theory of strong interactions between elementary particles including the interaction that binds protons and neutrons in the nucleus. The theory assumes that strongly interacting particles (hadrons) are made of quarks and that gluons bind the quarks together. Quarks interact via the strong force by exchanging gluons. In contrast to QED, where the photons exchanged are electrically neutral, the gluons of QCD also carry color charges. To allow all the possible interactions between the three colors of quarks, there must be eight gluons, each of which generally carries a mixture of a color and an anticolor of a different kind.

Two characteristics of QCD are asymptotic freedom and confinement. Asymptotic freedom means quark-quark interactions weaken as the energy gets higher, or, equivalently, as the quarks approach one another. This prediction of QCD was first discovered in the early 1970s by David Politzer and by Frank Wilczek and David Gross. For this work they were awarded the 2004 Nobel Prize in Physics.

Confinement is the physics phenomenon that color charged particles (such as quarks) cannot be isolated singularly, and therefore cannot be directly observed. Quarks, by default, clump together to form hadrons (a category of particles that includes one of two combinations of quarks: three quarks or three antiquarks (a baryon) or a quark and an antiquark (a meson). The constituent quarks in a group cannot be separated from their parent hadron, and this is why quarks can never be studied or observed in any more direct way than at a hadron level. Because of this, it would take an infinite amount of energy to separate two quarks; they are forever bound into hadrons such as the proton and the neutron. Although analytically unproven, confinement is widely believed to be true because it explains the consistent failure to find free quarks.

The Standard Model basically states that everything in the universe is found to be made from twelve basic building blocks called fundamental particles, governed by four fundamental forces. The Standard Model of particle physics groups particles in two categories: particles that carry force and particles that make up matter. Each particle has an antiparticle, such as an anti-quark. Ordinary matter is made of protons, neutrons, and electrons. Atomic nuclei are made of protons and neutrons, which in turn are made of quarks. The fundamental forces are communicated between particles by the exchange of quanta which behave like particles. These include four intermediate vector bosons the gluon (nuclear or strong force), the photon (electromagnetic force) and the W and Z bosons (weak force). The Standard Model is a final solution to the attempt started by Paul Dirac (Nobel Prize, 1933) to construct relativistically invariant quantum mechanics. With all its success the Standard Model falls short of being a complete theory of fundamental interactions because it does not yet include gravity.

Without quantum physics much of the technology of today would simply not exist. Perhaps the two most important technologies with the greatest impact to come from quantum physics are the transistor and the laser.

Dr. John Bardeen, Dr. Walter Brattain, and Dr. William Shockley discovered the transistor effect and developed the first device in December 1947, while the three were members of the technical staff at Bell Laboratories in Murray Hill, NJ. They were awarded the Nobel Prize in physics in 1956.

The transistor is a solid-state semiconductor device that can be used for amplification, switching, voltage stabilization, signal modulation and many other functions. It acts as a variable valve that, based on its input voltage, controls the current it draws from a connected voltage source. Transistors are made either as separate components or as part of an integrated circuit. The transistor is the building block of all modern electronics and computers (everything from a battery operated watch, to a coffee maker, to a cell phone, to a supercomputer). Microprocessors for modern personal computers, such as the Intel Pentium 4 Processor, contain around 55 million transistors each.

A LASER (Light Amplification by Stimulated Emission of Radiation) is an optical source that emits photons in a coherent beam. Laser light is typically near monochromatic, i.e. consisting of a single wavelength or hue, and emitted in a narrow beam. This is in contrast to common light sources, such as the incandescent light bulb, which emit incoherent photons in almost all directions, usually over a wide spectrum of wavelengths. Laser action is understood by application of quantum mechanics and thermodynamics theory.

In a laser, the atoms or molecules of a crystal, gas, liquid, or other substance are excited in a laser cavity so that more of them are at higher energy levels than are at lower energy levels. Reflective surfaces at both ends of the cavity permit energy to reflect back and forth, building up in each passage. The excited molecules bounce back and forth between two mirrors until coherent light escapes from the cavity. If a photon whose frequency corresponds to the energy difference between the excited and ground states strikes an excited atom, the atom is stimulated as it falls back to a lower energy state to emit a second photon of the same (or a proportional) frequency, in phase with and in the same direction as the bombarding photon. This process is called stimulated emission. The bombarding photon and the emitted photon may then each strike other excited atoms, stimulating further emission of photons, all of the same frequency and phase. This process produces a sudden burst of coherent radiation as all the atoms discharge in a rapid chain reaction.

Physicist Charles Townes built the first microwave laser in 1954 and physicist Theodore Maiman built the first optical laser in 1960. CD players, CD-ROMs, CD-burners, and DVD players all use lasers to read and write data. Without fundamental research in physics by Einstein, the inventors of the laser, and others, the CD and other applications of the laser such as fiber optics representing industries worth billions of dollars would not exist. It is ironic that, like so many other discoveries in physics, the laser was at first thought by many to have no practical uses whatsoever.

The other major scientific revolution of the 20th century was the biotechnology revolution. Biotechnology is technology based on the use of biological processes, organisms, or other biological derivatives to produce or modify products or processes for a specific use. Biotechnology uses techniques such as recombinant DNA, tissue culture-based processes, or gene transfer in living plants. Biotechnology combines the disciplines of genetics, microbiology, molecular biology, biochemistry, chemical engineering, information technology and bioinformatics. Most biotechnology applications have been developed for use in agriculture, and medicine but new advances have been made in the area of bio-fuels and gene therapy. Biotechnology products developed for medical purposes include insulin (stimulates glucose uptake from blood in people with insulin dependent Type 1 diabetes), tissue plasminogen activator (dissolves blood clots after heart attacks and strokes), growth hormone (somatropin), and various antibiotic and vaccine proteins.

The biotechnology revolution began with the discovery and structural determination of deoxyribonucleic acid (DNA). There were many contributors to the final determination of the molecular structure of DNA beginning in 1869 when the Swiss physician Friedrich Miescher discovered a substance containing both phosphorus and nitrogen in the nuclei of white blood cells found in pus. The substance, first named nuclein because it seemed to come from cell nuclei, became known as nucleic acid after 1874, when Miescher separated it into protein and acid components.

Phoebus Levene isolated the nucleotides, the basic building blocks of the nucleic acid molecule; and in 1909 he isolated the five-carbon sugar d-ribose from the ribonucleic acid (RNA) molecule. Twenty years later he discovered 2-deoxyribose (a sugar derived from d-ribose by removing an oxygen atom), which is part of the DNA molecule. He also determined how the nucleic acid components combine to form the nucleotides and how the nucleotides combine in chains.

Based on the fact that DNA contains phosphorous but no sulfur and sulfur is present in some proteins, the Hershey-Chase experiment provided decisive biochemical evidence that nucleic acids, not proteins are the hereditary material. Using a kitchen blender to separate radioisotope labeled bacteriophage (viruses that infect bacteria) that had infected bacteria from bacteriophage 'ghosts' which remained on the outside of the cells, Hershey and Chase showed that 32P (phosphorous radioisotope) labeled nucleic acids entered the cells whereas 35S (sulfur radioisotope) labeled proteins largely remained on the outside.

In 1950, Erwin Chargaff and his colleagues at Columbia University found that DNA from many different species and from different sources within a single organism exhibits certain regularities. In almost all DNA, the following rule holds: The amount of adenine equals the amount of thymine (A=T), and the amount of guanine equals the amount of cytosine (G=C). As a result, the total abundance of purines (A+G) equals the total abundance of pyrimidines (T+C). The structure of DNA could not have been worked out without this observation, now known as Chargaff's rule.

In 1953 James D. Watson and Francis Crick suggested what is now accepted as the first correct double-helix model of DNA structure in the journal Nature. Their double-helix, molecular model of DNA was then based on a single X-ray diffraction image taken by Rosalind Franklin and Raymond Gosling in May 1952, as well as information obtained through private communications from Erwin Chargaff that DNA bases were paired.

In 1957, Francis Crick proposed the "Central Dogma" of molecular biology, which foretold the relationship between DNA, RNA, and proteins. The central dogma states that DNA codes for the production of RNA, RNA codes for the production of polypeptides (proteins), and protein does not code for the production of protein, RNA, or DNA. A given gene is transcribed to produce a messenger RNA (mRNA) molecule complementary to one of the DNA strands, and transfer RNA (tRNA) molecules translate the sequence of bases in the mRNA into the appropriate sequence of linked amino acids during protein synthesis. Further work by Crick and coworkers showed that the genetic code was based on codons. A codon is a triplet of RNA or DNA bases that represents the code for a single amino acid, for example CGC (cytosine-guanine-cytosine) codes for the amino acid arginine, UGA (uracil-guanine-adenine) for tryptophan.

Along with the discovery of DNA the mapping of the human genome stands as one of the great advances in biology this century. Completed in 2003, the Human Genome Project (HGP) was a 13-year project coordinated by the U.S. Department of Energy and the National Institutes of Health. Project goals were to

- identify all the approximately 20,000-25,000 genes in human DNA
- determine the sequences of the 3 billion chemical base pairs that make up human DNA
- store this information in databases
- improve tools for data analysis
- transfer related technologies to the private sector
- address the ethical, legal, and social issues (ELSI) that may arise from the project

Though the HGP is finished, analyses of the data will continue for many years. The mapping of the human genome along with continued advances in molecular biology will bring about a revolution in medicine that should some day provide advanced gene therapies that will make cancer and other genetic disorders treatable diseases.

World War I (1914) began as a result of the assassination of Archduke Ferdinand, the heir to the throne of the Austro-Hungarian Empire, by a Slav nationalist by the name of Gavrilo Princip. Austria-Hungary blamed Serbia for the killing and because Europe was linked by a series of diplomatic alliances, the affair escalated into full-scale war. The alliances were Austria-Hungary, Germany, and Italy, referred to as the Central Powers, and Britain, France, and Russia, referred to as the Triple Entente or Allied Forces. The conflict truly became a 'world war' when Japan joined the Entente forces and the Ottoman Empire joined the Central Powers.

World War I was the first 'total war' with fighting occurring on land, sea, and in the air. The Battle of Verdun in 1916 was one of the costliest battles of the war. Verdun exemplified the 'war of attrition' pursued by both sides and which cost so many lives. Verdun was a Gallic fortress before Roman times and later a key asset in wars against Prussia. The Germans knew that the French would throw as many men as necessary into its defense, which would enable German forces to inflict the maximum possible casualties. Ultimately the Germans could no longer afford to commit new troops to

Verdun. At a cost of some 400,000 French casualties and a similar number of Germans the attack was called off.

Major German successes in the east contributed to two revolutions in Russia where Tsar Nicholas II was forced to abdicate and a Bolshevik regime under Vladimir Lenin was established. The October Revolution took Russia out of the war (an armistice was declared in December 1917 and a Russo-German peace treaty was signed at Brest-Litovsk in March 1918). This meant that German forces could concentrate more fully on the Western Front. In 1915, the British passenger liner the Lusitania was sunk by a German submarine, killing 128 Americans and further heightening tensions. With the sinking of the Lusitania and German attempts to entice Mexico to invade the United States, on April 6, 1917, the USA declared war on Germany.

Allied counter-offensives (August 1918) at the Marne and at Amiens in Northern France were successful and in the early autumn a 'hundred days' of semi-mobile warfare forced the Germans back beyond the Hindenburg line and freed much of occupied France and Belgium. Although an armistice was agreed in November 1918, it was not until June 28, 1919 that the Treaty of Versailles was signed between the Allied powers and Germany, thus officially ending the war 'to end all wars'.

The number of World War I casualties (military and civilian) was over 37 million - over 15 million deaths and 22 million wounded. This includes almost 9 million military deaths and about 6.6 million civilian deaths. The Entente Powers lost more than 5 million soldiers and the Central Powers more than 3 million.

The peace after World War I was short lived. World War II began on September 1, 1939 with the German invasion of Poland. France and the United Kingdom honored their defensive alliance of March 1939 by declaring war two days later. Australia and New Zealand declared war the same day and Canada followed a week later. The United Kingdom, France, Poland, and others were known as the Allies. Germany, Italy, and Japan, were jointly known as the Axis.

In June 1941, Germany invaded the Soviet Union, causing the Soviets to enter the war on the side of the Allies. On December 7, 1941, the Japanese bombed Pearl Harbor causing the United States to enter the war on the Allies' side as well. China, which had been at war with Japan since the mid-1930s, also joined the Allies, as did a number of other countries.

The turning point of the war come on "D-Day" (June 6, 1944) when the Western Allies invaded German-held Normandy in a pre-dawn amphibious assault spearheaded by American (82nd and 101st), British (6th) and Canadian 3rd Infantry Division forces, opening the "second front" against Germany. D-Day marked the beginning of the eventual Allied victory over the Axis powers. The landing included over 5,000 ships, 11,000 airplanes, and 150,000 service men. When it was over, the Allied Forces had suffered nearly 10,000 casualties, and more than 4,000 were dead.

On December 1944, the German Army made its last major offensive in the West, known as the Battle of the Bulge. The Allied forces, largely unprepared for this sudden attack, suffered heavy casualties. In addition, the poor weather during the initial days of the offensive favored the Germans because it grounded Allied aircraft. However, clearing skies allowed Allied air supremacy to resume; with the German failure to capture Bastogne; and the arrival of General Patton's Third Army, the Nazis were forced to retreat back into Germany and the offensive was defeated.

German forces in Italy surrendered on May 2, 1945; those in northern Germany, Denmark, and the Netherlands surrendered on May 4, 1945; and the German High Command under General Alfred Jodl surrendered unconditionally all remaining German forces on May 7, 1945 in Reims, France. The Western Allies celebrated Victory in Europe "V-E Day" on May 8th, and the Soviet Union "Victory Day" on May 9th.

In 1942 under the control of the U.S. Army Corps of Engineers, the Manhattan Project began. General Leslie R. Groves directed the project with its scientific research directed by physicist J. Robert Oppenheimer. In 1942, at the University of Chicago reactor, Enrico

Fermi oversaw the first controlled energy release from the nucleus of the atom, and by 1945 the Y-12 plant in Oak Ridge, Tennessee, began to produce bomb-grade U-235 (uranium), which was shipped to Los Alamos, New Mexico. U-235 was used in the Little Boy bomb and plutonium was used in the Fat Man bomb produced at Los Alamos.

On August 6, 1945, the Boeing B-29 Superfortress "Enola Gay", piloted by Colonel Paul Tibbets, dropped an atomic bomb "Little Boy" on Hiroshima, effectively destroying it. Little Boy was detonated at an altitude of 1,800 feet. It weighed about 9,000 lbs. and had an explosive force (yield) equal to about 20,000 tons of TNT.

On August 8, 1945, in an attempt to seize territory from an already defeated Japan, the Soviet Union declared war on Japan, and launched a large-scale invasion of Japanese occupied Manchuria (Operation August Storm). On August 9, 1945, a second atomic bomb "Fat Man" was dropped on Nagasaki, Japan.

The Japanese surrendered on August 15, 1945, Victory over Japan "V-J day", signing official surrender papers on September 2, 1945, aboard the USS Missouri in Tokyo Bay. Japan's surrender to the Allied powers did not fully end the war, however, because Japan and the Soviet Union never signed a peace agreement. In the last days of the armed conflict, the Soviet Union occupied the southern Kuril Islands, an area previously held by Japan and claimed by the Soviets. World War II was the largest and deadliest war to date in the sorry history of human conflict leaving approximately 62 million people dead.

During the war the Japanese were especially fanatical and displayed incredible brutality. Kamikazes 'divine wind' and the creed that went with the kamikazes in World War II is usually associated with those Japanese pilots who flew into American warships in an effort to sink them. However, there were other forms of kamikazes such as the human torpedoes that the Japanese used in the Pacific.

Japanese forces, after their defeat at the Battle of Midway in 1942, lost the momentum they had at the start of the Pacific War. Japan's fighter planes were becoming outnumbered and outclassed by newer US-made planes, especially the F4U Corsair and P-51 Mustang. Because of combat losses, particularly at the Battle of Midway, skilled fighter pilots were becoming extremely scarce. Finally, the low availability of parts and fuel made even normal flight operation a problem. The Japanese were losing the war and running out of options, when the 1st Air Fleet commandant, Vice Admiral Takijiro Onishi decided to form a suicide attack unit, the Kamikaze Special Attack Force.

According to the U.S. Air Force approximately 2,800 Kamikaze attackers sunk 34 Navy ships, damaged 368 others, killed 4,900 sailors, and wounded over 4,800. Despite radar detection and cuing, airborne interception and attrition, and massive anti-aircraft barrages, a distressing 14 percent of Kamikazes survived to score a hit on a ship; nearly 8.5 percent of all ships hit by Kamikazes sank.

The Bataan Death March began at Mariveles, Philippines on April 10, 1942. Captives were forced to march, about 100 kilometers north to Nueva Ecija to Camp O'Donnell, a prison camp. Any troops who fell behind were executed. Japanese troops beat soldiers randomly, denied the POWs food and water for many days, and routinely tortured the prisoners. One of their tortures was known as the sun treatment. The Philippines in April is very hot. The POWs were forced to sit in the sun without any shade, helmets, or water. Anyone who dared ask for water was executed. On the rare occasion they were given any food, it was only a handful of contaminated rice. When the prisoners were allowed to sleep for a few hours at night, they were packed into barbed wire enclosures so tight that they could barely move. There were no latrine facilities, everybody was sick with malaria and dysentery. The prisoners were finally freed when the war ended.

The war was responsible for the re-drawing of national boundaries and the creation of new nations, the end of Western colonialism, and the beginning of the Cold War. After World War II, Europe was informally partitioned into Western and Soviet spheres of influence. Western Europe largely aligned as NATO, and Eastern Europe largely as the Warsaw pact. There was a fundamental shift in power from Western Europe and the British Empire to the new superpowers, the United States and the Soviet Union, with significant boundary changes and displacement of people as Soviet imperialism absorbed land areas and countries in Eastern Europe. Technological innovations increased dramatically to help support the war effort. New inventions during this period include radar, long-range missiles, the jet engine, the atomic bomb, and the first computers.

In Asia, the United States' military occupation of Japan led to Japan's democratization. China's civil war continued through and after the war, resulting eventually in the establishment of the People's Republic of China. The former colonies of the European powers, such as India, Indonesia, and Vietnam, began their road to independence.

Mao Tse-tung (1893-1976) was the chairman of the Politburo of the Communist Party of China from 1943 and the chairman of the Central Committee of the Communist Party of China from 1945 until his death in 1976. Under his leadership, the Chinese Communist Party (CCP) became the ruling party of Mainland China after victory over Chinese Nationalists, the Kuomintang, in the Chinese Civil War.

Since the League of Nations had obviously failed to prevent the World War II, a new international order was constructed. In 1945, the United Nations was founded with the hope of preventing such a devastating war from occurring again and to establish a lasting peace. The United Nations (UN) is an international organization that describes itself as a "global association of governments facilitating cooperation in international law, international security, economic development, and social equity." As of 2005 there were 191 member states.

The Space Age began on October 4, 1957, when the Soviet Union successfully launched Sputnik I. The world's first artificial satellite was about the size of a basketball, weighed only 183 pounds, and took about 98 minutes to orbit the Earth on its elliptical path. That launch ushered in new political, military, technological, and scientific developments. While the Sputnik launch was a single event, it marked the beginning of the American – Soviet space race.

There was a fear that the Soviets' ability to launch satellites could be translated into the capability to launch ballistic missiles that could carry nuclear weapons from the Soviet Union to the United States. Then on November 3, 1957 Sputnik II was launched, carrying a much heavier payload, including a dog-named Laika. This mission was followed in 1961, when the Russian cosmonaut Yuri Gagarin, became the first human to orbit the earth.

The Sputnik launch led directly to the creation of National Aeronautics and Space Administration (NASA). In July 1958, Congress passed the National Aeronautics and Space Act (commonly called the "Space Act"), which created NASA from the National Advisory Committee for Aeronautics (NACA) and other government agencies.

Four years later on February 20, 1962, John Glenn piloted the Mercury-Atlas 6 "Friendship 7" spacecraft on the first manned orbital mission of the United States. Launched from Kennedy Space Center, Florida, he completed a successful three-orbit mission around the earth, reaching a maximum altitude (apogee) of approximately 162 statute miles and an orbital velocity of approximately 17,500 miles per hour. Glenn was celebrated as a national hero, and received a ticker-tape parade reminiscent of Charles Lindbergh, when in 1927, flying the "Spirit of St. Louis," he became the first aviator to make a solo, non-stop, transatlantic flight.

On July 20, 1969, the human race accomplished its single greatest technological achievement of all time when a human first set foot on another celestial body. Neil A. Armstrong took "one small step for man; one giant leap for mankind" when he stepped off the Lunar Module, named "Eagle," onto the surface of the Moon. "Buzz" Aldrin joined him, and the two astronauts spent 21 hours on the lunar surface and returned 46 pounds of lunar rocks. Michael Collins served as command module pilot on the Apollo 11 mission. He remained aboard the command module, Columbia, in lunar orbit while Armstrong, spacecraft commander, and Aldrin, lunar module pilot, descended to the lunar surface.

Planetary exploration began with the launches on August 20 and September 5, 1977 of the Voyager mission to the outer planets. The twin spacecraft Voyager 1 and 2 flew by and observed Jupiter and Saturn, while Voyager 2 went on to visit Uranus and Neptune. Both craft are now heading out of the solar system. In 1998, Voyager 1 became the most distant human-made object in space. The space age continues today with exploratory missions to Mars in preparation for a future manned mission to Mars, missions to investigate the origin and structure of comets, and the construction of the international space station.

Although Professor John Atanasoff, who had a Ph.D. in theoretical physics from the University of Wisconsin, and his physics graduate student Clifford Berry, built the first electronic digital computer in the basement of the physics department at Iowa State University in 1939, it is generally accepted that the Computer Age began in 1943 when computers were developed to aid the Allied World War II efforts. John Eckert and John Mauchly, of the University of Pennsylvania, began developing ENIAC (Electronic Numerical Integrator and Computer), for the U.S. Army in 1943. The ENIAC was one of the most complex electronic devices ever assembled incorporating 19,000 vacuum tubes, and using nearly 200 kilowatts of power. Two years later they began work on the EDVAC (Electronic Discrete Variable Automatic Computer), a computer that used a permanently stored program, which eliminated the necessity to program it using punched cards or paper tape.

A computer is any device capable of processing information to produce a desired result. Computers typically perform their work in three well-defined steps: accepting input, processing the input according to predefined rules (programs), and producing output. The road to the development of the modern computer began with the work of Charles Babbage and George Boole.

Charles Babbage (1792-1871) is the originator of the concepts behind the present day computer. In 1822, Babbage built a small machine, involving several linked adding mechanisms, which would automatically generate successive values of a simple algebraic function, using the method of finite differences. In the space of a few years he had developed the concept of a program controlled, mechanical, digital computer, incorporating a complete arithmetic unit, store, punched-card input and output, and printing mechanism, which he called an Analytical Engine.

George Boole (1815-1864) in 1854 published his most important work *An investigation into the Laws of Thought, on Which are founded the Mathematical Theories of Logic and Probabilities*. Boole approached logic in a new way reducing it to a simple algebra, incorporating logic into mathematics. He pointed out the analogy between algebraic symbols and those that represent logical forms. Thus began the algebra of logic called Boolean algebra, which now finds application in digital circuits, which are the foundation for modern computers. Whereas elementary algebra is based on the numeric operations multiplication xy, addition x + y, and negation -x, Boolean algebra is based on logical counterparts to those operations, namely conjunction (AND), disjunction (OR), and complement or negation (NOT).

In 1951, when the Remington Rand Corporation introduced the UNIVAC computer on a commercial basis, its first customers included the U.S. Bureau of Census, which used the UNIVAC computer to tabulate the 1950 census. This was the first use of a computer for business and marked the beginning of the "commercial" computer age.

International Business Machines (IBM) introduced its Model 650 which soon became the most widely used of all first generation computers, with hundreds delivered between 1955 and 1959. The IBM 650 was faster than most other magnetic drum computers, but the main reason for its great success was its well-integrated punched card input and output and its adaptability to existing punched-card systems.

After IBM entered the computer market in the 1950s, and advances in computer technology accelerated. This lead to a period of mainframe computing with large centralized computer systems accessed via "dumb" terminals. IBM introduced its third generation computer, the IBM 360, in April of 1964. The IBM 360 was tremendously successful with thousands of installations. Many features of the 360 became standards in large segments of the computer industry.

Modern computers did not become practical until the invention of the transistor and the integrated circuit. Jack Kilby has over 60 patents to his credit but is probably most famous for his invention of the monolithic (formed from a single crystal) integrated circuit (September 1958), for which he received the Nobel Prize in Physics in the year 2000. After his success with the integrated circuit Kilby stayed with Texas Instruments and, among other things, he led the team that invented the hand-held calculator.

The integrated circuit has come a long way since Jack Kilby's first prototype. His idea founded a new industry and is the key element behind our computerized society. Today the most advanced circuits contain several hundred millions of components on an area no larger than a fingernail. In November 2003, Intel used 65-nanometer (a nanometer is one-billionth of a meter) process to build a 4-megabit SRAM memory chip. Some 10 million of the transistors in this chip could fit in one square millimeter, roughly the size of the tip of a ballpoint pen.

Subsequent breakthroughs in electronic technology (transistors, integrated circuits, and memory chips) drove the development of increasingly reliable and more usable computers. The first widely used high-level programming language was FORTRAN, developed during 1954–57 by an IBM team led by John W. Backus. Advances in software continued when in 1968 Doug Engelbart demonstrated three now common applications, a word processor, an early hypertext system, and a collaborative (groupware) application.

The most spectacular growth area in the latter part of the third generation period was in the microcomputer field. At the time the largest company in this field was Digital Equipment Corporation, which is famous for its PDP and VAX (Virtual Address eXtension) series of computers. Ironically, it was a PC company, Compaq Computers that purchased Digital Equipment Corporation in 1998.

The next big revolution in computing was the personal computer (PC). The road to the modern day PC began when Gordon Moore and Robert Noyce formed Intel in 1968. Then in 1969, Xerox created its Palo Alto Research Center (PARC). PARC's mission was to explore the "architecture of information". Research at PARC led to the development of windows based operating systems, and the mouse.

Fairchild Semiconductor introduced a 256-bit Random Access Memory (RAM) chip in 1970, and in late 1970 Intel introduced a 1K RAM chip and the 4004, a 4-bit microprocessor. The 4004 was the brainchild of three engineers: Ted Hoff, Stan Mazor and Federico Faggin, and was designed to be a calculator component for a Japanese manufacturer, which initially owned all rights to the chip. At the time, most Intel executives saw little promise in the product. Two years later in April 1972, Intel introduced the 8008, an 8-bit microprocessor that was to become the basis for the original IBM PC. In 1972, Gary Kildall developed PL/M, the first high-level programming language for the Intel microprocessor. He created CP/M the same year to enable the 8080 to control a floppy drive, combining for the first time all the essential components of a computer at the microcomputer scale.

Popular Electronics featured the MITS Intel 8080 based Altair 8800 on its cover, in January 1975. It was hailed as the first "personal" computer. Thousands of orders for the 8800 rescued MITS from bankruptcy. Paul Allen and Bill Gates developed BASIC (Beginner's All-purpose Symbolic Instruction Code) for the Altair 8800. In 1975, Bill Gates dropped out of Harvard University and with his partner Paul Allen began writing software programs, including BASIC and MS-DOS the operating system for the original IBM Personal Computer. Their company, Microsoft Corporation, later became one of the world's largest sellers of computer software.

In 1977, college dropouts Steve Jobs and Steve Wozniak, working in Wozniak's garage, built and marketed the Apple II computer, the first computer with a television-like screen and useful keyboard. Their computer became the most famous ever built and spawned a multibillion computer hardware industry. Apple began selling its Apple II for $1,195, including 16K of RAM but no monitor. By 1980, Apple had captured 50% of the personal computer market. In 1980, IBM approached Microsoft to develop BASIC for its personal computer project. The first IBM PC was released in August 1981, priced at $2665.00 for a system with a single disk drive, 64 megabytes of RAM, and IBM DOS. Apple Computer responded with the Apple Macintosh making its debut in 1984. It featured a simple, graphical interface, used the 8-MHz, 32-bit Motorola 68000 CPU, and had a built-in 9-inch B/W screen. Microsoft Corporation followed with its own graphical interface, window based operating system, Microsoft Windows 1.0, which shipped in November 1985. Today the PC hardware and software market has grown to a multi-billion dollar industry, and over half of all American households have a computer and Internet access.

The Internet Age began with timesharing, the concept of linking a large numbers of users to a single computer via remote terminals, and was first developed at MIT in the late 1950s and early 1960s. While working at RAND Corporation on a scheme for U.S. telecommunications infrastructure to survive a "first strike," Paul Baran developed the ideas of distributed communications and digital packet switching, the Internet's underlying data communications technology. In 1964, Paul Baran published his ideas on computer networking in the paper *On Distributed Communications*.

The Defense Advanced Research Projects Agency (DARPA or ARPA) was interested in computer networks and funded a study through Lawrence Roberts at MIT's Lincoln Laboratory in late 1965. The study report, *A Cooperative Network of Time-Sharing Computers*, proposed the establishment of an experimental three-computer network to investigate the concepts of computer networking. In 1967, Lawrence Roberts published his proposal for an ARPANET to develop the computer network concept.

This was followed by ARPA request for proposals (RFP) to propose a research network. In December 1968, ARPA awarded the contract for ARPANET to Bolt, Beranek, and Newman (BBN). ARPANET went online in 1969, and by 1971 the ARPANET connected 15 sites and 23 host computers.

A time-slotted radio network, ALOHA Net, was developed by Norman Abrahamson at the University of Hawaii, which was connected into ARPANET in 1972. Robert Metcalf further refined the elements of this architecture in his 1973 doctoral thesis, which outlined the Ethernet architecture as the basis for a common broadcast Local Area Network (LAN) environment. Bob Kahn and Vincent Cerf made further refinements. The initial design of this protocol, first named *Kahn-Cerf protocol* after its major architects was later named Transmission Control Protocol / Internet Protocol (TCP/IP) and was presented in the paper, *A Protocol for Packet Network Interconnection*. In 1983, ARPANET was converted to run only TCP/IP and in 1984, ARPANET was split between MILNET (Military Network) and the ARAPNET for a research and development platform.

With the introduction in the 1980s of the IBM PC, and the Ethernet LAN, the catalyst for the exponential growth of the Internet was in place. The next major transition of the evolving Internet began with the deployment of NSFNET, a networking project funded by the National Science Foundation (NSF). The projects original goal was to link five supercomputer centers with an Internet backbone network to facilitate communications between the academic and research community. As the academic and research Internet gathered speed, so did the pressure to construct a more commercial friendly network. UUNET was one of the first commercial Internet Service Providers (ISPs) to meet this emerging demand. There are now thousands of ISPs, and as of March 2006, there were an estimated 1 billion world Internet users out of a total world population of 6.5 billion people.

In 1980, while an independent contractor at CERN (originally called European Council for Nuclear Research) from June to December 1980, Tim Berners-Lee proposed a project based on the concept of hypertext, to facilitate sharing and updating information among researchers. With help from Robert Cailliau he built a prototype system named

ENQUIRE. He used similar ideas to those underlying the Enquire system to create the World Wide Web (WWW), for which he designed and built the first web browser and editor, and the first Web server called HTTPD (short for Hypertext Transfer Protocol daemon). Browsers from Netscape and Microsoft followed, providing ease of use and new features.

From these humble beginnings the number of computers and software grew exponentially and the Internet Age flourished. Computers and computer technology now touch all aspects of our lives and culture and have led to large increases in productivity. New Internet innovations continue with social networking systems such as blogs, Internet radio and television, and unprecedented access to knowledge and information.

The rise of the Internet is already having an effect on other media outlets. The percentage of adults who report reading daily newspapers has fallen from 81 percent in 1964 to just 52 percent in 2004. Americans with Internet access are watching less television, according to the UCLA Internet Report 2001. The survey of 2,000 households also shows that, as users get more on-line experience, their television viewing declines further.

Most Internet users report that they spend about the same amount of time on non-computing activities at home as they did before they had the Internet. However, Internet users watch 4.5 hours less television weekly than do non-Internet users. And among users who have had Internet access for five or more years, almost 35 percent said their television viewing decreased, compared to about 30 percent among users who have been on-line for less than a year. There seems to be little doubt that the Internet will have as great of impact on society as the Gutenberg printing press did over 500 years ago.

The Cold War was the protracted geopolitical, economic, and ideological struggle that emerged after World War II between the global superpowers the Soviet Union and the United States, supported by their respective alliance partners. The Cold War endured over four decades, from 1947 until the decline and eventual collapse of East European and Soviet state communism in the late 1980s. The disintegration of the Soviet Union in 1991 is generally considered to mark the absolute end of the conflict.

The struggle was widely called the Cold War in that it did not involve direct-armed conflict between the main contestants (by contrast, a so-called "hot" war). The Cold War was instead waged by means of diplomatic maneuvering, economic pressure, selective aid, intimidation, propaganda, assassination, low-intensity military operations and full-scale proxy wars. The Cold War period produced the largest arms race (both conventional and nuclear) in history, leading to widespread global fears of a potential nuclear war.

In his second term, President Reagan met with Soviet leader Mikhail Gorbachev in Geneva, Switzerland in 1985 and Reykjavík, Iceland in 1986, the latter to continue discussions about scaling back their respective intermediate missile arsenals in Europe. The talks broke down in failure. Afterwards, Soviet policymakers increasingly accepted Reagan administration warnings that the U.S. would make the arms race a huge burden for them. The twin burdens of the Cold War arms race on one hand, and the provision of large sums of foreign and military aid, which their socialist allies had grown to expect, added to the failure of socialist economics, which left Gorbachev's efforts to boost production of consumer goods and reform the stagnating economy all but impossible. The result was a dual approach of cooperation with the west and economic restructuring (perestroika) and democratization (glasnost) domestically, which eventually made it impossible for Gorbachev to reassert central control and influence over Warsaw Pact member states.

One of the main reasons for the collapse of the Soviet Union was the massive spending on military technology that the Soviets saw as necessary in response to NATO's increased armament of the 1980s. Soviet efforts to keep up with NATO military expenditures resulted in massive economic disruption and the effective bankruptcy of the Soviet economy, which had always labored to keep up with its Western counterparts. The pace of military technology was advancing such that the Soviets were simply incapable of keeping up and still maintaining a healthy economy. The arms race, both nuclear and conventional, was too much for the underdeveloped Soviet economy of the time. It is for this reason that President Ronald Reagan, portrayed by some as a militarist or warmonger, is seen by many as the man who 'won' the Cold War by forcing the Soviets into bankruptcy through his aggressive pursuit of military expansion. In the end, it was proven once again that Marxist socialism is a failed system that simply cannot compete with capitalism.

The following is a summation of the events of 1989 as chronicled in the CIA report *At Cold War's End: US Intelligence on the Soviet Union and Eastern Europe, 1989-1991*

The USSR withdrew its last soldier from Afghanistan. Gorbachev demanded that the retreat be orderly and dignified--he didn't want television images reminiscent of the chaotic 1975 US pullout from Vietnam. "We must not appear before the world in our underwear or even without any," he told the Politburo inner circle. "A defeatist position is not possible." The withdrawal was intended as a sign of conciliation toward the West and reassurance to the East Europeans, but it encouraged the national minorities to challenge Soviet power.

The communist party lost its monopoly of power. In the USSR, multi-candidate elections were held for the first time. In Poland, Solidarity emerged from underground to win a stunning electoral victory over the communists and form the first coalition government in Eastern Europe since 1948. In Hungary, the communists agreed to multi-party elections, which occurred the next year.

Communism collapsed in Eastern Europe. The USSR renounced the "Brezhnev doctrine" and condemned the 1968 invasion of Czechoslovakia. As one historian noted, in Poland communism took ten years, in Hungary ten months, in East Germany ten weeks, and in Czechoslovakia ten days to disappear. In Romania--the bloody exception to the rule of peaceful transition--the end came with the execution of Nicolae Ceausescu and his wife on Christmas Day.

Nationalism trumped communism. The Soviets believed they had solved the problem of nationalism and ethnic conflict within their multinational state. But nationalism was in fact the gravedigger of the Soviet system. As the center disintegrated and Gorbachev opened up the political process with glasnost (openness), the old communist "barons" in the republics saw the handwriting on the wall and became nationalists; they "first of all attacked the USSR government . . . and subsequently destroyed the USSR." Asked when he decided to secede from the USSR, Ukrainian party boss Leonid Kravchuk replied: "1989."

The Soviets pondered the fate of their revolution as the French celebrated the bicentennial of theirs. The Soviets considered their revolution both the heir to and a superior version of the French Revolution of 1789 because it had solved the problem of class in-equality by eliminating private property and the irrationality of the business cycle by replacing the market with the plan. But as historian Francois Furet wrote: "It is 1917 that is being buried in the name of 1789." A protest banner summed up the Soviet experiment: "72 Years on a Road to Nowhere." The system's failure was evident. Then perestroika (restructuring) turned into katastroika, a neologism that was heard more and more on Moscow streets as Gorbachev's reform program faltered and then failed. The next year, a Soviet citizen could ask, only half-jokingly: "If there were socialism in the West, whom would we buy food from? The Ethiopians perhaps?"

The Berlin Wall, the paramount symbol of the Cold War and the division of Europe, fell. When Gorbachev visited East Berlin in October (ironically to celebrate the 40th anniversary of the East German state), his mere presence rocked the foundations of the Stalinist regime. Young marchers handpicked and bussed in from the countryside to present an image of unity and conformity spontaneously chanted: "Gorby! Gorby! Help us!" German unification a year later accelerated the Soviet political and military withdrawal from Europe. When it was over, Russia's borders had been pushed back to those of 1653, undoing more than 300 years of Tsarist and Soviet advance toward the West and leaving behind a country that was more Eurasian than European.

Gorbachev introduced glasnost (openness) to create popular support for his reforms. By doing so, however, he opened a Pandora's Box of revelations about the Gulag, the Great Terror, genocidal famines, mass deportations, and killing fields that had turned the USSR into one large charnel house in Stalin's time. Glasnost underscored Gorbachev's key dilemma: by allowing the truth to emerge, it destroyed the foundation of lies on which the communist system was built. One example: After releasing a map showing that the government had covered up the actual extent of contamination caused by the 1986 Chernobyl' nuclear reactor catastrophe, Moscow confiscated dosimeters from civil defense units so that people in the affected areas could not measure radiation levels.

The fall of the totalitarian communist Soviet state was accompanied by a sudden and dramatic decline in total warfare, interstate wars, ethnic wars, revolutionary wars, the number of refugees and displaced persons, and an increase in the number of democratic states, once again proving that freedom, individual rights, equality, free markets, and democracy are the basic elements of existence desired by most humans.

Science and Scientific Method

Natural law, in science, means the formulation of some uniform character, mode of behavior or uniform correlation of things or events; and it is frequently used in describing uniform relationships among various phenomena. Any such uniformity may be called a natural law, for example: all the laws formulated in physics and chemistry. On the other hand, the term "law of nature" is sometimes restricted to irreducible or primary laws (like the law of gravitation) as distinguished from derivative laws (like Johannes Kepler's laws of planetary motion). Laws with regard to nature are sequences of events or in human activities that have been observed to occur with unvarying uniformity under the same conditions.

Everything in nature follows certain patterns. For example, everything in nature is born. Once born; an entity lives, after a certain period of time it dies. If there are progeny, there is rebirth. This is true of everything in nature. A bacterium is born, it exists, and it dies. Humans are born, he or she lives, then death. The solar system was born, it lives, and it will die when the sun runs out of fuel and becomes a supernova, vaporizing the Earth and all the other planets. Stars, like the sun, are born, they live, and they die. It follows that the universe should also be evolutionary in that it is born, it lives, and it to will eventually die. This is the natural law of reciprocity or the cyclic nature of reality. Cyclic activity is seen in nature, it is seen in economics, it is seen in history and human behavior, and it is seen in organisms. In organisms it can be observed as the Krebs or citric acid cycle, and the pentose-phosphate cycle, which are mechanisms in carbohydrate metabolism.

Additionally, natural law is based on the concepts of uniformity, regularity and limitations. Uniformity and regularity describe the fact that entities behave according to specific causal conditions. For instance a human will not spontaneously begin photosynthesis. This is a biochemical function, and is only seen in entities, which have the correct biochemical makeup. Limitations are an integral part of the natural universe. Regularity in nature is the consequence of limitations; entities are limited in terms of their actions. Water runs down hill due to the force of gravity, it will not spontaneously change direction and in violation of the laws of gravitation start running up hill. The uniformity in nature permits the systematic study of reality (science) and the formulation of general principles of nature (natural laws), which are used in predicting future behavior.

Many things that are observable in the animal world and in nature are things that man has had to imitate, implement, or produce to insure his survival. For example, leaf cutter ants are as sophisticated and sometimes more sophisticated than many human civilizations. They engage in building roads to transport leaves that will be used to fertilize the crops they grow. They engage in excavation to build their homes and they have a waste disposal system to keep their community clean. The division of labor is also evident in many insect communities including the ants and bees. Violence is another feature of nature. Rhesus monkeys may exhibit violent and dictatorial behavior and even murder their own kind, but they do not possess reason, they are not self-aware, and they do not understand the concepts of self-interest or perpetuation of the species. The parallels between man, animals, and nature, and the moral application of the pursuit of happiness and self-interest are fascinating and important topics; unfortunately they must wait for another book.

All of these things that we see in nature follow patterns and order, and can be described mathematically. There is no need to create a God or a supernatural force to account for these phenomena. They stand on their own, for nature needs no master. The following from Lester Ward's, *Glimpses of the Cosmos*, is an eloquent summation of the conflict between science and theology.

Science is the great Iconoclast. Lord Bacon, the founder of inductive science, commenced the work of purification by breaking up the idols of the human intellect. He found it necessary before his "Great Restoration" could begin to destroy the Idols of the Tribe, the Den, the Market, and the Theater. Ever since his day, science has been continuing the work of image breaking. Steadily pursuing its course, turning neither to the right nor to the left, it has already revolutionized the world. But its especial tendency - we do not say its aim - is to purify, if not to supersede, the whole system of theology, which has so long prevailed over humankind. And though it does not attack theology, still it is today shaking its very foundations. The aim of science, preeminently and exclusively, is to know the truth. It has no prejudices; it rides no hobbies; it clings to no pet ideas. It is ready to sacrifice its most cherished theories the moment they are found not to square with that one great standard, truth. It is willing to labor; it is not sluggish, or delicate, or puffed up. It digs its treasures out of the bowels of the earth, or seeks them amid the hazy nebulae of heaven. It toils and delves and asks no praise from man, no favor shown of God. But this is perhaps no more than the stoics did; no more than the pilgrim or the monk has done. But a tree is known by its fruits.

The candid world is beginning to compare the fruits of theology with those of science. And what does it find? It finds that theology, though as old as human history, has brought few if any beneficial results; while on the other hand, its manifold evils lie scattered all along its pathway. Take from its history all the details of its wars, its conquests, its persecutions, and its massacres, and there would be nothing left but the graves of its hundred million victims, and the magnificent temples and costly tombs which it has taken the bread from the mouths of a starving world for four thousand years to erect.

Turning from such a picture to the result of scientific labor, behold the contrast! Scarce three hundred years have sufficed to transform the whole aspect of society. To enumerate the results of the application of the power of steam and electricity, so apparent to all, and so often alluded to as to have almost become hackneyed, would give but a meager idea indeed of what science has done to elevate, enlighten, and happify humankind. Its magic wand has touched almost every known object in nature - and many but for it unknown - and they have taken forms of beauty, of convenience, and of usefulness. Brilliant gas jets have superseded the dim and unsightly tapers and candles of the past; elegant fuel-saving stoves have supplanted the ancient chimney places; a thousand laborsaving machines relieve the weary limbs of toiling men and women, while countless factories, mills, and machine shops are supplying fabrics of every description to enhance the comfort and increase the enjoyment of humankind.

We can scarcely fix our mind upon one temporal blessing that we enjoy today, from the luxury of good food to the luxury of good health, for which we are, not indebted to science.

But besides these countless physical blessings science affords the highest and purest intellectual delight. It has led us into the arena of the infinite universe, and taught us to contemplate the wonders of nature, from the vast firmament of revolving spheres to the infinitesimal world of moving atoms; from the sparkling crystal to the living organism, the contemplation of which sublime truths yields to the mind a holier ecstasy than any reflections upon the character and attributes of anthropomorphic deities, or any selfish hopes of a future eternity of bliss. And when we remember that which is the crowning glory of science, that with all these blessings she has never cost one human life, one drop of human blood, one pang of human suffering; how long will the world hesitate to pronounce its decision?

The pursuit of science is the search for truth, knowledge and understanding through the formulation of the laws of nature. The word science is derived from the Latin word *scire*, which means, "to know." The formal definition of science is systemized knowledge derived from observation, study and experimentation carried on in order to determine the nature or principles of what is being studied. Science consists of the following activities:

- Classification and measurement
- Deduction and inductive inference
- Observation and generalization from experience
- Developing hypotheses and theories
- Experimentation and experimental verification of theory
- Verification, refinement and improvement of scientific knowledge through mathematics and empirical evidence

Science is the most exact, most carefully verified, and the most general knowledge available to man. Science seeks to comprehend the laws of nature independently of the bias and emotions of man. This is accomplished by using logic and reason rather than prejudices and passion.

Scientific method is the procedure by which knowledge is gained through empirical studies. Historically, in the tradition of Plato and Aristotle scientific method is analogous to mathematics. That is, all asserted propositions, which are not in themselves self-evident, should be derived from others that are self-evident. Aristotle also introduced the notion of induction and deductive reasoning.

Induction is general inference from particular instances, or drawing conclusions from several known cases. In induction, we observe a sufficient number of individual facts, and, on the grounds of analogy, extend what is true of them to others of the same class, thus arriving at general principles or laws.

Deduction is reasoning from a known principle to an unknown, from the general to the specific, or from a premise to a logical conclusion. In deduction we begin with a general truth, and seek to connect it with some individual case by means of a middle term or class of objects known to be equally connected with both. Thus we deduce the specific from the general, attributing to the former the distinctive qualities of the latter. As it relates to scientific method and logic, deduction is a formal structure based on a set of unproved axioms and a set of undefined objects. Axioms are statements that are accepted without proof. New terms are defined in terms of given undefined objects, and new statements, or theorems, are derived from the axioms by proof. A model for a deductive theory is a set of objects that have properties stated in a set of axioms. The deductive theory can be used to prove theorems that are true for all its models. The axioms of a mathematical system are the basic propositions from which all other propositions can be derived. A set of axioms is inconsistent if it is possible to deduce from these axioms that some statement is both true and false.

Francis Bacon and J.S. Mill further developed science and scientific method under the assumption that the empirical scientist was to establish universal propositions about causal connection. In J.S. Mill's *System of Logic* (1843) he defined a cause as an invariable antecedent and modeled his account of induction on Bacon's. In this work Mill defined what is known as Mill's Methods, or the five principles for the determination of causal connections.

1. The Method of Agreement - The factor (or complex of factors) always present in the circumstances in each instance in which the phenomenon is present, is causally connected with the phenomenon.
2. The Method of Difference - That factor (or complex of factors) which is present in the circumstances in the one instance in which a phenomenon is present but is always absent in each instance, which the phenomenon is absent, is causally connected with the phenomenon.
3. Joint Method of Agreement and Difference - That factor (or set of factors) which is always present in the circumstances in each instance in which the phenomenon is present, and which is always absent in each instance in which the phenomenon is absent, is causally connected with the phenomenon.
4. The Method of Concomitant Variation - That factor (or set of factors) which always varies in the circumstances in a direct or inverse relationship with the degree to which the phenomenon is present is causally connected with the phenomenon.
5. The Method of Residues - When one factor (or set of factors) of a compound phenomenon is always associated with a certain part of the factors constituting the circumstances, then the remaining factors of the circumstances are causally connected with the remaining (residual) factors of the phenomenon.

Since consistent, accurate, and unbiased evaluations are what we are striving for, it is important to have a foundation from which to approach all evaluations. Thus we will begin with a brief explanation of the stages of scientific method.

1. Observation - Through careful and systematic observation, the basic facts regarding the phenomena to be investigated are determined.
2. Hypothesis - Based on these observational data, a hypothesis is formulated that would (if accepted as true) account for the observed phenomena. A hypothesis is a supposition; a proposition, or principle, which is supposed or taken for granted, in order to draw a conclusion or inference for proof of the point in question. The hypothesis is the starting point of any experiment. It is an idea, phrased as a general or tentative statement about a relation between two or more events, which the scientist wishes to test in an experiment. A hypothesis can be confirmed by showing that what is deduced from it with certain initial conditions is actually found under those conditions, and that no other hypothesis will work, or can replace it as valid.
3. Verification - The fitness of this hypothesis as an acceptable theory is tested by its employment in relation to new and experimental circumstances and situations. The general pattern of such tests is as follows: First, the predictive consequences of the theory in such new circumstances are determined by (deductive) inference from the theory. Then a check is made on whether the actual observations in these cases are in accord with the expectations based on inference from the theory.

The modern implementation of scientific method consists of four major steps.

1. Identify the problem and formulate hypothetical cause-and-effect relations among variables. This step involves classifying variables into the proper categories and describing the relations among variables in general terms.

2. Design and execute an experiment. This step involves manipulating independent variables and observing dependent variables. Both variables must be operationally defined and the independent variable must be controlled so that definitive conclusions can be made. The independent variable does not depend upon another quantity for its value, while the dependent variable depends on another variable for its value. It is the independent variable that the experimenter manipulates and the dependent variable that it is measured.
3. Determine the truth of the hypothesis by examining the data from the experiment. This step often involves special mathematical procedures to determine whether an observed relation is statistically significant.
4. Communicate the results. This is usually accomplished by producing a scientific paper and having it published in the appropriate publication were it can be reviewed, scrutinized, checked for accuracy, disproved if possible, and analyzed by the scientific community. This provides the means for seeking the truth and it allows others to use the information to produce new theories or to improve the current theory.

What science is ultimately searching for is the truth. Truth is what really separates science from faith and belief, which are not based on facts. The meaning of truth is the state or quality of being true and being true means that the statement or knowledge is in accordance with fact or reality. To be a fact there has to be evidence.

Evidence is data that furnishes or tends to furnish proof. It is that which brings to the mind a just conviction of the truth or falsehood of any substantive proposition, which is asserted or denied. Evidence includes all the means by which any alleged matter of fact, the truth of which is submitted to investigation, is established or disproved. This proof must establish the grounds for belief. Without demonstration and affirmation of fact there is no proof. This is what science in fact does. It provides evidence for theory. Based on this evidence the theory is judged to be true or false. In religion and non-scientific belief systems there is no equivalent, there is only faith without evidence.

Just because you want to believe something does not mean it is true. False beliefs do not correspond to facts. Scientists, unlike their religious counterparts, follow the facts wherever they take them. If the facts take them down a different road they will throw out the old theory and pursue the facts until the truth is known. Reason does not demand that human knowledge be closed to further investigation. On the contrary, it demands that the frontiers of human knowledge must always remain open.

One of the basic tenants of science is disproof. All attempts possible are made to disprove scientific theories. A good example of this is the continuous attempts to disprove Einstein's theories of general and special relativity. In 1916 when Einstein published his work on relativity people thought he was crazy and no one believed him. Einstein himself stated that his ideas had to pass three crucial experimental tests.

1. The advance of Mercury's perihelion (closest point to the sun) by about 43 arc seconds per century after subtracting out the effects of precession (The wobble of the Earth's rotational axis) and the other planets.
2. The gravitational bending of starlight at the limb of the sun.
3. The gravitational red shift or time dilation.

The first was an effect that had been long known but unexplained until relativity. It was due to the warping of space near the sun. The second was observed during a solar eclipse in 1919, making Einstein world famous. The last crucial experiment is based on relativity's prediction that gravity will cause time to slow down. The stronger a gravitational field, the slower a clock will run. Once the technology existed for a clock that was accurate enough to detect this effect the third test could be carried out. In 1976 Robert Vessot of the Harvard-Smithsonian Center for Astrophysics and Martin

Levine now with Frequency and Time Systems, in collaboration with NASA, carried out an experiment using a hydrogen maser clock. At 10,000 kilometers above earth where gravity is weaker, a clock would gain one second every 73 years. This experiment verified Einstein's prediction to an accuracy of .014 percent. Without proof, scientists would not even believe Einstein. Experimental verification of theory is what makes science, science, not faith.

Science requires a great deal of intellectual labor and knowledge to acquire real proficiency, but this is no reason to ignore it, or deny its reality. And instead, believe dogmatic nonsense merely on faith. When people deny science and reality, they do so because they are too lazy to learn the facts of natural phenomena, and develop their own worldview based on facts and reason.

Logic and Mathematics

Logic and mathematics are the sciences of reasoning, the operations of understanding which are subservient to the estimation of evidence, and include the process of proceeding from known truths or axioms to unknown variables. An axiom is a first principle, premise, or basic assumption that is assumed to be a self-evident truth for the purpose of further analysis or deduction and provide a basis for logical reasoning. An axiom is synonymous with a postulate.

An axiom or postulate differs from a theorem in that a theorem is a proposition deducible from basic postulates, which can be proven to be true. An example of a postulate from geometry is through any two points there is exactly one line. From this postulate the theorem that a line segment has exactly one midpoint can be derived.

Logic is the study and evaluation of arguments. An argument is a group or series of statements, one or more of which, (the premises) are claimed to provide support for, or reasons to believe, one of the others, (the conclusion). A statement is a sentence that is either true of false. An example of an argument is as follows:

> All humans are mortal.
> Socrates is human.
> Therefore, Socrates is mortal.

Arguments can be divided in two groups, deductive and inductive. A deductive argument is an argument in which the premises are claimed to support the conclusion in such a way that it is impossible for the premises to be true and the conclusion false. An inductive argument is an argument in which the premises are claimed to support the conclusion is such a way that is that it is improbable that the premises are true and the conclusion false. The difference between impossible and improbable is that deductive arguments are those that involve necessary reasoning, and inductive arguments are those that involve probabilistic reasoning.

Aristotle was the father of logic, with the *Organon*, Aristotle's collected works on logic, being the most extensive treatment on the subject. Francis Bacon further developed logic in his work *Novum Organum*, with further developments by Immanuel Kant in *Introduction to Logic* and Rene Descarte's *Discourse on Method*. Logic today is the systematic study of valid inference, and the science of correct reasoning. It includes the fields of mathematical logic, set theory, and syllogistic logic.

Mathematics is the collective name applied to all those sciences in which operations in logic are used to study the relationship between quantity, space, time, and magnitude. Mathematics employs a special kind of language using symbols, numerals, and letters. Their use is determined by the rules of logic within each of the fields of study and serves as a means of abbreviation, both in thinking and in visual representation.

Learning mathematics is like learning a second language. To become proficient in a second language you have to speak the language, to become proficient in mathematics you have to solve problems. Deliberate practice solving large numbers of mathematical problems with pencil and paper is how you get good at mathematics. As a mathematics professor once stated, math is a motor skill. Fine motor skill involves deliberate and controlled movements requiring both muscle development and maturation of the central nervous system. Just as children develop fine motor skills as they age, math skills are developed though the use of eye-hand-brain coordination.

Reasoning with numbers and symbols began with the introduction of problem solving and proofs. Historically the two main branches of mathematics were arithmetic and geometry. These branches both originated about the same time in Egypt and Babylonia as applied mathematics. In the 6th century B.C., the Greeks, including Pythagoras, Euclid, Archimedes, and Thales transformed arithmetic and geometry into systems of logic. In the Middle Ages Arabic mathematicians, through the abstraction of arithmetic, developed algebra and trigonometry. Then in the 19th century, Rene Descartes combined algebra and geometry to create analytic geometry. Analytic geometry provided the foundation for new disciplines in higher mathematics including calculus, which was developed independently by Isaac Newton and Gottfried Leibniz. The development of modern mathematics continued with probability theory, non-Euclidean geometry, topology, set theory, game theory, and fractal geometry.

Mathematics to the Greeks was not only a useful method of calculating quantitative relations; it was also a divine science, almost a religion having to do with eternal things. They felt this way because mathematics is so useful in describing nature. The formulas that describe nature are symmetrical, have an underlying simplicity, and are beautiful in their structure. With these attributes it is no wonder that the Greeks held mathematics in such high esteem. Mathematics continues to provide the basis for advanced reasoning. Whereas people in different cultures and geographical areas all have their own interpretation of the various religions, mathematics is universal. Its structure and logic are the same no matter where it is practiced or what language it is written or spoken in.

Mathematics is the science of numbers and their operations, interrelations, combinations, generalizations, and abstractions, and of space configurations and their structure, measurement, transformations, and generalizations. Mathematics is a science of pattern and order. Mathematics, as a major intellectual tradition, is a subject appreciated as much for its beauty as for its power. The enduring qualities of such abstract concepts as symmetry, proof, and change have been developed through 3,000 years of intellectual effort. The process of mathematics is more than just calculation or deduction; it involves observation of patterns, testing of conjectures, and estimation of results. Mathematics is both a foundation of truth and a standard of certainty. In addition to theorems and theories, mathematics offers distinctive modes of thought, which are both versatile and powerful, including modeling, abstraction, optimization, logical analysis, and inference from data, and use of symbols.

When children first start studying math, and they have to learn addition and subtraction, then multiplication and division, most kids start asking, "Why do I have to learn this stuff?" They probably got a response something like; "You have to learn your arithmetic so you can advance to the next grade." Well, that really isn't the reason. You need to learn math because if you want to succeed in modern society you have to know mathematics.

Expertise in mathematics provides the basis for careers in many of the fastest growing fields including, actuarial sciences, statistics, bio-informatics, quantitative research in equities and derivatives, computer science, and math instruction. In the relatively new field of mathematical finance, people with a PhD. in mathematics first-year compensation can range between $100,000 and $300,000, or more depending on background and experience.

Mathematics is fundamental to knowledge and is critical to success in the modern world. Once you learn advanced mathematics you can learn any other field of study. Do yourself and your children a favor, and study mathematics. It will not only help your career it will help your brain. To help get you started and to show the importance of mathematics in the development of today's modern technological society, a brief history of mathematics is provided below.

A Brief History of Mathematics

Mathematics arose from the need to catalog and count property and people, and the practical needs of agriculture and trade. It seems reasonable that the earliest humans used fingers to count and communicate numbers and the widespread use of the decimal system is the result of the fact that humans happen to have ten fingers and ten toes. Decimal refers to the base ten number system, which uses the characters 0 through 9 to represent values.

The first record of the use of mathematics beyond mere counting comes from the Egyptians and Babylonians. Building on the concept of counting, arithmetic was developed. Today, arithmetic refers to numerical computation involving the four fundamental operations of addition, subtraction, multiplication and division, which are performed in accordance with the axioms for real numbers.

Most of our knowledge of Egyptian mathematics comes from the Rhind papyrus written by the scribe Ahmes about 1650 B.C., and the Moscow papyrus. Papyrus is an early form of paper made from the papyrus plant. The Rhind Papyrus was named after the Scottish Egyptologist Alexander Henry Rhind, who purchased it in 1858. The Rhind papyrus, which now resides in the British Museum, consisted of a collection of practical mathematical problems and solutions. Many of the problems were in the form of what we would today call "story problems." The Rhind papyrus also includes several tables of fractions. The Moscow Papyrus has several of the same type of problems and solutions found in the Rhind papyrus. It also includes a description of the truncated pyramid. A truncated pyramid has a square base, which narrows to a square top. In other words, a normal pyramid with the top cut off.

The Babylonians used the cuneiform system of writing. Cuneiform used a reed to impress wedge-shaped marks onto the surface of clay tablets. These cuneiform symbols were used to create tables to aid calculation. Babylonian mathematics included the development of a sexagismal (base 60) positional notation number system, and the use of the Pythagorean theorem many years before its formal proof. The innovation of positional notation streamlined the process of representing numbers and kept the number of symbols to a minimum. By contrast the Roman numeral system, which was not a place value system, required a large number of symbols, such as I, V, X, L, C, D, M, and was very cumbersome to work with.

Sexagismal measure is the degree system of measure in which a complete revolution is considered to be 360 degrees. The unit of measure, or 1 degree, is equal to 1/360 of a complete revolution. The degree is divided into 60 minutes (60') and the minute into 60 seconds (60").

Place value, or positional notation, is a numeration system in which a real number is represented by an ordered set of characters where the value of a character depends on its position. Each position is related to the next by a constant multiplier called the base of that numeral system. The resultant value of each position is the value of its symbol or symbols multiplied by a power of the base. The total value of a positional number is the sum of the resultant values of all positions. In the base ten number system, the first place from right to left is the units digit, the second place is the tens digit, the third digit is the hundred's digit, and so on; when necessary zero is used as a placeholder. The number 364 means 3 hundreds, plus 6 tens, plus 4 units, or $300 + 60 + 4$.

The Greek Period produced some of the greatest mathematicians and philosophers the world has known. Greek mathematicians developed the foundations of modern mathematics, and had a profound influence on philosophy and scientific method. Greek geometry in particular stands as one of the greatest achievements of the human intellect.

During the Greek period mathematics advanced from arithmetic to abstraction. To abstract is to consider apart from application to or association with a particular instance. Abstraction in mathematics is the process of extracting the underlying essence of a mathematical concept, removing any dependence on real world objects with which it might originally have been connected, and generalizing it so that it has wider applications.

Many areas of mathematics began with the study of real world problems, before the underlying rules and concepts were identified and defined as abstract structures. For example, geometry has its origins in the calculation of distances and areas in the real world; statistics has its origins in the calculation of probabilities in gambling; and algebra started with methods of solving problems in arithmetic.

Abstraction is an ongoing process in mathematics and the historical development of many mathematical topics exhibits a progression from the concrete to the abstract. As mathematics becomes more advanced it also becomes more abstract. The first steps in the abstraction of geometry were made by the ancient Greeks, with Euclid being the first person to document the axioms of plane geometry.

Thales of Miletus (c. 624–548 B.C.) was one of the Seven Wise Men of Greece, and is often referred to as the first true mathematician. Although historical evidence of the life and times of Thales is minimal, he is attributed with providing the first geometrical proof. His proof of the theorem that an angle inscribed in a semicircle is a right angle is known as the Theorem of Thales. He is also regarded as the originator of the deductive organization of geometry and for providing additional important geometric proofs.

Like Thales, historical evidence for the works of Pythagoras (c. 580-500 B.C.) is elusive. Despite a lack of hard evidence of the accomplishments of Pythagoras, it is evident that the Pythagoreans played an important role in the history of mathematics. Pythagoras was the founder of a school of mathematicians and a religion. The main tenets of the Pythagorean religion were the transmigration of souls and the sinfulness of eating beans. Pythagoras made remarkable contributions to the mathematical theory of music. Pythagoras noticed that vibrating strings produce harmonious tones when the ratios of the lengths of the strings are whole numbers, and that these ratios could be extended to other instruments. Pythagoras believed that all relations could be reduced to number relations. This generalization stemmed from Pythagoras's observations in music, mathematics and astronomy.

The greatest discovery of Pythagoras, or his disciples, was the proposition about right triangles, that the sum of the squares on the sides adjoining the right angle is equal to the square on the remaining side, the hypotenuse. The Egyptians had known that a triangle whose sides are 3,4,5 contains a right angle, but it was the Greeks who were first to observe that $3^2 + 4^2 = 5^2$, and to discover a proof of the general proposition. Unfortunately for Pythagoras, this theorem led to the discovery of incommensurables, which appeared to disprove his whole philosophy. Incommensurable means not having a common measure.

The Pythagoreans believed that any two lengths are "commensurable" (that is, measurable) by integer multiples of some common unit. They believed that the whole (or counting) numbers, and their ratios (rational numbers or fractions), were sufficient to describe any quantity. The discovery of surds (the square roots of numbers that are not perfect squares) undermined the Pythagoreans belief that reality is essentially mathematical and based on whole numbers.

The earliest known use of irrational numbers was in the Indian Sulba Sutras composed between 800-500 B.C. The first proof of irrational numbers is usually attributed to the Pythagorean Hippasus of Metapontum, who produced a proof of the irrationality of the square root of 2. The story goes that Hippasus discovered irrational numbers when trying to represent the square root of 2 as a fraction. However, Pythagoras believed in the absoluteness of numbers, and could not accept the existence of irrational numbers.

He could not disprove their existence through logic, but his beliefs would not accept the existence of irrational numbers and so he sentenced Hippasus to death by drowning.

An irrational number is a number that cannot be expressed as a fraction p/q for any integer's p and q. Irrational numbers have decimal expansions that neither terminate nor become periodic. All transcendental numbers, such as pi are irrational.

The period from 440 B.C. to 300 B.C. saw a number of Greek philosophers contribute significantly to the development of mathematics. Among them were Plato (427–347 B.C.) and Eudoxus (c. 408–355 B.C.). Plato considered mathematics to be the perfect training for the mind, its logical rigor demanding the ultimate in concentration, cleverness, and care. Eudoxus is remembered for two major contributions to mathematics. One was his theory of proportion, and the other his method of exhaustion. The general strategy of the method of exhaustion was to approach an irregular figure by means of a succession of known elementary ones, each providing a better approximation than its predecessor. Archimedes used this method when he determined the area of a circle by inscribing within the circle a square, then doubling the number of sides to get an octagon, and doubling again, and so on. These simple polygons approach and eventually approximate the circle itself.

Euclid of Alexandria (c. 325-265 B.C.) is best remembered for *The Elements*, which is a systematic development of most of the Greek mathematics known up to that point. Generally considered the greatest textbook on mathematics of all time, it is divided into 13 books and contains 465 propositions on plane and solid geometry, and number theory.

Euclid begins with a list of 23 definitions so the reader would know precisely what his terms meant. Building on his defined terms, Euclid presented five postulates to serve as the foundations of his geometry, and the starting points from which all would follow. The geometry of Euclid starts with axioms, which are self-evident and proceed, by deductive reasoning, to arrive at theorems that are often very far from self-evident.

In Book IX of *The Elements*, Euclid proves that there are infinitely many prime numbers. This is one of the first proofs known which uses the method of contradiction to establish a result. Euclid also gives a proof of the Fundamental Theorem of Arithmetic: Any positive integer (other than 1) can be written as the product of prime numbers in one and only one-way.

In 250 B.C. Greek mathematician and astronomer Eratosthenes (276–194 B.C.), director of the great library at Alexandria, calculated the circumference of the Earth and completed the first calculation of the distance of earth from the sun. Eratosthenes compared the noon shadow at midsummer between Syene (now Aswan on the Nile in Egypt) and Alexandria. He assumed that the sun was so far away that its rays were essentially parallel, and then with knowledge of the distance between Syene and Alexandria, he gave the length of the circumference of the Earth as approximately 26,600 miles, which is fairly close to the modern estimate of 24,894 miles. Eratosthenes also invented a method of separating the prime numbers by eliminating the multiples of each successive prime. This method is called the sieve of Eratosthenes. Prime numbers are natural numbers that have no integral factors except 1 and itself.

Archimedes of Syracuse (c. 287-212 B.C.) was one of the greatest mathematicians of all time and can well be called the father of mathematical physics for his two books *On the Equilibrium of Planes* and *On Floating Bodies*. In his treatise *On the Equilibrium of Planes* Archimedes deduced and provided the mathematical laws of the lever and developed the concept of center of gravity. *On Floating Bodies* contained Archimedes work on hydrostatics including the principle of buoyancy.

Archimedes contributions to mathematics included his works *Measurement of a Circle*, *On the Sphere and Cylinder*, and *The Method*. The *Measurement of a Circle* contains three propositions, the first one being the most important. In the first proposition Archimedes proved the famous formula for the area of a circle, which is known today as $A = p \, r^2$ and in the third proposition he provided a remarkably accurate estimate of the number p, which today is approximately 3.14159 . . . on to infinity.

In his treatise *On the Sphere and Cylinder* Archimedes determined the surface area and volume of the sphere. He had also discovered and proved that the ratios of the volumes of a cylinder and sphere are the same as the ratios of the areas - that is three-to-two. In *The Method* Archimedes pioneered the use of infinitesimals, demonstrating that breaking a figure down into an infinite number of small parts could be used to determine area and volume. Archimedes is the first to explicitly use infinitesimals to solve problems that would now be treated by integral calculus. In mathematics, an infinitesimal or infinitely small number, is a number that is greater in absolute value than zero yet smaller than any positive real number.

During the Second Punic War, in the sack of Syracuse, a Roman soldier killed Archimedes despite orders from the Roman general, Marcellus that he was not to be harmed. The Greeks said that he was killed while drawing an equation in the sand engrossed in his diagram and impatient with being interrupted, he is said to have muttered his famous last words before being slain by an enraged Roman soldier: "Don't disturb my circles."

Apollonius of Perga (c. 262-190 B.C.) in his famous book *Conics* first introduced terms, which are familiar to us today such as parabola, ellipse and hyperbola. Conic sections are the curves that are formed by the intersection of a plane and a right circular cone. The parabola is a plane curve generated by a point moving so that its distance from a fixed point is equal to its distance from a fixed line (called the directrix). The directrix is a straight line the distance to which from any point of a conic section is in fixed ratio to the distance from the same point to a focus. The ellipse is a closed plane curve generated by a point moving in such a way that the sums of its distances from two fixed points are a constant. The hyperbola is a plane curve generated by a point so moving that the difference of the distances from two fixed points is a constant.

The Greek astronomer and mathematician Hipparchus of Nicaea (180–125 B.C.) compiled the first trigonometric table and thus earned the right to be known as "the father of trigonometry." Hipparchus produced a table of chords, an early example of a trigonometric table. The purpose of this table of chords was to give a method for solving triangles, which avoided solving each triangle from first principles. He also introduced the division of a circle into 360 degrees into Greece.

Trigonometry means triangle measurement. Trigonometry includes the study of solutions of triangles by computation and trigonometric functions. The six trigonometric functions, sine, cosine, tangent, cotangent, secant, and cosecant, can be defined using three different approaches: as ratios of the sides of a right triangle, in a coordinate system using angles in standard position, and as arc lengths on a unit circle. Trigonometry has applications in surveying, navigation, construction, and many branches of science, and is essential in the study of calculus.

Perhaps the discovery for which Hipparchus is most famous is the discovery of precession, which is due to the slow change in direction of the axis of rotation of the earth. This work came from Hipparchus's attempts to calculate the length of the year with a high degree of accuracy. There are two different definitions of a year. One based on the time that the sun takes to return to the same place amongst the fixed stars, the other based on the time interval between one vernal equinox (the vernal equinox marks the first day of the season of spring) and the next. The first is called the sidereal (expressed in relation to stars) year while the second is called the tropical year.

As the Earth travels around the Sun in its orbit, the north-south position (declination) of the Sun changes over the course of the year due to the changing orientation of the Earth's tilted rotation axes with respect to the Sun. It is this change in the position of the sun that is responsible for seasons. The dates of maximum tilt of the Earth's equator correspond to the summer solstice and winter solstice, and the dates of zero tilt to the vernal equinox and autumnal equinox. The summer and winter solstices are the longest and shortest days of the year.

As Rome ascended Greek mathematics declined. The Hindu and Arabic scholars served as a bridge to the modern world. Al-Khwarizmi was a Persian scientist, mathematician, and astronomer. Al-Khwarizmi encountered the Indian numeral system (0, 1, 2, 3, 4, 5, 6, 7, 8, 9), and wrote a treatise on what we call Arabic numerals. It was translated into Latin in the twelfth century as *Algoritmi de numero Indorum* or *Al-Khwarizmi on the Hindu Art of Reckoning,* and was crucial in the introduction of Arabic numerals to medieval Europe. It may well represent the first use of zero as a positional placeholder. From the title of this treatise, we have the word "algorithm" (a procedure for solving a mathematical problem in a finite number of steps).

Al-Khwarizmi's most important work, however, was the treatise called *al-Kitab al-mukhtasar fi hisab al-jabr w'al-muqabala* or *The Compendious Book on Calculation by Completion [or Restoring] and Balancing.* This book is an explanation of the solution to quadratic and linear equations of six varieties. Al-jabr refers to the process of moving a subtracted quantity to the other side of an equation; al-muqabala involves subtracting equal quantities from both sides of an equation. *Al-Kitab al-mukhtasar fi hisab al-jabr w'al-muqabala* was translated into Latin in 1140 A.D. as *Liber algebrae et almucabala,* from which we have the word "algebra" for the whole process of solving equations, consequently some have considered Al-Khwarizmi the father of algebra.

For almost one thousand years after the extraordinary development of the Greek mathematicians, with the exception of Al-Khwarizmi's algebra there were no major developments in mathematics. One other notable development came from Leonardo Pisano (1170-1250 A.D.) who is better known by his nickname Fibonacci. Fibonacci's best-known work was *Liber abaci*, published in 1202 after his return to Italy. The book was based on the arithmetic and algebra that Fibonacci had accumulated during his travels. The book, which went on to be widely copied and imitated, introduced the Hindu-Arabic place-valued decimal system and the use of Arabic numerals into Europe.

Fibonacci is best known for his development of the Fibonacci sequence 1,1,2,3,5,8,13,21... where each term after the first two is the sum of the two terms immediately preceding it. This sequence has been found to have many significant properties. As you go farther and farther to the right in this sequence the ratio of a term to the one before it will get closer and closer to the golden ratio. The golden ratio is an irrational number, approximately 1.618, that possesses many interesting properties. Shapes defined by the golden ratio have long been considered aesthetically pleasing in Western cultures, reflecting nature's balance between symmetry and asymmetry. Fibonacci numbers are common in nature and appear in the spirals of pinecones, pineapples, and sunflowers and in the logarithmic spiral (like the one in a nautilus shell) where all the angles are equal based on the Fibonacci sequence.

The next great expansion of mathematical thought came during the Renaissance period. The Renaissance was an influential cultural movement, which brought about a period of scientific revolution and artistic transformation, at the dawn of modern European history. It marks the transitional period between the end of the Middle Ages and the start of the Modern Age. The Renaissance is usually considered to have begun in the 14th century in Italy and the 16th century in northern Europe.

The High Renaissance was the culmination of the artistic developments of the Early Renaissance, and one of the great explosions of creative genius in history. It is notable for three of the greatest artists in history: Michelangelo Buonarroti, Raphael Sanzio, and Leonardo da Vinci. Even today, there are few artists that can match the works of the great Renaissance masters. One of the reasons for the fine art of this period was the development of the theory of perspective. Perspective, when used in the context of vision and visual perception, refers to the way in which objects appear to the eye based on their spatial attributes, or their dimensions and the position of the eye relative to the objects. For example, the parallel lines of a railway track are perceived by the eye of a standing human being as meeting at a distant point at the horizon. The person who is credited with the first correct formulation of linear perspective is Brunelleschi. He appears to have made the discovery in about 1413. He understood that there should be a single vanishing point to which all parallel lines in a plane, other than the plane of the canvas, converge. Also important was his understanding of scale, and he correctly computed the relation between the actual length of an object and its length in the picture depending on its distance behind the plane of the canvas.

The first person to actually write down an explanation of how the rules of perspective work was Alberti (1404–1472) in his treatise *On Painting*. The most mathematical of all the works on perspective written by the Italian Renaissance artists in the middle of the 15th century was by Piero della Francesca (1410–1492). In his three-volume treatise *On Perspective for Painting* Piero begins by establishing geometric theorems in the style of Euclid but unlike Euclid, he also gives numerical examples to illustrate them.

In 1545 Cardan (1501–1576) published his greatest mathematical work *Ars Magna*. In it he gave the methods of solution of the cubic and quartic equation. A cubic equation is an equation of third degree such as $x^3 - x^2 - 9x + 9 = 0$. Cubic equations can be solved by graphing, factoring, or by a combination of these methods, or through the use of Cardan's formula. A quartic equation is an equation of fourth degree. The degree of a polynomial is the highest degree of any term in the polynomial.

The development of algebra continued with Francois Viete's (1540–1603) introduction of literal notation in algebra, which is the systematic use of letters to represent both coefficients and unknown variables in algebraic equations. In his treatise *In artem analyticam isagoge*, Viete demonstrated the value of symbols by introducing letters to represent unknowns. He suggested using letters as symbols for quantities, both known and unknown. He used vowels for the unknowns and consonants for known quantities. Descartes introduced the convention where letters near the beginning of the alphabet represent known quantities while letters near the end represent unknown quantities.

John Napier (1550–1617) was a Scottish mathematician who invented logarithms. After 20 years of work, in 1614 he published his *A Description of the Marvelous Rule of Logarithms*. Henry Briggs followed with his table of common logarithms (base ten) of the numbers 1 to 1000 carried out to fourteen places. A logarithm is the exponent used to indicate the power to which a base must be raised in order to obtain a given number. In the expression $3^4 = 81$, 3 is the base and 4 is the power to which 3 must be raised to obtain 81. Thus 4 is the logarithm of 81 to the base 3.

In 1637, Rene Descartes (1596–1650) published his treatise *La geometrie*, which described analytic geometry. Analytic geometry is geometry in which coordinates express position and the method of reasoning is primarily algebraic. For example, in analytic geometry a circle, of radius r whose center is at the origin in a x-y coordinate system is described by the equation $x^2 + y^2 = r^2$. The x-y coordinate system, often referred to as the Cartesian coordinate system named after Descartes, is a system in which ordered pairs of real numbers in the form of (x, y) represent the locations of points from two perpendicular axes that intersect at the origin.

Pierre Fermat (1601-1665) contributed to the development of analytic geometry, differential calculus, minima and maxima, and to the foundations of probability theory. Fermat is best remembered for this work in number theory, in particular for Fermat's Last Theorem. This theorem states that $x^n + y^n = z^n$ has no non-zero integer solutions for x, y and z when $n > 2$. Three hundred years later in June 1993, the British mathematician Andrew Wiles proved the truth of Fermat's assertion.

In 1653 Blaise Pascal (1623–1662) wrote his *Traité du triangle arithmétique* in which he described a convenient tabular presentation for binomial coefficients, the "arithmetical triangle", now called Pascal's triangle. Yang Hui, a Chinese mathematician of the Qin dynasty, had independently worked out a concept similar to Pascal's triangle four centuries earlier. Pascal's triangle is a triangular arrangement of numbers which gives the numerical coefficients of $(a + b)^n$ for any value of n.

In 1654, prompted by a friend interested in gambling problems, he corresponded with Fermat on the subject, and from that collaboration was born the mathematical theory of probabilities. Probability is a branch of mathematics that measures the likelihood that an event will occur. For equally likely outcomes, the probability of an event is the number of favorable outcomes divided by the total number of possible outcomes of an experiment. Probabilities are expressed as numbers between 0 and 1. The probability of an impossible event is 0, while an event that is certain to occur has a probability of 1. If the probability is .5 the event has a 50 percent chance of a favorable outcome.

John Wallis (1616–1703) contributed substantially to the origins of calculus and was the most influential English mathematician before Newton. Wallis developed methods in the style of Descartes analytical treatment and was the first English mathematician to use these new techniques. His work is also famous for the first use of the symbol ∞ which was chosen by Wallis to represent a curve which one could traced out infinitely many times. This symbol is still used today to represent infinity.

Wallis had a great ability to do mental calculations. He slept badly and often did mental calculations, as he lay awake in his bed. One night he calculated the square root of a number with 53 digits in his head. In the morning he dictated the 27-digit square root of the number, still entirely from memory.

Isaac Newton (1642–1727) was one of the greatest scientists and mathematicians of all time. Newton was the single greatest contributor to the development of modern science. He added mathematical rigor and created a new methodology for scientific method, which were the foundations of the Age of Reason, and for the technological civilization of today.

Newton's treatise *Philosophiae Naturalis Principia Mathematica* (Mathematical Principles of Natural Philosophy) written in 1687, described universal gravitation and the three laws of motion, laying the groundwork for classical mechanics. The three laws of motion are:

1. (Law of inertia): A body at rest remains at rest and a body in motion continues to move at a constant velocity unless acted upon by an external force.
2. A force F acting on a body gives it an acceleration a, which is in the direction of the force and has magnitude inversely proportional to the mass m of the body: or $F = ma$.
3. Whenever a body exerts a force on another body, the latter exerts a force of equal magnitude and opposite direction on the former.

By deriving Kepler's laws of planetary motion from this system, he was the first to show that the motion of bodies on Earth and of celestial bodies is governed by the same set of natural laws. The unifying and deterministic power of his laws was integral to the scientific revolution and the advancement of heliocentrism.

Among other scientific discoveries, Newton realized that the spectrum of colors observed when white light passes through a prism is inherent in the white light and not added by the prism (as Roger Bacon had claimed in the 13th century), and notably argued that light is composed of particles.

From his work in optics he concluded that any refracting telescope would suffer from the dispersion of light into colors, and invented a reflecting telescope (today, known as a Newtonian telescope) to bypass that problem. By grinding his own mirrors, using Newton's rings to judge the quality of the optics for his telescopes, he was able to produce a superior instrument to the refracting telescope, due primarily to the wider diameter of the mirror. Newton also developed a law of cooling, describing the rate of cooling of objects when exposed to air, and enunciated the principles of conservation of momentum and angular momentum.

Newton shares credit with Gottfried Leibniz for the development of integral and differential calculus, which he used to formulate his physical laws. Newton developed calculus using as fundamental notions fluxions (time derivatives) and fluents (inverse of fluxions), fluents being interpreted as areas. He also made contributions to other areas of mathematics, having derived the binomial theorem in its entirety. The binomial theorem is an important formula giving the expansion of powers of sums.

Calculus is the branch of mathematics studying the rate of change of quantities, which can be interpreted as slopes of curves and the length, area, and volume of objects. Calculus is sometimes divided into differential (derivatives) and integral (integrals) calculus.

Differential calculus is the study of the rate at which a function changes relative to a change in the independent variable. Geometrically, the derivative is interpreted as the slope of the line tangent to a curve at a point. Integral calculus is the study of the limit of a sum of elements when the number of such elements increases without bound while the size of the elements diminishes.

Gottfried Wilhelm Leibniz (1646–1716) is often described as the last universalist, having contributed to virtually all fields of scholarly interest of his time, including law, history, theology, politics, engineering, geology, physics, and perhaps most importantly philosophy, mathematics, and logic. His study of logic and intellectual quest for order continued throughout his life and became a basic principle to his method of inquiry.

Leibniz is also known for his independent development of calculus. Leibniz based his calculus on the finding of differentials, which he understood as infinitesimal differences, and defined the integral as an infinite sum of infinitesimals (infinitely or immeasurably small). The operation of summing and of finding the differences was mutually inverse. His vision of a universal symbolic language led him to devise notation for calculus that is still used today, such as d for differential and $\int$ for integral. Leibniz also published a paper that is the basis for the modern binary number system. Leibniz's uses 0 and 1, like the modern binary numeral system. The binary numeral system (base 2 numerals) represents numeric values using two numbers, zero and one. Binary is a positional notation with a radix of two. Due to its relatively straightforward implementation in electronic circuitry, virtually all-modern computers use the binary system.

Johann Bernoulli (1667–1748) was in continual competition with his brother Jacob in what turned into a bitter rivalry. Bernoulli proposed the problem of the brachristochrone (curve of fastest descent) in 1696 and challenged others to solve it. The brachistochrone problem was one of the earliest problems posed in the calculus of variations. Newton was challenged to solve the problem in 1696, and did so the very next day. In fact, the solution, which is a segment of a cycloid, was found by Leibniz, L'Hospital, Newton, and the two Bernoullis. Johann Bernoulli showed that the curve of quickest decent was the cycloid, thereby solving the first problem of the calculus of variations.

Jacob Bernoulli's (1654–1705) work led to advances in algebra, the infinitesimal calculus, the calculus of variations, mechanics, the theory of series, and the theory of probability. In 1689, he published important work on infinite series and published his law of large numbers in probability theory. The phrase "law of large numbers" is also sometimes used to refer to the principle that the probability of any possible event (even an unlikely one) occurring at least once in a series increases with the number of events in the series.

Leonhard Euler (1707-1783) was the most prolific writer in the history of mathematics. He proved many original and difficult theorems in nearly every branch of mathematics. Euler also helped standardize the symbol i for the square root of negative one. Using this notation a complex number is defined to be one of the form $a + bi$, where a and b are real numbers.

Carl Friedrich Gauss (1777–1855) is considered along with Archimedes and Newton to be one of three greatest mathematicians of all time. Gauss was a German mathematician and scientist of profound genius who contributed significantly to many fields, including number theory, analysis, differential geometry, geodesy, magnetism, astronomy and optics.

In a feat that even the great mathematician Euler was unable to accomplish, Gauss in his 1799 doctoral dissertation from the University of Helmstadt furnished the first proof of the fundamental theorem of algebra. The fundamental theorem of algebra states that any n^{th} degree polynomial equation written in the complex numbers will have n (perhaps repeated) solutions, all of which must themselves be complex numbers. In other words, in the field of complex numbers every polynomial equation has a root.

Augustin-Louis Cauchy (1789–1857) determined the first correct definition of limits in his *Cours d'analyse* (1821). This work also contained the first systematic study of convergence of series and the first theory of function of functions of a complex variable. He defined the derivative and integral in terms of limits. In mathematics, the concept of a "limit" is used to describe the behavior of a function, as its argument gets "close" to either some point, or infinity; or the behavior of a sequence's elements, as their index approaches infinity. Limits are used in calculus and other branches of mathematical analysis to define derivatives and continuity.

Cauchy was the first to produce a rigorous study of the conditions for convergence of infinite series and a rigorous definition of an integral. His treatise *Cours d'analyse* was concerned with developing the basic theorems of calculus as rigorously as possible and in 1829 in *Leçons sur le Calcul Différentiel* he defined for the first time a complex function of a complex variable.

During the period of 1829–1832, Nikolai Lobachevskii (1793–1856) and Janos Bolyai (1802–1860) independently developed the first non-Euclidean geometries including hyperbolic geometry in which a plane is regarded as part of a hyperbolic surface, shaped like a saddle. The term non-Euclidean geometry describes both hyperbolic and elliptic geometry, which are contrasted with Euclidean geometry. The essential difference between Euclidean and non-Euclidean geometry is the nature of parallel lines. In non-Euclidean geometry, the parallel line postulate (through a given point not on a line, there is one and only one line parallel to that line) does not hold true.

Georg Friedrich Bernhard Riemann (1826-1866) was a German mathematician who made important contributions to analysis and differential geometry, his work on non-Euclidean geometry paved the way for the later development of general relativity. Georg Riemann was also the first to propose higher spatial dimensions.

Evariste Galois (1811–1832) was a French mathematician who developed new techniques to study the solubility of equations, which are now called group theory. Simultaneously with Abel, he showed that the general quintic equation (equations of the fifth degree) and polynomial equations of higher degree are not soluble in terms of a finite number of rational operations and root extractions. Unfortunately, Galois judgment did not match his brilliance in mathematics and he was killed in a duel at the young age of twenty.

In 1854 George Boole (1815-1864) published *An investigation into the Laws of Thought, on Which are founded the Mathematical Theories of Logic and Probabilities.* Boole approached logic in a new way reducing it to a simple algebra, incorporating logic into mathematics. He pointed out the analogy between algebraic symbols and those that represent logical forms, which was the basis of the algebra of logic known today as Boolean algebra. Boolean algebra is a system of symbolic logic, which uses Boolean variables and logical operations such as AND, OR, and NOT, and is primarily used in computer science and in expressing the relationships between sets (abstract collection of numbers or symbols). Boole also worked on differential equations, including the influential *Treatise on Differential Equations,* which appeared in 1859, and the calculus of finite differences *Treatise on the Calculus of Finite Differences* (1860), and general methods in probability. He published around 50 papers and was one of the first to investigate the basic properties of numbers, such as the distributive property, that underlie the subject of algebra.

Karl Weierstrass (1815–1897) lectured at the University of Berlin for over thirty years. He gave the modern definition of a limit, eliminated the remaining vagueness in the concepts of calculus, introduced the idea of uniform convergence, and found the theory of functions of a complex variable on power series.

Arthur Cayley (1821-1895) was a brilliant English mathematician who primarily worked in algebra. He had difficulty obtaining a job after graduation, so became a lawyer for 14 years. During his free time, he published more than 200 mathematical papers. He initiated analytic geometry of n-dimensional spaces and was one of the first to study matrices in *On the Theory of Linear Transformations* (1845). A matrix is a rectangular array of numbers. He also developed the theory of invariants, and studied the geometry of plane curves. In mathematics, an invariant is something that does not change under a set of transformations.

Georg Cantor (1845-1918) was a German mathematician who established the importance of one-to-one correspondence between sets, defined infinite and well-ordered sets, and proved that the real numbers "are more numerous" than the natural numbers. In fact, Cantor's theorem implies the existence of an "infinity of infinities." He defined the cardinal and ordinal numbers, and their arithmetic. A cardinal number is a number that is used in simple counting that indicates how many elements there are in an assemblage. An ordinal number is a number assigned to an ordered set that designates both the order of its elements and its cardinal number.

Richard Dedekind (1831–1916) was a German mathematician who did important work in abstract algebra and the foundations of the real numbers. While teaching calculus for the first time at the Polytechnic, Dedekind came up with an idea now called a Dedekind cut, which is today a standard definition of the real numbers. The idea behind a cut is that an irrational number divides the rational numbers into two classes (sets), with all the members of one class (upper) being strictly greater than all the members of the other (lower) class.

The development of topology began with Jules Henry Poincare (1854-1912) and Johann Benedict Listing (1802-1882) who was the first to use the word topology. In 1861, Listing published a paper in which he described the Möbius strip (a continuous closed surface with only one side) four years before Möbius and studied components of surfaces and connectivity.

Henri Poincaré is often described as the last Universalist in mathematics. He made contributions to numerous branches of mathematics, celestial mechanics, fluid mechanics, and the philosophy of science. Poincaré's *Analysis situs*, published in 1895, is an early systematic treatment of topology. He is the originator of algebraic topology and claimed that his research in many different areas such as differential equations and multiple integrals had all led him to topology. Forty years after Poincaré published the first of his six papers on algebraic topology essentially all of the ideas and techniques in the subject were based on his work. Even today, the Poincaré conjecture remains as one of the most baffling and challenging unsolved problems in algebraic topology. Topology is the branch of pure mathematics that deals only with the properties of a figure X that hold for every figure into which X can be transformed with a one-to-one correspondence that is continuous in both directions.

Karl Pearson (1857–1936) was one of the founders of modern statistics and was instrumental in the development of linear regression and correlation, the classification of probability distributions, and chi square testing. From 1893 to 1912 he wrote 18 papers entitled *Mathematical Contributions to the Theory of Evolution*, which contains his most valuable work. These papers contain contributions to regression analysis, the correlation coefficient, and include the chi-square test of statistical significance (1900). His chi-square test was produced in an attempt to remove the normal distribution from its central position. Pearson coined the term 'standard deviation' (a statistical measurement of dispersion around an average or mean) in 1893, and made significant contributions to the development of mathematical statistics, with applications in the fields of biology, epidemiology, anthropometrics, medicine, and sociology. In 1901, with Weldon and Galton, he founded the journal *Biometrika* whose objective was the development of statistical theory. He edited this journal until his death.

David Hilbert's (1862-1943) work on integral equations in 1909 led directly to 20th-century research in functional analysis (the branch of mathematics in which functions are studied collectively). This work also established the basis for his work on infinite-dimensional space, later called Hilbert space, a concept that is useful in mathematical analysis and quantum mechanics. Making use of his results on integral equations, Hilbert contributed to the development of mathematical physics by his important memoirs on kinetic gas theory and the theory of radiations. Hilbert's famous 23 Paris problems challenged (and still challenge today) mathematicians to solve fundamental questions. Hilbert's famous speech The Problems of Mathematics was delivered to the Second International Congress of Mathematicians in Paris.

Bertrand Russell (1872–1970) and Alfred North Whitehead (1861–1947) published *Principia Mathematica* (1910-1913) a three-volume work on the foundations of mathematics. *Principia Mathematica* was an attempt to derive all mathematical truths from a well-defined set of axioms and inference rules in symbolic logic.

John Von Neumann (1903-1957) was a Hungarian-German mathematician who made important contributions in quantum physics, functional analysis, set theory, computer science, economics, and many other mathematical fields. Most notably, Von Neumann was a pioneer of the modern digital computer, the application of operator theory to quantum mechanics, member of the Manhattan Project Team, and with Oscar Morgenstern (1902-1977) creator of game theory, and the concept of cellular automata.

Meteorologist Edward Lorenz (1917-) discovered a mathematical system with chaotic behavior leading to a new branch of mathematics known as chaos theory. As Lorenz studied weather patterns he began to realize that the weather did not always change as predicted. Minute variations in the initial values of variables in his primitive computer weather model (c. 1960) would result in grossly divergent weather patterns. This sensitive dependence on initial conditions came to be known as the butterfly effect.

Benoit Mandelbrot (1924-), while working at IBM's Watson Research center, developed new concepts in geometry and the computer programs to generate the graphical representations of his geometry. His work was elaborated in *The Fractal Geometry of Nature* in 1982. Fractals are geometrical entities characterized by basic patterns that are repeated at ever decreasing sizes. They are relevant to any system involving self-similarity repeated on diminished scales (such as a fern's structure) as in the study of chaos. The Mandelbrot set is a connected set of points in the complex plane.

One of the major achievements in mathematics in the twentieth century was the proof of Fermat's Last Theorem. Fermat claimed that for the general family of equations $x^n + y^n = z^n$ where n is greater than 2 and x, y, z, are not equal to zero, it is impossible to find a solution. This problem had been unsolved by mathematicians for 300 years. The equation is deceptively simple in appearance, and yet all the great mathematicians in history couldn't solve it, until Andrew Wiles proved it in 1995.

Fermat's Last Theorem is one of several examples of problems that, on the surface, appear to have simple solutions, but are in fact incredibly complex. Other examples of problems that at first glance appear simple but are very complex include the four-color theorem, the sphere-packing problem, and the traveling salesman problem.

The four-color theorem states that any map in a plane can be colored using four-colors in such a way that regions sharing a common boundary (other than a single point) do not share the same color. This problem is sometimes also called Guthrie's problem after Francis Guthrie, who first formulated the theorem in 1853. The conjecture was then communicated to de Morgan. In 1878, Cayley wrote the first paper on the conjecture. The problem remained open until Kenneth Appel and Wolfgang Haken produced a computer-assisted proof in 1976.

The traveling salesman problem is a problem in discrete or combinatorial optimization. It is a prominent illustration of a class of problems in computational complexity theory, which are hard to solve. The traveling salesman problem asks, "given a number of cities and the costs of traveling from any city to any other city, what is the cheapest round-trip route that visits each city once and then returns to the starting city?" No general method of solution is known at the present time.

The traveling salesman problem is of considerable practical importance, apart from evident transportation and logistics applications. A classic example is in printed circuit manufacturing: scheduling of a route of the drill machine to drill holes in a printed circuit board (PCB). In robotic machining or drilling applications, the "cities" are parts to machine or holes (of different sizes) to drill, and the "cost of travel" includes time for retooling the robot (single machine job sequencing problem).

The sphere-packing problem asks, "What is the most efficient way to pack equal-sized spheres together in a large crate?" This four hundred year mathematical problem posed by the famous astronomer Johannes Kepler has finally been solved. Mathematician Thomas Hales of the University of Michigan after six years effort in 1998 proved that a guess Kepler made back in 1611 was correct. Kepler's guess, known as the Kepler conjecture, states that no arrangement of equal spheres filling space has a greater average density than that of the cubic close packing (face centered cubic) and hexagonal close packing arrangements. The density of these arrangements is a little over 74 percent.

The culmination of mathematics in the twenty first century was the solving of fifteen of Hilbert's 23 problems. Hilbert's problems are a set of (originally) unsolved problems in mathematics proposed by Hilbert. Hilbert's problems were designed to serve as examples for the kinds of problems whose solutions would lead to the furthering of disciplines in mathematics. As such, some were areas for investigation and therefore not strictly "problems."

There are still many unanswered problems to challenge mathematicians in the new millennium. The Clay Mathematics Institute of Cambridge, Massachusetts (CMI) has named seven Prize Problems. The Scientific Advisory Board of CMI selected these problems, focusing on important classic questions that have resisted solution over the years. The Board of Directors of CMI designated a $7 million prize fund for the solution to these problems, with $1 million allocated to each. The Millennium Prize Problems are as follows:

 Birch and Swinnerton-Dyer Conjecture
 Hodge Conjecture
 Navier-Stokes Equations
 P vs NP
 Poincaré Conjecture
 Riemann Hypothesis
 Yang-Mills Theory

Religion and Religious Belief

Religion is a system of beliefs and practices by which a group of people interprets and responds to what they feel is supernatural and sacred. Supernatural phenomena are phenomena that are unexplainable by natural law. Religion includes a belief in a divine or superhuman power or powers, which are to be obeyed and worshipped as the creator and ruler of the universe. This belief is generally accompanied by a code of ethics and a philosophy of life. Features of religion include the following:

1. Religion centers on issues such as salvation and the meaning of life and death.
2. Religion is future oriented, concerned with life in the hereafter, or the coming of a savior.
3. Religion is oriented towards supernatural powers, obedience and supplication involving sacrifice and prayer, such as asking the appropriate deity or spirit to act on one's behalf.
4. Religion is generally a group activity, with groups of people collectively engaged in rituals and worship.

Religion, like all customs and traditions based on myth, has evolved over time, beginning with the early primitive belief in multiple Gods (polytheism) and nature worship, followed by the worship of a single god (monotheism) with established rituals, which eventually led to the elaborate monotheistic religions of today.

The first signs of religious thought began with the tribal band, whose religion was animistic, and involved shamans and totems. Animism is the attribution of conscious life to objects in and phenomena of nature or to inanimate objects. Since the group was tribal (hunter / gatherers), there were no permanent sanctuaries. The cultic rites of the animists centered on appeasing spirits and on identification with animals.

As society developed into Chiefdoms and small kingdoms, religious rites began to serve different functions. Agriculture became important and so fertility gods (often female) were introduced. The status of the chief was supported with mythic tales of heroes and demigods, whom he may be descended from. When these small kingdoms merged into larger groups (often through conquest), different cults merged. The conquest of one group by another is therefore recorded in an epic tale of the conquest of the conquered group's god by the victor's.

Finally, the growth of the city-state brought about progression to ethical monotheism. This was partly due to the role of a hierarchical society with a god-like absolute ruler. A more powerful social force was the isolation of the individual as he moved from the clan to a more cosmopolitan lifestyle. Questions of justice and value that had been previously answered by the family and small tribe were now to be pursued independently. The relative anonymity of the city afforded the opportunity for not only "sin" but also loneliness. Ethical monotheism answered society's need for a moral guide and motivation, while a unique personal God who was sovereign over all areas of life answered people's feelings of isolation and powerlessness.

The Egyptians had traditionally worshipped a whole pantheon (the official gods of a people) of gods who were represented in human or animal form or as animal-headed humans. Some gods were specific to particular towns or places; others had broader appeal. From early periods solar gods such as Re had played an important role in Egyptian state religion because the distant but universal power of the sun fitted well with prevailing ideas of the supreme power of the king both within Egypt and beyond its borders.

In the New Kingdom (Egyptian 18th Dynasty), solar gods again became prominent, among them the Aten, the visible sun disk that can be seen traversing the sky each day. Akhenaten raised the Aten to the position of 'sole god', represented as a disk with rays of light terminating in hands, which reach out to the royal family, sometimes offering the hieroglyphic sign for life. Akhenaten's religion is probably not strictly speaking monotheistic, although only the Aten is actually worshipped and provided with temples. The majority of traditional gods were not tolerated, however, and teams of workmen were sent around the temples of Egypt where they chiseled out the names and images of these gods wherever they occurred.

Considered by many to be the first true monotheistic faith, Zoroastrianism is thought to have originated between the 18th and the 11th centuries B.C. in the Eastern part of present-day Iran or in Bactria, and is still practiced today. Zoroastrianism is based on many of the concepts found in the major Abrahamic religions such as monotheism (the belief in one god), heaven and hell, the Last Judgment (God will decree the fates of all men according to the good and evil of their earthly lives), Satan and evil spirits (dualism - the war between good and evil), prophecy, the coming of the Messiah (millenarianism – the belief in a coming ideal society and especially one created by revolutionary action), and angels.

From Zoroastrianism the Abrahamic religions evolved. Three world religions honor Abraham as their ancient patriarch and a model of faith in one God. In Judaism, the 12 tribes of Israel trace their lineage to Abraham through his son Isaac and grandson Jacob. In Christian scriptures, he is a spiritual ancestor, "justified by faith." In Islam's Koran, he and another son, Ishmael, build the Kaaba at Mecca, which by decree of Allah through Muhammad remains the holiest destination for Muslim pilgrims worldwide.

The biblical book Genesis describes Abram's birth in Ur (near modern Nasiriyah, Iraq), his marriage to Sarai, and God's promise to make of him "a great nation." God sends them on a long, dramatic, Middle Eastern journey, eventually renaming them Abraham and Sarah and periodically giving Abraham guidance and commands. The hardest of these is to offer his son Isaac as a human sacrifice; an angel stops Abraham at the last minute. Muslims believe that Arabs are descended from Abraham and Hagar (in the Book of Genesis, the handmaiden of Sarah and wife of Abraham) through their son Ishmael. Abraham is further regarded as an ancestor of Muhammad.

In the major Abrahamic religions, there exists the expectation of an individual who will herald the end of the world, and/or bring about the Kingdom of God on Earth. Judaism awaits the coming of the Jewish Messiah (the Jewish concept of Messiah differs from the Christian concept in several significant ways despite the same term being applied to both). The Jewish Messiah is not a "God" but a mortal man who by his holiness is worthy of that description, and will make his appearance only during an era of peace and holiness. Christianity awaits the Second Coming of Christ. Islam awaits both the second coming of Jesus (in order to complete his life and die, since he is said to have been risen alive and not crucified) and the coming of Mahdi (for Sunnis in his first incarnation, for Shi'as the return of Muhammad al-Mahdi).

Christianity originated in Judea, at the end of the 1st century, as a radically reformed branch of Judaism. Islam originated in the 7th century, in the Arabian cities of Mecca and Medina. Although not a dissident branch of either Judaism or Christianity, it explicitly claimed to be a continuation and replacement for them, and echoed many of their principles. According to the Muslim belief, the Koran was the final word of God and its message was that of all the prophets. As an example of the similarities between the faiths, Muslims believe in a version of the story of Genesis and in the lineal descent of the Arabs from Abraham through Ishmael, who was conceived through Abraham's servant Hagar.

In all major religions including Christianity, Buddhism, Judaism, and Hinduism, there is a belief that either God himself or some cosmic, supernatural force intervened in history, altered the normal course of events, and deliberately added to what had been previously known. This intervention could occur by personal contact with the divine power, an experience with an intermediary such as an angel, sudden inspired insight, or the discovery of secret written messages. Regardless of the form of intervention, it is the direct intrusion of a supernatural power with new knowledge, and insight for man.

It is important to realize that such revelation explanations for the origins of religion concern what believers consider being the only "true" religion, that being their own. Proponents of the revelation hypothesis refer only to their religion as the one revealed by God. Other religions may exist, but their source is something else, an inferior source, although other religions are ultimately trying to find the very truth that God has given only to proponents of a particular religion.

Some have argued that religion was essential for the development of civilization. For without a central force and uniform belief system people would never have come together to form a cohesive group. There are also those who believe that without the Reformation and Puritanism, capitalism would not have developed. Others believe that market forces, human nature, and increased education among the masses devoid of religion would have yielded similar or perhaps superior results.

Puritanism was a 16th and 17th century movement for reform in the Church of England. The movement opposed the ecclesiastical establishment and aimed at purifying the church; hence the name Puritans. The Puritans were Calvinists and adhered to Calvin's advocacy of sobriety, diligence, thrift, and lack of ostentation; they regarded contemplation as mere laziness, and poverty either as punishment for sin or evidence that one did not have God's grace. The Puritans believed that only the elect could expect salvation. They considered themselves the elect but could not be sure unless they were given a sign. They believed their way of life was ethically correct and that it led to worldly prosperity. Prosperity was accepted as the sign. Goodness came to be associated with wealth, and poverty with evil; not to succeed in one's calling seemed to be clear indication that the approval of God was being withheld. The behavior that once was believed to lead to sanctity led the descendants of the Puritans to worldly wealth.

The modern day proponents of religion obviously believe that religion is beneficial to humankind. They site such things as its role in strengthening marriage and the family, inspiring voluntarism, reducing crime and drug use, and reducing premarital teenage sex. They also claim that consistent religious worship significantly reduces rates of suicide and depression and there is no doubt that some religious organizations such as the Salvation Army in the U.S. and others perform admirable services to help the poor and victims of natural disasters. As pointed out by Rodney Stark co-author of *Theory of Religion*, religion can deter juvenile delinquency in American communities with high rates of church membership, but not in communities with low rates of church membership. That is, the religious faith of an individual teenager is impotent to guide that individual's behavior, unless it is supported by social control.

The Socialization of Religion

Sociology (from Latin: *socius*, "companion"; and the suffix *-ology*, "the study of", from Greek, *logos*, "knowledge") is an academic and applied discipline that studies group behavior, human social interaction, and societal and cultural phenomena. The sociology of religion is the study of the practices, social structures, historical background, development, universal themes, and roles of religion in society. There is particular emphasis on the recurring role of religion in nearly all societies today and throughout recorded history. Sociologists of religion attempt to explain the effects that society has on religion and the effects that religion has on society.

The socializing intent of religious groups is summarized in a classic manner by Jesus: and Jesus came and said to them, "All authority in heaven and on earth has been given to me. Go therefore and make disciples of all nations, baptizing them in the name of the Father and of the Son and of the Holy Spirit, and teaching them to obey everything that I have commanded you. And remember, I am with you always, to the end of the age," Mathew 28:18-20. This intent materializes in the form of missionaries who are sent all over the world in an attempt to convert non-believers, and the believers of other religions, into believers of the one so-called "true religion". The factors involved with religious socialization are as follows:

1. The group convinces the newcomer to make a commitment to the group and what it stands for, often on the basis of very little knowledge or contact.
2. There is the core process of building on that commitment through teaching the newcomer the norms of the group, its beliefs and appropriate behaviors and rituals.
3. The group tries to extend its influence over the person to those situations where he or she is not in direct contact with the group or its members. That is, the group tries to influence all the individuals' values.
4. There is the reinforcement and encouragement aspect of continuing socialization. This effectively means that through rituals, coercion, and constant repetition of religious dogma, the individual is brainwashed until they are no longer capable of thinking for themselves.

Religious socialization takes on many forms and uses various techniques to gain adherents. One of these techniques, which are a direct violation of natural law, is the idea that the meek shall inherit the earth. Natural law tells us that it is the fittest that will inherit the earth. Believing anything else is again not facing up to the reality of nature and the world. Max Weber in his book, *The Sociology of Religion*, calls turning poverty into a virtue a "theodicy of disprivilege", that is, a rationalization and justification of one's disprivileged economic and social status as an advantage so far as salvation is concerned. Weber identifies three different forms release from earthly disprivilege might take:

1. The expectation of a better life in the hereafter (paradise or heaven).
2. Hope for one's self, or at least for one's progeny, in a new world to be created by God for the faithful called the Messianic Age or "the millennium."
3. Hope for another life or rebirth in this world that will be better or higher than the present one (for example, the concept of transmigration of souls in Hinduism)

Stark and Bainbridge in their treatise *Theory of Religion*, define religion as systems of general compensators based on supernatural assumptions. Compensators are postulations of reward according to explanations that are not readily susceptible to unambiguous evaluation. Compensators vary according to the generality, value, and kind of rewards for which they substitute. Compensators, which substitute for single, specific rewards are called specific compensators. Compensators, which substitute for a cluster of many rewards and for rewards of great scope and value, are called general compensators. Primary compensation substitutes a compensator for a reward that people desire for themselves. Secondary compensation substitutes a compensator for a reward that a person is obligated to provide to another person.

It has been observed that social or political movements that fail to achieve their goals will often transform into religions. As it becomes clear that the goals of the movement will not be achieved by natural means (at least within their lifetimes), members of the movement will look to the supernatural to achieve what cannot be achieved naturally. The new religious beliefs are compensators for the failure to achieve the original goals. Examples of this include the counterculture movement in America: the early counterculture movement was intent on changing society and removing its perceived injustice and boredom; but as members of the movement proved unable to achieve these goals they turned to Eastern and new religions, and Marxism as compensators.

Most religions start out their lives as cults or sects. For example, groups in high tension with the surrounding society. Over time, they tend to die out, or become more established, mainstream and in less tension with society. Cults are new groups with a new novel theology, while sects are attempts to return mainstream religions to (what the sect views as) their original purity. Mainstream established groups are called denominations. The comments below about cult formation apply equally well to sect formation.

According to the Bainbridge and Stark theory, the three models of compensator generation, or cult formation, include the psychopathology model, the entrepreneur model, and the subculture-evolution model. Although presented as three different ways in which new religious cults could emerge in the modern world, these models were really theories about religious innovation in general, including the original emergence of religion in human history.

The psychopathology model states that individuals suffering from certain forms of mental illness invent religious innovations. During a psychotic episode, the individual will experience a vision, discovering a new package of compensators to meet his or her own needs. After the episode, the individual will return more-or-less to normal, and be able to communicate the vision to other people. If some of these people are themselves experiencing unresolved psychological strain, they may adopt the new package of compensators for their own use. If the society as a whole happens to be undergoing a significant crisis, there may be a large enough constituency for the religious innovations to catch hold, modifying the existing religious tradition or even establishing an entirely new tradition.

According to the Entrepreneurial Model, founders of religions act like entrepreneurs, developing new products (religions) to sell to consumers (to convert people). According to this model, most founders of new religions already have experience in several religious groups before they begin their own. They take ideas from the pre-existing religions, and try to improve on them to make them more popular.

The subculture-evolution model notes that profound innovations can occur in a large number of small steps. Individually, these steps may be like tiny examples of psychopathology and entrepreneurship. We all have mental lapses, and we all exaggerate from time to time. In a social system, such as a family, tribe, or small group, there is an active exchange of hopes and demands, rewards and suggestions about how to obtain rewards. In the absence of a desired reward, sometimes rumors can grow about algorithms (a step-by-step procedure for solving a problem or accomplishing some end) to obtain it. Some of those algorithms can readily be tested and found valueless. Some others, including those that rest upon supernatural assumptions, are harder to test and will not fail so obviously. These rumors will remain in the culture, unless of course someone finds an algorithm that is really effective in obtaining the desired reward.

Major Religions of the World

Religions take on many forms, each with its own set of beliefs, its own set of rituals, its own manifest God or gods, and its own methods of recruitment. In order to understand religion, it is helpful to see what the major religions are based on, how they developed, and their common features. The major religions that are reviewed represent 95% of the world's population and include Judaism, Christianity, Islam, Hinduism, and Buddhism. Of the Earth's estimated 6.5 billion people roughly 2 billion are Christians, 1 billion are Muslims, another 1.3 billion are Hindu and Buddhist and 14 million are Jewish.

There are hundreds of small sects in the United States alone which claim to have between 2 - 5 million adherents, and many more divisions of larger bodies of the five main organized religions, most of which are all very similar in content and will not be discussed. According to the Encyclopedia of American Religions there are 1,187 primary denominations in the United States alone.

The major religions have many things in common including common rituals to perform, prayers to recite, places to frequent or avoid, holy days to keep, means by which to predict the future, a body of literature to read and study, truths to affirm, charismatic leaders to follow, and ordinances to obey. Many have buildings, sites, and statues set aside for worship and activities such as prayer, sacrifice, and contemplation.

The founders of the major religions all claimed to be either divinely inspired or that God or one of his agents had delivered to them the true word of God, whether it is the angel Gabriel revealing God's message to humanity through the prophet Muhammad in Islam, the Torah being received from God by Moses on Mount Sinai in Judaism, Jesus Christ speaking the word of God in Christianity, or the angel Moroni who directed Joseph Smith to the golden plates of Mormonism. With so many prophets, religious divergence was inevitable.

Judaism

Judaism is one of the world's oldest monotheistic religions (the belief in the one and only god) and the parent religion of both Christianity and Islam. The name derives from the Latin Judaeus and the Hebrew Yehudhi, meaning descendant of Judah who was the fourth son of Jacob. The founder of Judaism was Abraham, who lived about 1500 B.C. It is important to point out that Abraham was not the first to develop the concept of monotheism.

Abraham made a covenant with God that he and his descendants, as the Chosen People (supposedly meaning that God had chosen the Jews because God's love for them was unique, and God was counting on them to make his will known and bring healing to all nations), would carry the message of one God to the world. The Israelites base their dominant, expansionist viewpoint on this belief, that God has chosen them to be morally and religiously superior, and that they have a unique destiny in the world.

Abraham is said to have learned by reflection and revelation of the existence of the one, everlasting God, maker of heaven and earth, who rules the world and whose way is the doing of "righteousness and justice" [Genesis XVII, 19). Classic Judaism is a revealed religion, and follows the Talmudic notion that the lawgiver Moses on Sinai dictated every word in the Torah. And that further interpretation and later writings have been guided by divine inspiration.

The new nation was given structure by Moses, who in the 13th century B.C. led the Israelites out of slavery in Egypt, received the Ten Commandments from God on Mt. Horeb (Sinai), and brought his people to the edge of the land of Canaan, which had been promised to Abraham as part of the covenant. Under the dominating personality of Moses, the formerly enslaved Hebrew tribes, now known as the children, or people, of Israel, became a nation and Hebrew monotheism was organized and developed.

Once in the Promised Land, the Israelites built a temple, established priesthood, and began offering sacrifices in accordance with the teachings of Moses - practices that survived the 6th-century Babylonian Exile. But in 70 A.D., when the Roman army destroyed the temple in Jerusalem, study and prayers in synagogues supplanted sacrificial worship.

Although Judaism has no specific creeds, its sacred writings consist of laws, prophecies, and traditions that reflect 3500 years of spiritual experience. The principal text is the Torah or Pentateuch, which consists of the first five books of Moses, which include Genesis, Exodus, Leviticus, Numbers and Deuteronomy. The rest of the Hebrew Bible, which shares some of the same books as the Christian Bible's Old Testament, includes writings which comprises Psalms, Proverbs, Job, Ecclesiastes, and writings of the major and minor prophets. The Torah or "Law" denotes teaching and includes doctrine and practice, religion and morals. The Torah was a necessary consequence of the covenant. Its objective was to train the people in holiness, in conformity with the covenant. With divine will as the common source of all these laws, the violation of any of them was a sin against God that could not go unpunished. The Torah accordingly provides a system of penalties, varying in accordance with the gravity of the offense and the intent with which it had been committed. Promises of rewards, primarily temporal and national, are also made for obedience. This amounts to the use of fear of God's punishment and the hope of his reward as the motives for obedience.

Another authoritative work is the Talmud, a collection of laws that include the Mishna, a Hebrew compilation of the Oral Laws (in Hebrew), and the Gemara, a collection of comments (in Aramaic) on the Mishna by rabbis. There are actually two Talmuds, one that emanated from Palestine in the 5th century and one from Babylonia a century later.

The basis of Judaism is belief in the living God who is transcendent, omnipotent, and just, and who reveals himself to mankind. The faith rests on the words of Deuteronomy 64: "Hear, O Israel, the Lord our God, the Lord is one."

For Jews the oneness of God implies the brotherhood of men, and religious knowledge is considered inseparable from the ethical injunction "to do justly, and love mercy, and to walk humbly with thy God." Judaism's elaborate system of laws and rituals, such as dietary regulations, are designed to give sacred meaning to every aspect of daily life. The main features that distinguish Judaism from other religions include the following:

1. Divine transcendence. The substitution of the covenant relation for the nature bond has as its corollary the idea of the transcendence of God. Everywhere else the divine is comprehended as immanent, as compounded with nature; in Hebrew monotheism God is conceived as transcendent, unbounded by any form or manifestation of physical existence.

2. God as ground of all existence. Transcending every phenomenon, God is the only ground of all existence, the sole creator of all things. The creative principle is thus no longer to be looked for as elsewhere in the regenerative powers of some natural element, from which the deity itself was said to emerge, but in the enlivening spirit and free will of God himself.

3. Ethical conception of God. As the transcendent creator, God is not force but character, a free personality possessed of ethical attributes. The moral qualities ascribed to the deity in some of the nature religions do not necessarily make the god ethical, as these qualities are invariably identified with the selfish interests of the tribe, not with the cause of ethical virtue itself, as is the case in Hebrew monotheism.

4. Concern for individual moral culture. Hebrew monotheism not only affirms the ethical character of God but also makes conformity to the divine pattern the supreme task of man (Leviathan. XIX 2). This is in contrast to nature religions in which the gods worshiped, even when conduct comes under their control, are at best mere custodians of tribal custom and morality, with no concern for individual moral character.

5. Universalism. The transcendental ethical conception of God implies universalism, alike in religion and morality. All men are bound to seek God, the creator of the world and the maker of them all, and to obey his moral law.

6. Election for service. Universality of true religion and morality demands for its realization knowledge of God and his law. Hence the Hebrew doctrine of election by virtue of which a people or individuals become the recipients of the divine revelation, which they are called, to share with all men. The idea of divine choice and mission that is found throughout the ancient near east has nothing in common with the Hebrew conception where, alone, election is not for domination but for service.

7. Unity of history in the purpose of God. This universal quest for the one and only God imparts a unity to all history in the purpose of God. Everywhere else history is at bottom meaningless, a mere repetition of sin and misery; in Judaism it is full of meaning and significance, every fresh phase in the historical process being a further stage in the development of the purpose of God for the establishment of his universal rule among all the sons of men.

Jews have an ordained clergy and observe the Sabbath, which runs from sunset Friday to sunset Saturday, and is observed with services of prayer and readings in local synagogues. Major festivals include Pesach (Passover, celebrating the Exodus), Shabuoth (Pentecost), Rosh Hashana (New Year), Yom Kippur (Day of Atonement), and Sukkoth (Feast of Tabernacles).

Judaism has generated numerous internal sects and movements, including the Sadducees and Pharisees during the early Christian era. In the 12th century, Maimonides tried to relate Judaism to Western philosophy, especially that of Aristotle. Modern religious movements developed from Moses Mendelssohn, a rationalist of the 18th-century Enlightenment, and Hasidism, which preaches piety and mysticism.

Present-day American Judaism is divided among three major denominations. The orthodox stresses strict adherence to the Torah. Reform Jews, in the tradition of Mendelssohn, have repudiated legalism and emphasize the compatibility of Judaism with liberal secular values. Conservative Judaism reflects a middle road acceptance of the Torah but also a willingness to adapt it to modern conditions. In recent years, a Reconstructionist movement, which was originated by Mordecai M. Kaplan and developed out of the Conservative wing, has stressed Judaism as an evolving religious civilization. Since the destruction of their nation in 70 A.D., Jews have once again dreamed of having their own state.

The first Zionist Congress was held in 1897 in Basle and, in the wake of the Nazi holocaust, which took the lives of 6 million Jews, the State of Israel came into being in 1948 after the British Mandate of Palestine. Zionism is a movement formed for the establishment and advancement of the Jewish national state.

Christianity

Christianity developed among first-century Jews out of the conviction that Jesus of Nazareth, who according to Christian belief lived from about 4 B.C. to 29 A. D., was the long awaited Hebrew Messiah. The name Jesus is Greek for the Hebrew Joshua, a name meaning Savior, while Christ derives from the Greek Christos, meaning Messiah, or Anointed. Jesus was a Jew, as were all the apostles. Early Christianity was in fact a movement within Judaism. The acknowledgement of Jesus as "the Christ" means that he is the fulfillment of the promises originally made to Abraham, Isaac, and Jacob.

Traditional Christianity says that Jesus was God made man, wholly divine, wholly human. He was born to Mary, rumored to be a virgin, and died on the cross to atone for mankind's sins. His supposed resurrection from the dead provides man's only hope for salvation. The principal sources for his life are the four Gospels of Matthew, Mark, Luke, and John.

According to Christian theology, Jesus was born a Jew in Bethlehem of Mary, wife of Joseph, a carpenter of Nazareth. His date of birth is believed to be between 8 B.C. and 4 B.C. When he was about 30 years old Jesus began a three-year mission as a preacher. His activity was centered on Galilee, and he gathered a small band of disciples. Jesus preached the coming of the Kingdom of God, and called on his listeners to repent. The Gospels also describe miracles he performed. His uncompromising moral demands, his repeated attacks on the Pharisees and scribes, and his sympathy for social outcasts and the oppressed kindled popular enthusiasm. In the third year of his mission, while in Jerusalem for Passover, he was betrayed to the authorities by one of his companions, Judas Iscariot. After sharing the Last Supper (a Passover Seder) with his disciples, he was arrested. The Gospels indicate that he was interrogated by Jewish authorities and handed over to the Romans, who crucified him, perhaps as an agitator. On the third day, his tomb was found empty, and an angel (or a man) announced that he had risen from the dead. According to the Gospels, Jesus later appeared to several of his disciples, and after 40 days he ascended into heaven.

The collections of the sayings and deeds of Jesus were combined with the writings of the apostles to form a body of Christian sacred writings. The Christian Bible includes most of the Hebrew Bible, which is called the Old Testament, and the New Testament, which contains 27 additional books and was formalized by the 4th century. Central are the four Gospels of Matthew, Mark, Luke, and John, which describe the life and teachings of Jesus. Some Christians also accept the 14th book appendix to the Authorized Version of the Old Testament, known as the Apocrypha, as canonical.

The essence of traditional Christian theology is that Jesus was the son of God who came to save the world, was crucified, resurrected, and will come again to judge mankind. The core of the Christian ethic is the commandment: "Thou shalt love the Lord thy God with all thy heart and thy neighbor as thyself." The main theological concepts, on which Christianity is based, include the idea of the incarnation of the Son of God, original sin, redemption through the cross, and the life of divine grace and the sacramental system of the universality of the Gospels.

Missionaries, notably Paul, spread Christianity throughout the Roman Empire. A turning point in Christian history occurred at the Council of Jerusalem in 49 A.D. when Paul convinced other church leaders to spread the faith to non-Jews. Early Christians endured severe persecution, but in 313 A.D. Constantine I officially tolerated Christianity in the Roman Empire.

Fundamental theological issues such as the divinity of Jesus Christ were thrashed out at a series of ecumenical councils during the first eight centuries. The early church was plagued by heresies concerning the nature of Christ (e.g. Arianism, Nestorianism, and Monophysitism), which were condemned at councils such as the First Council of Nicaea in 325 A. D. Doctrinal statements emanated from these councils, such as the Nicene Creed and the teaching of the Trinity, which asserts that God has appeared to man as the Father, the Son, and the Holy Ghost.

In 1054, Christianity was split into a Western or Roman Catholic Church, which acknowledges the pope - the bishop of Rome - as Christ's supreme vicar on earth, and the Eastern Orthodox Churches, which reject the jurisdiction of the pope, and recognize the patriarch of Constantinople as the preeminent ecclesiastical figure. The split between the East and the West began in the 5th century and became definite with the condemnation of the patriarch of Constantinople by Pope Leo IX. In the fifth century the Protestant Reformation further divided the Roman Catholic Church.

The ecumenical movement of this century has now shifted momentum toward a quest for unity among Christian churches. An important development was the founding in 1948 of the World Council of Churches, which has more than 220 Protestant and Orthodox churches as members.

Islam

Islam is the religion founded by the prophet Mohammed (570 - 632 A.D) in 622 A.D. at Yathrib (now Medina) in Arabia. Mohammed's message to the Meccans was simple and forthright. He proclaimed the existence of only one absolute Lord and Creator, whose name Allah was known but almost buried in the Arabic pantheon. This God was sole master of mankind, whose final judgment would be a terrible vengeance on the ungodly. Man's only hope before the Deity was a blind abandonment (Islam) to the divine will, and a life of prayer and resistance to one's sinful inclinations. The Arabic word Islam means submission to God and followers call themselves Muslims.

Mohammed was a caravan conductor and Mecca shopkeeper of the Koreish tribe who experienced a prophetic calling at the age of 40. After founding his religion, he also acted as a governor general and judge. Mohammed is regarded as the "Seal of the Prophets" the last in a series of messengers from God, consisting of Adam, Noah, Abraham, Moses and Jesus.

The sacred text of Islam is the Koran (Quran in Arabic), which means "reading", and contains the revelations of Mohammed over a period of 20 years; it also deals with manners, religious laws, and morals. The Koran has supplemented the Sunna (the way or custom), which is a collection of Traditions (moral sayings and anecdotes). Both are reinforced by the principle of Ijma (unanimous consensus or agreement), which states the belief that a majority of Muslims cannot agree in error. The Koran, the Sunna, and the Ijma are the three foundations of Islam. Islam is radically theistic, and the essence of its faith (shahada) is simply stated: "There is no God but Allah, and Mohammed is the messenger (or Prophet) of Allah." Mohammed rejected the Trinitarianism of Christianity, but he incorporated a number of Judeo-Christian concepts into his system. For example the creed states: "I believe in God, his Angels, his Books and his Messengers, the Last Day, the Resurrection, Predestination by God, Good and Evil, the Judgment, the Balance, Paradise and Hell-fire." The Muslim Theological Creed consists of five articles of faith:

1. A belief in one and only one God
2. Faith in angels
3. Faith in the revealed books
4. Faith in the prophets
5. Faith in the Day of Judgment

To these was added, during the early development of the dogma, the belief in God's predetermination of good and evil.

The Five Pillars of Islam - These are the five obligatory duties:

1. Reciting the profession of faith. The profession of the faith must be recited, at least once in a lifetime, aloud, correctly, purposively, with a full understanding of its meaning and with an assent from the heart.
2. You must pray. Muslims pray five times a day - at dawn, noon, mid-afternoon, dusk and at night. The prayers, which consist primarily of thanksgiving and praise of Allah, are performed facing Mecca and involve traditional physical postures (kneeling on the ground). The principal public service takes place at midday on Friday usually in a mosque.
3. The paying of the Zakat tax - or the "purification" tax, the payment of which renders the remaining property religiously and legally legitimate and is payable on food grains, money, etc., each year after one year's possession.
4. Fasting - this fast, during which all eating and drinking is forbidden, starts at daybreak and ends at sunset and is generally observed during the night of 26-27th Ramadan.
5. The pilgrimage to Mecca - it is incumbent on every Muslim to perform this pilgrimage once in a lifetime provided they can find support during the journey and can also arrange for the provision of his dependents during his absence.

Early disputes over the "caliph" or successor of Mohammed, led to sectarian divisions within Islam. The most important were the Sunnites, Shiites, and Khawaij who differed over matters of ceremony and law. Other modern movements have included the Babis and the Wahabis.

The great schism of Islam arose over the issue of the caliph, or the successor of Muhammad, as the temporal and spiritual head of Islam. The Shi'a supported Ali, Muhammad's son-in-law for caliph. They believe that the divine line of descent from Muhammad will culminate in the twelfth imam, hidden from usurpers, the so called "hidden Imam," will appear on the Last Day as the messiah to bring divine justice to the world.

In Shi'a Islam the imam is fundamental to the theology. The Shi'a imam must be of direct descent of either Husayn or his brother Hasan. The imams are supposed to be divinely appointed, sinless, infallible successors of Muhammad, and provide guidance for the human race in both religious as well as secular matters. Due to this quality, there can only be one imam at a time. The imam is the only one who fully understands all aspects of Islam. He is infallible, and the only one who can give interpretations of the Koran.

In Sunni Islam the term imam is used principally as a title and is the person who performs the congregational prayer. The imam is considered the most learned and most respected person in the assembly, and each mosque has their own imam.

Islam is a missionary religion though Muslims do not regard Jews and Christians as pagans and have normally permitted them to keep practicing their faiths after conquests. In centuries past Muslim armies took over large sections of India and once came within 100 miles of Paris. This tolerant outlook has changed in the 20th century, to bitter hatred of the Jews by the majority of devout Muslims.

The principal areas of Islamic influence today are the Middle East, North Africa, and Western Asia and there are substantial communities in the Philippines, Indonesia, and Malaysia. Islam is currently increasing rapidly in African countries south of the Sahara. Considerable theological activity has gone on during this century toward discrediting such Islamic practices as polygamy, slavery and intolerance thus making Islam more acceptable under modern conditions.

Hinduism

Known to its followers as Santana Dharma (the Eternal Religion), Hinduism is the religion of the majority of Indians today. It has developed gradually over a period of 5,000 years, making it possibly the world's oldest faith, and is thought to have developed from the synthesis of sacrificial cults brought in by the Aryan invaders of 1500 B.C. with the religions of the various indigenous peoples they conquered.

Hinduism has no ecclesiastical organization and there are no beliefs or practices universal to all Hindus. Religious activity is mainly centered in the home. With each home having at least one sacred image before which puja (rite of worship) in the from of prayers, hymn singing, the offering of flowers, and the burning of incense are performed.

Hinduism has no fixed canon of sacred books. The principal text is the Veda (meaning divine knowledge), which is a collection of 1,200 hymns and incantations addressed to various deities, including those of fire and wind. Some of this material is believed to date from the arrival of the Aryans in India c. 1500 B.C. There are four Vedas, which together form the Samhitas (collections), of varying length and are concerned with a different aspect of faith and practice. The oldest part of the Vedas consists of songs (mantra) and ritual formulas that exist in three anthologies, the Rig Veda, the Sama Veda, and the Yajur Veda. A fourth book, Atharva Veda contains directives for Hindu priests and only much later obtained recognition. More philosophical works that have also gained wide acceptance include the Brahamanas, the Upanishads, and the poem "Bhagavad-Gita" (Sanskrit for song of the Lord).

Hinduism is polytheistic in the extreme, with literally hundreds of thousands of gods and some forms of animal life worshiped. The principal gods are Brahma, the unapproachable creative spirit, and the two popular gods, Siva and Vishnu - both of which have spawned innumerable cults. The main distinguishing features of Hinduism include the following:

1. The doctrine of the transmigration of souls, with its corollary that all living beings are of the same essence.
2. Hindus emphasize the divinity of the soul and the harmony of all religions with a propensity to assimilate rather than to exclude.
3. Life is seen as a series of lives in which a man's position is determined by his Karma, or deeds, in previous lives. Hinduism postulates a cosmology based on a universe of immense size and immensely long in duration, passing through a continuous process of development and decline. This led to the general view that life is essentially unsatisfactory, since man is enmeshed in this universal scheme by the process of samsara or continued reincarnation. The Hindu finds existence a vale of tears, and his long-term aim is to achieve salvation or release from the round of birth, death, and rebirth. The achievement of this goal generally involves a series of many lives and demands a long course of spiritual discipline, meditation and devotion.
4. The idea of a caste system. A caste is a system based on social, racial, and hereditary class distinctions each of which are formerly excluded from social dealings with the others. The social "caste" into which a person is born is thus an indication of his spiritual status. Traditionally the origin of castes goes back to the Rig Veda, which states that, "One fourth of the supreme being constitutes all beings, while three fourths of him are immortal and stand above. With the one fourth below, he extended on all sides into the animate and the inanimate. His face became the Brahmin. His arms were made into the Kshatryia. His thighs became the Vaisya. From his feet the Sudra was born.

Historically India, when ruled by the Aryans, was a theocracy that was ruled by divinely appointed kings (Kshatryia), assisted by priests and ministers who explained the code of laws (Brahmins). The Vaishyas handled arming and trade. The aborigines (Sudras) were reduced to slavery by the upper three classes. For the ordinary man, Hinduism involves careful observance of food and marriage rules, pilgrimages to sacred rivers and shrines, participation in festivals, and worship in the temples and shrines that are found in every village. Entry to ultimate truth comes not from the acceptance of certain dogmas but from worship and religious experience.

Over the centuries Hinduism has produced numerous reform movements, including Buddhism and Sikhism. Modern social and cultural conditions are also bringing about modification of the caste system and other changes such as increased social status for women. Some of the reform movements such as Sikhism have produced violent clashes in India with the result being hundreds of deaths.

Buddhism

Buddhism is the way of life based on the teachings of Siddhartha Guatama, an Indian prince of an aristocratic warrior caste, who lived in the sixth century B.C. and came to be known as the Buddha, or the "enlightened one." Dissatisfied with the formalism of the Hinduism of his day and vowing to find an explanation for evil and human suffering, the prince left his family, three palaces, and forty-thousand dancing girls, and wandered as a hermit for six years in search of the mystery of human existence and the truth that would liberate mankind. He studied philosophy under two Hindu masters of Yoga, engaged in fasting and eating repulsive herbs, and tried repressing his natural emotions.

Finally Guatama found what he was looking for after several weeks of meditation under a bodhi tree (pipal or sacred fig, the tree of enlightenment) and began preaching and sending missionaries forth to spread his discovery. From that time on he was the Buddha. The Buddha taught that the path beyond sorrow and suffering was the "middle way." The two extremes that are not to be followed are between the profitless life of indulgence in sensual pleasure (sensuality) and the equally profitless way of self-mortification (austerity). This enlightenment consists in the realization of the four basic truths, known as the Four Noble Truths:

1. The Noble Truth of Pain (or Suffering): birth is pain, old age is pain, sickness is pain, and death is pain. Union with the unpleasant is pain, separation from the pleasant is pain, and not obtaining what one wishes is pain. In short, the five groups of clinging to existence are pain.
2. Noble Truth of the Cause of Pain: the craving that leads to rebirth accompanied by delight and passion, rejoicing at finding delight here and there, namely, the craving for lust, for existence, for non-existence.
3. Noble Truth of the Cessation of Pain: the complete cessation of that craving - its forsaking, relinquishment, release and detachment from it.
4. Noble Truth of the Path that Leads to the Cessation of Pain: This is the Noble Eightfold Path, namely, right view, right thought, right speech, right action, right livelihood, right effort, right mindfulness, and right concentration.

The motive of this first sermon is to awaken recognition of the universality of suffering inherent in existence, to indicate its cause in craving and to teach a way of deliverance through rightness in thought, conduct and inner discipline. The description of the Path covers the whole training of the disciple. The steps of this path are:

1. Right view is understanding the Four Truths.
2. Right thought is free from lust, ill will, cruelty and untruthfulness.
3. Right speech is abstaining from lying, tale bearing, harsh language and vain talk.

4. Right conduct is abstaining from killing, stealing, and sexual misconduct.
5. Right livelihood is earning a living in a way not harmful to any living thing.
6. Right effort is to avoid evil thoughts and overcome them, to arouse good thoughts and maintain them.
8. Right attentiveness is to pay vigilant attention to every state of the body, feeling, and mind.
9. Right concentration is concentration on a single object so as to induce certain special states of consciousness in deep meditation.

By following the Path a disciple aims at complete purity of thought and life, hoping to become an arahat, one freed from the necessity of rebirth ready for Nirvana. The final goal is Nirvana, which is a transcendent state free from craving, suffering, and sorrow. It is the state of perfect blessedness achieved by the extinction of individual existence and by the absorption of the soul into the supreme spirit, or by the extinction of all desires and passions.

The Buddha did not speak of God, and his teachings constitute, in the ordinary Western sense, more of a philosophy and system of ethics than a religion. Buddhism affirms the law of Karma, by which a person's actions in life determine his status in future incarnations. The object of the Buddhist life is to achieve Nirvana, a condition of enlightenment and detachment from the world by which the cycle of successive rebirths comes to an end.

The simple life of the Buddha and his followers gave way after his death to the creation of monasteries, shrines, and temples. Buddhism eventually split into numerous branches. The two major ones today are Mahayana (greater vehicle) Buddhism, which is practiced in China, Korea, and Japan and has an elaborate theology in which the Buddha is regarded as a divine savior, and Hinayana (lesser vehicle) Buddhism, which is concentrated in Southeast Asia and preserves the earlier monastic tradition. Zen Buddhism, a Japanese variation of Mahayana Buddhism, stresses contemplation, while the Lamaism of Tibet represents a mixture of Buddhism with local demonolatry.

As can be seen, all these religions have the same things in common. They are all based on an individual who claims to have figured out the world and the purpose of man's existence. They all lay claim to the only "real truth." They all have a book or a series of books that purport to contain all of these truths and all of the knowledge that man needs. They all claim that their religion is the only true religion and the other religions are wrong or evil. They are all based on faith with no basis in scientific fact.

Atheism

"All natural institutions of churches whether Jewish, Christian, or Turkish, appear to me no other than human inventions set up to terrify and enslave humankind and monopolize power and profit" Thomas Paine

Atheism is defined as the doctrine or belief that there is no God, or a lack of belief in the existence of God or gods. There is no scientific evidence for any of the divine attributes normally associated with God. These divine attributes, omnipotence (having unlimited power), omniscience (having infinite knowledge), and omni-benevolence (the property of being perfectly good), do not exist any where in nature, and there is no evidence that they exist in a supernatural existence. Omnipotence is maximal power. In its true meaning, it would mean that the person, god, or force, would have the power to do absolutely anything, including the logically impossible. The possessor of omnipotence could change the past, present, and future, and change the laws of nature at will. If a god cannot do all these things and has limited power then it follows that there is no god.

Atheists believe that any group of people, who believe that suffering in the world, is purification for sin and is therefore good, is only rationalizing sadism. The idea that by dying you are going to meet God or going to a better world is equally barbarous. There is no better world than the world of the living, of being alive, and being able to enjoy the pleasures and joys of life. There are just too many wondrous things in nature to waste time on religion. Going through existence without studying and appreciating life and nature is truly a shame.

Would you believe a fairy tale to be a true and accurate description of reality? What about ancient Greek mythology? For the atheist, believing in the sacred text of the world's religions is like believing in the Greek God Zeus or Santa Claus. The main reason most people believe in God is the same reason that they believe in Santa Claus, that is, they have been taught from early infancy to do so. How can anyone base all their beliefs on one book of fiction, the origin of which is questionable, when the universe of facts is made up of thousands of books?

The problem with the evolution of religion is that there is no evidence that Abraham, Moses, or Jesus Christ actually existed. There is no exact date for the birth, life span, and death of any of the most important figures of religion. There is substantial evidence that all religious books are works of fiction, authored by many individuals, some claiming to have received the direct word of God. Obviously, many portions of the Torah seem to imply more than one author, and like the Bible, contain numerous inconsistencies.

No one can place a solid date, location, or definitively state who authored the Torah, the Bible, or the Koran. God did not need human messengers, agents, and authors to decipher and record his words. A true God would have no need to reveal himself to humans, a true God would have just created a single volume of the knowledge and laws needed by humans and handed it to someone. Since this is not the case, there is no universal religion.

Why is humankind still involved with the logical fallacy of argumentum ad populum, where the prejudices and passions of humans are appealed to rather than reason? The scientific evidence is overwhelmingly against all religions. Religion is filled with contradictions and mindless efforts at understanding the universe and the role of humankind in the universe. There is just no valid reason to suppose that any religion is true. Why then would anyone base his or her sense of reality on religion?

Blind acceptance of dogmatic and doctrinal beliefs as the sole and eternal truth has led man away from fact and logic and towards a mindless wasteland. The less satisfaction we derive from being independent free thinker's content with reason and logic, the greater our desire to be like others and blindly follow the herd. Religion is a concept, a mere man-made invention like the Greek gods and myths, to which devotion and faith is unworthy of free men. What is more contemptible than a coward who cannot face the perils of life without the help of myths, and blind faith in a fictitious supernatural savior? To the atheist religion is nothing more than a crutch for the weak of mind; for those that lack intestinal fortitude, and for those that do not have a belief in themselves.

Choosing not to believe scientific facts and natural law is choosing to disregard reality. If you deny natural law and scientific facts, you deny the existence of reality. Just as the world is finally waking up to the fact that natural market forces, competition, and freedom are the only way to organize an economic system, they will wake up to face the realities of life according to natural law and the pursuit of reason. Many of the past difficulties on the road to reason arose from the timid treatment and arguments put forth by many philosophers and theologians. The philosopher and theologian's problem has been, and still is, that they start from the premise that there was or is, a reason to believe in a God or gods. They started with God's existence and then tried to explain everything else from this basic tenet. This is an invalid premise. There has never been any scientific evidence that a God or gods existed, exists now, or will exist in the future. The rational person would start from the premise that there is no gods or God until there is some evidence for their existence.

For thousands of years humans own weaknesses, fears, and doubts in themselves have held them back from their true potential. The atheist's goal is to free humankind from the slavery of fear and the unknown. It is time modern man evolves from primitive man and ceases following the nonsensical dogma laid down by a group of outdated and uninformed philosophers and theologians. Life is finite, there is no life after death, and on a universal scale life is but a mere second in time. The statement life after death is a contradiction. Death by definition means the permanent cessation of life. People should enjoy their short finite existence while they can, rather than counting on the promise of infinite salvation and a utopian existence in paradise.

The Atheist response to the theologians and religious philosopher's main arguments for religion is as follows:

The cosmological argument - St. Thomas Aquinas and modern theologians argue that each effect must have a cause and that an endless chain must proceed back to a primordial first cause or prime mover, that being God. Since matter and energy are equivalent and the conservation of energy and matter laws state that energy and matter can neither be created nor destroyed there was no creation therefore, no creator. Even if the conservation of energy and matter laws turn out to be invalid, and it is shown that matter can in fact be created from nothing, it does not follow that there has to be intelligent design for this to occur. Because of these conservation laws, everything in the universe merely exists, and it follows that it has always existed. It has never been shown that matter can in fact be created out of nothing. Currently the two leading candidates for answering initial conditions are chaotic inflation and quantum cosmology.

Genesis from The Old Testament is certainly wrong, it states that God created the heavens and the earth at the same time and in six days. The heavens and the earth were not created simultaneously and it took longer than six days for their formation. Following the creation of the heavens and earth God said, "Let there be light". Light actually existed before the formation of earth. Additional processes and the sequential order of events described in Genesis are not consistent with scientific evidence.

The moral argument - This argument is based on the theologian's faith in the universal signs among mankind of conscience, of some moral law, and of each person's inability to keep it satisfactorily, all of which cannot be explained as mere conditioning or self-interest. The source of that spark or conscience according to theists is God. This doesn't even make sense. Morals and ethics are learned behavior; they are not innate qualities of the brain. Conscience is thought and is nothing more than the biochemical action of neurons in the brain. People with no morals or ethics still have thoughts and a conscience, they just don't care if they hurt someone or do something that another person or society thinks is wrong. Interestingly enough, people who believe in God are no more moral than non-believers.

The mental argument - in this argument, an all-intelligent being is offered as the only explanation for the power of reason and for humanity's other non-material qualities of mind and imagination. The power of reason and imagination, like man's development, is evolutionary. It derives from generations of past philosophers, free thinkers, researchers, and scientists, and ultimately from genetics and biochemical reactions in the brain.

The experiential argument - This argument states that because religious experiences are so widespread, there must be something or someone inspiring them. For the atheist this is a fallacy. Mental illness is also widespread, but that doesn't mean that someone or something is out inducing neurosis. In addition, there is no universal religion and therefore, there is no universal religious experience.

The teleological argument - In this argument the complexity of the structure of the universe is used to argue the necessary existence of an intelligent designer. This argument is the basis of creationism and intelligent design theory. It attempts to establish that natural entities act in such a way as to achieve ends or goals, and that these ends cannot be the result of chance or random events. The physicists and philosophers of old thought that the world was deterministic and that man was merely determining mathematically the order of nature that was already pre-defined by God. This has been shown by science to be an incorrect assumption. Natural selection is differential success and involves random mutations, and quantum physics is based on probabilities of the random motion of particles. These are not designed or pre-determined events. If all events were designed you would be able to predict the future course of everything that occurs or is going to occur.

The universe is so complex that no one supernatural being or force could control it. This becomes apparent when one considers that there are more than a trillion trillion particles in the universe and there are over 10 trillion cells per human. Interstellar space has an average gas density of one-hydrogen atom per cubic centimeter. Nebulae can have gas densities of 1000 hydrogen atoms per cubic centimeter. One cubic centimeter of air contains some 2.7×10^{19} molecules. Combined with all the other chemical reactions that are constantly taking place, and the fact that there are probably thousands of other civilizations in the universe, these large scale attributes preclude the chance that a single being (supernatural or otherwise) could be tracking and directing all of these interactions. Have you ever thought about what the odds of human evolution are compared to the odds that there's a guy with a beard sitting on some cloud somewhere directing every molecule in the universe? What would the theologians say if there were additional planetary systems with human or other life forms inhabiting them? What about multiple universes? Would they have the same God?

The intelligent design theory often uses the perfection of the human eye and body as examples. The human eye is far from a perfect device one would expect for an all knowing, all-powerful God. Human vision diminishes with age as the protective fluid of the cornea becomes less transparent over time. The muscles that control the opening of the Iris and the focusing of the lens atrophy (degenerates) and lose responsiveness, and the lens thickens and yellows, impairing visual acuity and color perception. The retina, which is responsible for transmitting images to the brain, can detach fairly easily from the back of the eye, leading to blindness. Contrary to any sensible design, blood vessels and nerves traverse the inside of the retina, creating a blind spot at their point of exit. Additionally, there is huge variety of different eyes in the animal kingdom, none of which are perfect. An intelligent omnipotent designer would have designed the perfect eye for all creatures. The human immune system cannot adapt and destroy many of the smallest entities known to man, the viruses and bacteria, and no God would have created mosquitoes, tics, and other disease spreading organisms. This is hardly the picture of intelligent design by an infallible designer. Although man and the universe are extremely complex, they are not beyond human understanding or scientific description. Because they are complex it is going to take time to figure everything out on a scientific basis, but man will eventually come to a complete understanding of life, the universe, and nature.

The ontological argument - This argument is totally metaphysical, and assumes that God's non-existence does not admit to an explanation, and that if it is possible that a highest conceivable being exists, then he must exist in actuality. Anselm's ontological argument attempts to use semantics and a purely logical argument to reach the conclusion that God exists. It is a fallacy to say that because you understand the definition of a term that this infers that the term exists in reality or that because a term exists in your understanding that it exists in reality. Understanding is the process of comprehending while to understand is to comprehend. There is an explanation for existence and it does not require the existence of a God or a highest conceivable being.

For the atheists all religion is an escape from reality. It is an escape from facing up to your own problems and being strong enough to solve those problems yourself. The way you solve problems is through self-discipline and rational thinking. Only the individual can make the decision to make their life worth living. It is in one's self that the power of the individual lies, not in some false god. The greater the belief in yourself, the more you can achieve. All it requires is patience, perseverance, discipline, and willpower.

Religious insanity is a global phenomenon. In the Philippines in one year, 17 people, including a convicted murderer, were nailed to crosses in bloody re-enactments of the Crucifixion. Thousands of others beat their bare backs with bamboo reeds, whips and glass-studded bats in a ritual of penitence introduced to the Philippines by 16th century Spanish missionaries. In Muslim countries, the Shiites commemorate the martyrdom of the Imam Hussein, grandson of the prophet Mohammad, in a battle in 680 A.D. by the shedding of blood by beating their heads and chests with chains and hitting themselves in the head with swords.

In a survey of Lutherans, done by the National Opinion Research Center for the Lutheran Council in the United States, of those people who attended church regularly, 82 percent believed that the devil exists and is active in the world. Eighty percent believed that Jesus would return to earth someday. And in a dangerous idea that permeates all Christian religions, 53 percent definitely agreed that a child is already sinful at birth.

The people that believe in the literal interpretation of the Bible and the Koran have declared war against reason, science, logic and reality. They use scripture to justify their bizarre acts and views. Religion turns people into automatons. Like sheep they blindly follow faith or some charismatic leader. This leaves them mentally dormant, with no independence of thought, no imagination, and no will of their own. They are stuck living in the past, seemingly helpless in facing up to the truth or preparing for the future. Can there really be any hope for mankind when people continue to live in the past, worship false gods, and participate in foolish acts that defy reason?

Paul Kurtz, a member of the Committee for the Scientific Investigation of Claims of the Paranormal sums up false belief very well when he says: "There is always the danger that once irrationality grows it will spill over into other areas. There is no guarantee that a society so infected by unreason will be resistant to even the most virulent programs of dangerous ideological sects."

Religious myths continue to be shattered. The theologians held the view that earth was the center of the universe, and that this had to be so because Man and Earth are central in God's plan for the universe. It turns out that the theologians were wrong again. The earth is not the center of our solar system. The solar system is not even in the center of our galaxy, and our galaxy isn't in the center of the universe. Earth is just another planet, one of the millions of planets that exist throughout the universe, so much for theological centrism and the chosen people. There can no longer be a religious philosophy of reality. Present day knowledge allows us to know how the universe was formed, and how life evolved. This knowledge tells us that life could occur anywhere in the universe given the right temperature gradients and the existence of water. Although science has not yet provided all of the exact details of the evolution of the universe and humans, this is no reason to believe in a creator or creation. Only the tools of science and reason can provide the ultimate truth.

If after reading this section you still believe in God then you will probably always believe in God. It is hard to give up something you have believed in your whole life. You can continue to use faith as a support system. If it helps you to live a better life that is fine, at least now you know the other side of the argument, and as with everything in life, it is your decision. Regardless of your decision, it is worth remembering the atheist viewpoint, that religion is nothing more than primitive superstition and a crutch for the weak.

Faith and Reason

"Belief in thyself is far better than belief in a non-existent deity" Anonymous

The existence of religion is rooted fundamentally in human ignorance and fear of the unknown. People do not know the answers to basic questions such as: If the conservation of energy law, which states that matter, can neither be created nor destroyed is correct, how did the universe begin? Does the universe have a purpose? How did life begin? Some of the explanations to these questions must be devised on the basis of incomplete evidence, which leads people to rely on faith instead of reason.

One of the first things everyone must do is obtain fulfillment and a state of happiness. This is generally accomplished by determining whether they believe in God, multiple Gods (Pantheism), or choose not to believe in any God. Most people were raised to believe in God and to worship under a particular type of religion. Since the majority of the world's population still has religious beliefs of one form or another it is obvious that religion is here to stay for quite some time. This leads to the following questions: Why is there no universal religion? Will there ever be peace among the various competing religions? Once humankind's ignorance on the questions of creation, death, and reality has been answered, will religion disappear? The following sections give the case for and against God and organized religion, and atheism or science based non-belief.

The conflict between religious theism and atheism is fundamentally a conflict between faith and reason. Faith and reason are opposites, two mutually exclusive terms. Faith is belief without a fundamental basis in reality, and without, or in spite of, reason. Faith is the commitment of one's consciousness to beliefs for which one has no sensory evidence or rational proof. Explicit atheism is the consequence of a commitment to rationality - the conviction that man's mind is fully competent to know the facts of reality, and that no aspect of the universe is closed to rational scrutiny. Reason is the faculty by which humans acquire knowledge; rational demonstration is the process by which they verify knowledge claims. A belief based on reason is a belief that has been examined for evidence, internal coherence, and consistency with previously established knowledge. There can be no propositions beyond the "limits of reason." To advocate that a belief can be accepted without reason is to advocate that a belief be accepted without thought and without verification. People follow faith because it is easier than investigating the truth. The criteria for a belief to claim the status of knowledge or fact are as follows:

1. A belief must be based on evidence.
2. A belief must be internally consistent (not self-contradictory).
3. A belief cannot contradict previously validated knowledge with which it is to be integrated.

This section is not a treatise on the nature of reality; it is only an attempt to give some perspective to the issue of existence and reality. Many philosophers have spent their whole careers trying to explain reality; most of them have totally missed the point. The state of being real is a state of existence, not something that is imagined, or only in the minds of humans. The universe exists independent of consciousness. Mental processes cannot change the laws of nature. The function of consciousness is not to create reality, but to comprehend it. Many people believe that if an entity is something that is not in the mind of humans, it does not exist. This is false. There was a universe before humans evolved. There were bacteria before humans evolved. These entities may not have been called a universe or bacteria before the existence of humans nonetheless they still existed. It seems that humans have just been unable to face up to the fact that the universe would do just fine without the human species.

Although humans get most of their data from the outside world in the form of sense perceptions, many things that are proven facts lay beyond the senses, and there are many things, such as quantum physics, that are contrary to common sense. These areas of knowledge are developed through logic, reason and mathematics. Even those things, which are not directly verifiable through the senses, have been verified through experiment. The space-time experiments of relativity and the wave-particle duality experiments of quantum physics are two good examples.

Empirical evidence is evidence that is capable of being verified or disproved by observation or experiment. This is what science is all about. Even things that defy common sense, and the ability of humans to perceive directly through the senses, can be discovered and a proof provided by experimental evidence. Due to the advances in the scientific disciplines and the knowledge that has been gained since the beginnings of human thought, and thanks to the philosophers of old such as Locke, Berkeley, and Hume (the empiricists), and Descartes, Spinoza, and Leibniz (the rationalists) man is now at the verge of understanding the whole of nature and reality. This will undoubtedly take another century or two, but man will eventually understand the universe in its totality. The task ahead for the human species is to spread this knowledge and to start working on the great adventure of discovery rather than wasting time and effort fighting over disagreements on the nature of reality and existence, and humans place in the universe.

Atheists View of Body Mind and Soul

The mind is the brain. The brain contains the perceptions, realities, thoughts, and knowledge of the individual. There is not a collective consciousness. When the individual dies, all of what was the biochemical make-up of the brain dies with the individual. The only way for the contents of the brain to exist beyond death is to communicate its contents to someone else. This communication can be either through the spoken or the written word.

Even if a person could be regenerated from their own DNA they still would not have all of the same mental characteristics, because they could not live their life over exactly as they had lived it before. Genetically, they would still have the same mental capacity, but their environment and life experiences could not be duplicated. What all this means is that you should make the most out of the one life you have to live. There is no other. When you die you are just organic matter, nothing transcends death, and death is final. This is not easy for most people to accept, so they believe in a multitude of crazy ideas. Some of these ideas include the concept of a soul, life after death, the spirit world, or reincarnation. You might as well face up to the facts. There are no distinct entities within man. The idea that man is made up of a soul, or contains a spiritual part is nonsense. There is only one whole made up of many physical parts, the mind and body are one. The idea of a spiritual life is escapism. There is no evidence that spirits and souls exist.

To keep both the brain and body in shape and at optimum levels of performance they both have to be exercised. It has been shown that exercising your body enhances your health and can actually slow or reverse aging. The same is true with the mind. Studies have shown that the advent of senility can be delayed if the mind is exercised through reading, problem solving, creative activities, and reasoning. These are the ways to superior development, not through trying to enhance a non-existent inner spirit or soul.

Technology has progressed so far that with devices such as the scanning-tunneling microscope we can now see individual atoms. With atomic and molecular transitions serving as references, measurement precisions near 10^{-15} seconds are possible. The second is determined by a resonance in the cesium atom. Bell Laboratories has measured a pulse of light to a time of 30 femtoseconds. A femtosecond is 1×10^{-15} of a second or a thousand million-millionths of a second. Ferenc Krausz and his colleagues at Vienna University have recently published in *Nature* the measurement of the shortest time interval ever recorded, a mere 100 attoseconds. An attosecond is one quintillionth, or 10^{-18} of a second. The National Bureau of Standards has developed an instrument that provides an accuracy of 6 parts in 1 billion - enough to detect the change in gravity over a vertical height of 2 centimeters.

The theoretical limits of physical systems are being reached and there is still no evidence of gods, souls, spirits, ghosts, or other mythical entities. These systems have allowed man to definitively say that there is no such thing as a soul or supernatural being or force. If such things exist we should be able to detect them. So far no such entities have been detected, and there is no reason to believe that any will ever be detected. Admitting or believing that there are superior beings or entities is admitting defeat. If humans are ever going to take their place as survivors and superior beings in the universe they will have to start using their heads for something besides a hat rack and start studying science, not scripture.

Established religions have spent centuries perpetuating myths and indulging in brainwashing and behavior modification techniques to keep the masses in line. They don't believe that humans are capable of facing up to reality and controlling their own destiny. Religions were formulated at a time when ignorance prevailed, and people just did not know any better. Thousands of year's later people continue to persist in a state of primitive ignorance. For atheists it is clear that religion is an error of past generations, and has become an obsolete anachronism. All religious teachings should be discarded and replaced with the teaching of a realistic and correct picture of natural law and the universe.

The Terrible Costs of Religion

> *"Billions of dollars and hundreds of religions later,*
> *Man's existence is still filled with despair, misery, poverty, and starvation."*
> *Anonymous*

Due to the vast number of religions and sects, each with their own varying and unique viewpoints of existence, it is difficult for believers to coexist without conflict. Religion and socialism have caused more deaths and suffering than any other human inventions. Instead of helping the world and being man's salvation, as the religious leaders all claim as their mission, they are instead fighting and killing both each other, and thousands of other innocent people. Atheists believe that religion must be eliminated if there is ever to be a unified world.

The loss of life due to religion comes in many forms. These incidents range from the 1978 cult tragedy in Guyana where 900 followers of the Rev. Jim Jones died in a mass murder-suicide, to the deranged activities of individuals who torture and kill babies they believe are possessed by the devil. There have been hundreds of cases of people dying because they thought faith alone would cure them of diseases. The Christian Scientists and other faith healers are famous for these crimes. In 1978, a group of Islamic extremists set fire to a crowded theater in Abadan, Iran. The moviegoers were violating Islamic beliefs by watching movies during the Islamic month of Ramadan. The fire killed over 400 women and children.

Death and torture at the hands of religious gangsters has gone on since the beginning of human worship of gods. Human sacrifice using women and children was commonplace. People who offended the gods were killed instantly. All over the world at a certain stage of religious evolution sacred animals and human beings were ceremoniously killed and eaten. Even the Olympian gods of Greek religion had demanded occasional human sacrifice until the 7th and 6th century B.C.

It was only 755 years ago in 1235 A.D. when the Inquisition was instituted by Gregory IX to inquire into offenses against the Roman Catholic Church. In 1252 A.D., Pope Innocent IV first authorized torture, as a means of extracting recantations or evidence. In 1478, Pope Sixtus IV established the Spanish Inquisition at the request of Ferdinand and Isabella. The first Inquisitor General was Toma's De Torquemada. Torquemada's name, as part of the Black Legend of the Spanish Inquisition, has become a byword for cruelty and fanaticism in the service of the Catholic Religion. The Inquisition's procedures were secret, and suspects were not told the identity of their accusers.

To get information, torture was used routinely, and penalties ranged from reprimand and warnings to being burnt at the stake. Other penalties included floggings, life imprisonment, and confiscation of property. The confiscation of property could be imposed on the heirs of those who died in heresy, as well as those who had acquired the possessions of deceased heretics by purchase. The proceeds from these confiscations went to defray the expenses of the Inquisition and to the ecclesiastical authorities. The Inquisition was suppressed in 1808 and its successor, the Tribunal of Faith, was abolished in 1834. These institutions are no longer in existence, but the pain, agony and suffering that is synonymous with religion still persists in many parts of the world.

The history of religion is a history of violence, hatred, and war. The military history given below is just a small sample of the historical and present day mayhem that is directly attributable to religion. Some of the excerpts below are from *The Encyclopedia of Military History*.

Palestine and Syria during the period of 1200-700 B.C.

c. 1200- c. 800. Between the decline of the Egyptian and Hittite empires, and before the height of Assyrian power, the various tribes of Palestine and Syria coalesced into a number of petty, independent, constantly warring states. Outstanding among these were the Jewish nation, the Philistines of Southwestern Palestine, the Phoenician cities of Northern and Western Syria, and the Aramean kingdoms of Eastern Syria, of which Damascus was the most important.

c. 1100. Gideon, the most famous of the early Jewish warriors temporarily united most of the independent Israelite tribes in repelling the incursions of the Midianites, an Arabic people living east of the Jordan.

1080-1025. The rise of the Philistines - Israel was invaded and dominated by the Philistines.

1028 - 1013. The reign of Saul - The Jews rose against their oppressors. Despite many successes, internal squabbles prevented Saul from driving the Philistines completely out of Israel. They killed him in the Battle of Mount Gilboa (1013).

1010-973. The reign of David - He checked, then destroyed, resurgent Philistine power, reunited the Jews, conquered all Palestine, and apparently dominated most of Syria. He defeated all the external councils of the Jews, but the later years of his reign were marred by several bloody internal insurrections, one led by his son Absalom.

973-933. The reign of Solomon, a period of peace and prosperity - After his death, the Jewish kingdom split into two parts, the kingdom of Israel and the kingdom of Judah. For two centuries, Jewish history was a succession of wars in which these two rival kingdoms were either pitted against each other or against their many small neighbors.

854. The Battle of Qarqar - The temporary alliance of Ahab of Israel and Ben Hadad II of Damascus postponed Assyrian conquest by a victory over Shalmaneser III.

c. 750. Assyrian Conquest - Palestine and Syria remained under foreign control for the next 27 centuries.

724-722. Revolt in Israel - Assyrian King Shalmaneser V heavily besieged Samaria. Upon his death Sargon II stormed the city and suppressed the revolt.

1187-1192 A.D. Saladin's Jihad (Holy War) - Saladin conquered Jerusalem and most of Palestine, and caused the Third Crusade. Despite some defeats, Saladin retained Jerusalem and most of his Palestine conquests; but in a treaty with Richard I of England, granted the Christians special rights in Jerusalem (1192).

The Wars of Religion 1560–1598

The First war of Religion 1562-1563 - The principal Protestant (Huguenot) leaders were Prince Louis of Bourbon and Conde' and Count Gaspard of Coligny, Admiral of France. The principal Catholic leaders were Guise, Constable Montmorency, and vacillating ex-Protestant Antoine of Bourbon and Navarre (brother of Conde', father of Henry of Navarre). Because of the recent peace with Spain and the Empire, France was full of unemployed soldiers, ready and eager for fighting and loot. Some important dates of the First war of religion include the following:

1562 - March 1 - Massacre of Vassy. A number of Protestants were massacred by Guise troops.

1562 - December 19 - Battle of Dreux. A Huguenot army of nearly 15,000 men unexpectedly ran into a Catholic army of about 19,000. Losses on each side were an estimated 4000 men.

The Second War of Religion 1567 - 1568 - More death and destruction.

The Third War of Religion 1568 - 1570 - More death and destruction.

1569 - October 3 - Battle of Moncontour. A combined attack by Catholic cavalry and the Swiss infantry put the Huguenot cavalry to fight. The Catholics crushed the Huguenot infantry, the Swiss being particularly ruthless in slaughtering the landsknechts. Huguenot losses were nearly 8,000 men, the Royalists losses probably no more than 1,000.

The Fourth War of Religion

1572 - August 23-24 - Massacre of St. Bartholomew's Eve. A massacre of the Huguenots, initiated by Catherine de' Medici. Estimates of casualties are 50,000 people killed. Catherine de' Medici received the congratulations of all the Catholic powers, and Pope Gregory XIII commanded bonfires to be lighted and a medal to be struck in her honor.

The Fifth War of Religion 1575-1576

The Sixth and Seventh Wars of Religion 1576-1580

The Eighth War of Religion 1585-1589

As if 38 years of religious warfare were not enough, another thirty years of war were only a few years away.

The Thirty Years' War 1618-1648 - This was primarily a religious war and was fought with the characteristic bitterness of such wars. It was a product of the struggle between Roman Catholics and Protestants in Germany. The physical devastation of this war, the loss of thousands of soldiers, and heavy civilian casualties, were the most severe in Europe since the Mongol invasion. And it was all due to the ambitions of Catholic Imperialism.

The battle between the Protestants and Catholics continues even today. The Protestant and Catholics have been battling each other for 20 years in Northern Ireland with hundreds of lives lost, and scores of innocent people killed and wounded.

1969-1974. Continuous Violence in Ulster - Catholic-Protestant terrorism kept the province in a bloody turmoil barely controlled by the equivalent of a British division plus local police. The Irish Republican Army (IRA) terrorist group, outlawed in Eire, was nonetheless based in Eire and attempting to force the British to agree to succession of Ulster to Eire. Some violence, in the form of bombings, spread to Britain. Ostensibly religious, economic, social, and political issues are also contributing factors.

1972 - January 30. "Bloody Sunday" in Londonderry - Thirteen unarmed civilians were killed by British troops when attacked by Catholic demonstrators. In response, an Irish mob in Dublin stormed and burned the British Embassy.

1972 - July 28. British Army Occupies Catholic Areas of Belfast and Londonderry - Barricaded enclaves previously considered too dangerous to enter were swept in a 3-day operation. British forces in Northern Ireland were at a 17,000-man peak.

1972-1990. Terrorist attacks by the IRA claim hundreds of lives. The struggle continues with no end in sight.

The Arab-Israeli Wars 1945–1973

108

As we have seen the conflict between the Jews and the Moslem Arabs dates back to the 1st century A.D. after the Roman subjugation of rebellious Palestine. The complete story of the religious hostilities between these peoples is beyond the scope of this book; only the more recent conflicts will be discussed. The years since 1945 have been marked by seven distinct periods of hostility:

1. The beginning of guerrilla warfare sparked by Jewish terrorism. In 1948, the massacre of Deir Yassin occurred. During the fighting for control of the Tel Aviv-Jerusalem Road, units of two Jewish Zionist paramilitary groups, the Irgun Zvai Leumi and the Stern Gang, slaughtered over 100 noncombatant Arab men, women, and children.
2. The First Arab-Israeli War or the War of Independence 1948-1949.
3. The Second Arab-Israeli or Sinai-Suez War 1956.
4. The Third Arab-Israeli War or the Six-Day War 1967.
5. The War of Attrition 1968-1970.
6. Guerilla warfare sparked largely by Arab terrorism 1970-1973.
7. The Fourth Arab-Israeli War, or the October War 1973.

Acts of terrorism, violence, and killings continue in the region today, especially in the Israeli occupied areas of the Gaza Strip and the West Bank, and in fighting between various religious factions in Lebanon and Beirut. These warring factions include Christians, Moslems, and Jews. Hundreds of Palestinians and Jews are still being killed on a daily basis. Since September 2000, more than 1800 Palestinians and 700 Israelis have been killed as a result of the ongoing conflict.

In Uganda, the Lord's Resistance Army's (LRA) brainwashed child-fighters seem determined to fight to the death. In 16 years, the LRA has abducted 15,000 children from northern Uganda, to use as fighters and sex slaves. The children's resolve is consistent with their leader's policy of bloodying new recruits, some as young as six, by making them bludgeon to death anyone who tries to surrender or escape. A self-declared spirit medium, Joseph Kony claims to be possessed by the Holy Spirit and to have been called by God to replace the Ugandan constitution with the Ten Commandments. A former altar boy, he preaches a blend of Catholicism, traditional spirit worship and the occult. Some 500,000 people have been displaced by his movement's terror attacks.

The above examples are just a few of the many conflicts that have arisen in the name of religion. Hundreds of other cases of uprisings, sectarian violence, assassinations and exterminations continue today. This violence includes both major religions and minor sects such as the Sikhs in India and the Sunnis vs. the Shiites in the Moslem nations. In India, an anti-Sikh massacre was triggered by the assassination of Indira Gandhi on October 31, 1984. Over the next four days, as many as 3000 Sikhs were killed in retaliatory attacks. In 1992, more than 1,000 people died in riots, after a 16th century mosque was pulled down by Hindus who believe the site to be the birthplace of the Hindu God-king Rama. Recently, 57 more people, including forty women and children, were burned alive when a Muslim mob set fire to a train carrying Hindu activists. According to official figures tabulated in the parliament, more than a thousand people were killed (790 Muslims and 254 Hindus) in the violence after the train incident.

When are these people going to learn? War has been going on in the Middle East for almost 3,000 years over what is basically the same disagreement on the nature of reality. How can humans possibly evolve with ignorance such as this leading to perpetual conflict?

Death and religious belief go hand in hand. In a recent pilgrimage to Mecca, the Moslem holy city and shrine, 1426 people were killed in a stampede by panicking pilgrims. Riots several years earlier killed an additional 500 people. All this death due to faith alone, or if you believe the Saudi leader King Fahd, it was really just a matter of "God's will, which is above everything. They are all better off, for they are martyrs for Allah." Can anyone really believe that being dead is better than being alive?

How much death and destruction does one have to list to prove a point? Does anyone really believe the religious violence that has been going on for thousands of years is going to stop without the end of all religious belief? To see the devastation all one has to do, is on any given day, pick up a newspaper and there will be another story of violence, war, and death that can be directly attributed to religion. An attempt has to be made to try to regain some sanity in the world, so that the so called "civilized" world can in fact finally become civilized.

The costs of religion go far beyond the killings and violence mentioned above. Additional costs to civilization include the wasted mental energies of the peoples that study and worship religious entities. This misdirected energy comes in the form of time spent praying, reading and studying the Bible, the Koran, the Torah, and other religious texts, the millions of man-hours per year wasted attending religious ceremonies and services, and the billions of dollars that are wasted on religion that could have been used for scientific research, education, health, and assistance for the poor.

Despite the religious propaganda from the true believers death, destruction, and war continue unabated. The propaganda of religion is like all propaganda, including Nazi propaganda, in that it is based on attacking people's minds with false information by appealing to emotions, lack of knowledge, and fear. The word propaganda is derived from the Catholic Church's Congregatio De Propaganda, or the Congregation for Propagating the Faith. It is used then as it is now, to mislead the masses and to bring in new converts.

Propaganda is defined as the deliberate attempt by some individual or group to form, control, or alter the attitudes of other groups by the use of the instruments of communications, with the intention that in any given situation the reaction of those so influenced will be that desired by the propagandist. The propagandist is the individual or group who makes any such attempt.

The missionaries of these religious institutions are corrupting the minds of millions. Church broadcasts now reach an estimated 990 million people a month around the world. These broadcasts are carried on television and radio including many stations utilizing the short wave frequencies. It has been stated by theologians that some 6,850 of the 8,990 ethnic or linguistic groups on earth have now been penetrated to some extent by the gospel. Many times this religious corruption has been against the will of the indigenous peoples. Many cultures, including tribes in Africa and South America, have become extinct due to harassment by these missionaries. The goal of these groups is the evangelization (meaning brainwashing) of the world in this generation. What this means is that an entire generation will grow up believing what their parents and other misdirected people have told them to believe, rather than using their own minds and independent free thought to determine their own view of reality.

Additional harm comes to the citizens of the world through the constant attempt by these groups to monopolize the information and knowledge of the world. Censorship, media control and book burning is on the rise, especially in the United States. Fundamentalist Evangelicals are trying to ban books, films, art, and anything else that they personally feel is not something that is appropriate. These people want nothing less than a monopoly on the ideas and thoughts of individuals. They have already succeeded in the banning of such classics as *Catcher in the Rye*, *Brave New World*, *To Kill a Mockingbird* and even dictionaries from schools, because they don't like certain words and ideas that they contain.

As unbelievable as it may seem, in 1981 a Federal Appeals court ruled that the school board in Warsaw, Indiana was within its rights when it ordered five books "destroyed and forbidden to be used" in a high school English class. After the verdict a group of knowledge destroyers burned a pile of the volumes outside the school. In another case, a federal judge in Mobile Alabama banned 36 books from virtually all public schools in Alabama, on the grounds that they illegally promoted what he referred to as the "religion of secular humanism." Secular humanism is not a religion. It is not based on faith. It contains no belief in the supernatural, and worships no deity. The definition of secular humanism is discussed further in the glossary. Some of the books that were banned include: *History of a Free People*, Henry W. Bragdon 1981, *Our Land*, Rand McNally, 1980, and *Understanding Regions of the Earth*, 1981. This is the sort of thing that one might expect in a totalitarian state such as Nazi Germany, the Soviet Union, or Communist China, but certainly not in the United States.

The fundamentalists would like to see us revert back to the times of Charles II and the Licensing Act of 1662. This act ordered that no person shall presume to print any heretical, seditious, schismatical, or offensive books or pamphlets, wherein any doctrine or opinion shall be asserted or maintained, which is contrary to the Christian faith, or the doctrine or discipline of the Church of England. There is no quicker way to ruin people's minds and to abolish freedom and free thought than to ban books that are contrary to the states, the churches, or individuals' preferences. We might as well be living in the Dark Ages. Just as the Inquisition wanted to censor Nicolaus Copernicus's book *De Revolutionibus Orbium Coelestium* (*On the Revolutions of Heavenly Spheres*) published in 1543 so that it could teach the heliocentric solar system as hypothesis rather than fact, the 16th century attitude is alive and well in California were the Creationists wish to use the same arguments to censor the presentation of evolution in biology textbooks.

Political Economic Systems

Everyone should know by now that socialism doesn't work and that capitalism is the only system that does work. History has proven this over and over again. Even though there is overwhelming evidence for the superiority of the capitalist system, Marxists and socialists refuse to believe it. They are the true believers, and again, faith is their guide not reason and fact. They keep hoping that one-day socialism will work and that Marx, their savior, will be right.

The main types of political economic systems are pure socialist economies, mixed socialist economies and capitalist economies. Unfortunately, pure Laissez-faire (leave us alone) capitalist systems no longer exist even in the United States. The U.S. is already a mixed economy and is heading towards a socialist economy. This will cause serious damage to America's standard of living, the ability to compete on a global basis, and will have a significant adverse effect on the future of the country.

Signs of the movement towards socialism can be seen by the calls for a classless egalitarian society "from each according to his ability, to each according to his need," the redistribution of capital, more government control, media and government attacks on business, and the class warfare practiced by the left and the socialist Democratic Party. The rich "limousine liberals" of today are no different than Marx and Engels. By virtue of a special privilege, the logic of certain elect bourgeois is not tainted with the original sin of being bourgeois. Karl Marx was the son of a well-to-do lawyer, married to a daughter of a Prussian noble, and his collaborator Frederick Engels, a wealthy textile manufacturer, never doubted that they were above the law and, notwithstanding their bourgeois background, were endowed with the power to discover absolute truth. The mendacity and hypocrisy of the rich socialists is sickening, they only want to redistribute other peoples money to the poor, not their own.

The socialists, with their never ending quest for the demise of capitalism, and using the stealth tactics they are known for, have come up with a new term for their socialist ideology, economic democracy. Instead of referring to procedures for choosing officials, as democracy normally does, it implies an equalization of wealth in society. This was to be achieved through redistribution policies enacted by governments mainly by means of taxation. The goal was to assure everyone a decent standard of living not necessarily related to whether they earned it or not. Other goals, such as housing, health care, schooling, and retirement care were included in this corrupted definition of democracy.

These and other social issues have also been renamed to become rights. For example, the right to health care, the right to a college degree, the right to have housing, the right to have everything paid for you by the government. Of course, these are not rights. There are only the rights of man. No one has a right to any of these things unless they earn it. There is no free lunch. Someone always has to pay. Taking money from one person, who through hard work and thrift happens to have more than someone else, and giving it to someone who doesn't work and lacks thrift hardly seems fair or equitable. Yet this is what socialists do. They take from the most productive citizens and give to least productive citizens. This is known as the Robin Hood syndrome. They steel from the rich and give to the poor.

Economic democracy was embraced by Communist nations, where people were barely permitted basic human rights and include the former Soviet Union and its Eastern European satellites, China, Cuba, and North Korea, as well as by such liberal democratic welfare states as Sweden, France, Great Britain, Canada, and the United States. For those who think they are entitled to free education and health care they can always move to Cuba. Of course, if you need auto parts or brake fluid for your car, or electricity for your home, forget it. The socialist economy in Cuba is so bad that people in Cuba are forced to use shampoo for break fluid because real break fluid cannot be found. Cuba's national electric grid is notoriously unreliable. Due to a shortage of spare parts at power plants, they rarely work at more than 60 percent of capacity. If free education and health care contribute so much to a utopian society, why are Cubans risking their lives to leave Cuba and come to the United States?

Whether by revolution or legislation, history shows that attempts to create economic democracy are destined for failure. Economic forces absolutely defy political legislation aimed at equality. History has shown that the stronger the attempt by governments to force economic equality the greater the failure of the economy itself, with the general result being an equality of poverty. Demanding the same level of prosperity for everyone is the unobtainable communist utopian ideal.

Socialism and Communism

Karl Marx (1818–1883) will be mentioned first because his ideas mark the beginning of what is known as scientific socialism. His ideas, presented in the works *Das Capital* and the *Communist Manifesto*, helped shape the former Soviet Union into the global leader of the socialist-communist movement. Marx believed in an idea known as the unchangeable law of history which he claimed to have discovered scientifically, although scientific method as we know it was not used in this discovery. This theory assumes that history runs in progressive stages until it reaches a final stage, that being when total communism is achieved. This final stage marks the end of history (not the end of time) in which society has reached its highest obtainable level, that being a global communistic utopia. There are six of these progressive stages, beginning with a primitive, communal state. From this state, society then progresses to a slave state, a feudal state, a capitalist state, a socialist state, and finally, to a communistic state. This simply means that each new stage of history replaces the previous stage of history until a utopian society comes into existence. Behind this process is a philosophy known as dialectical materialism, which was first, conceived of by the German philosopher George Wilhelm Friedrich Hegel (1770-1831). Dialectical materialism is the concept of progress in terms of the conflict of contradictory interacting forces called the thesis and the antithesis. It is materialist in that it denies transcendence and affirms the ultimate reality of the physical world. Since matter is the only reality everything, including human behavior, can be explained in terms of matter and everything has its origins in the material universe. Fundamentally, dialectical materialism means that these two opposites (the thesis and the antithesis) clash, maybe even violently, until there is a synthesis. Out of this synthesis emerges something that is better than what existed before.

As it applies to scientific socialism this process of synthesis-clash-synthesis continues until the final synthesis, that being communism begins. What this theory describes is a concept of revolutionary social change. For Marx, the thesis and the antithesis were the Bourgeois and the Proletariat respectively; the Bourgeois being the owners of the means of production, and the Proletariat being the workers who do not own the means of production. From the *Communist Manifesto*, Marx states, "The other Proletarian parties, formation of the Proletariat into a class, overthrow of the Bourgeois supremacy, and conquest of political power by the Proletariat."

Following this idea of the dialectic, where opposites clash resulting in a synthesis, today the two major forces in conflict are capitalism and communism. The Soviet communists saw communism and capitalism locked in a deadly conflict that they planned to win at all costs. To achieve their goal of winning the communist-capitalist conflict they were prepared to use any and all means available to them. As another Soviet hero, Vladimir Lenin (1870-1924) once said, "We must use any ruse, dodge, trick, cunning, unlawful methods, deceit, and veiling of the truth...for as long as capitalism and socialism exist we cannot live in peace."

Since Lenin's ideas contribute so much to the overall ideology of the Soviets, it is worthwhile to look at a few more of his ideas. One of the major contributions of Lenin was to give the Soviets the self-proclaimed role as the world's premier communist power and leader. Another statement from Lenin that sums up the Soviet intentions and shows them in their true light is as follows: "The victorious Proletariat in one country...after organizing its own Socialist production, should stand up against the remaining capitalist world, attracting to itself the oppressed classes of other countries, raising revolts in those countries against the capitalists, and in the event of necessity, coming out even with armed force against the exploiting classes and their governments." This was a declaration of war against all governments that were not socialistic and did not adhere to the ideals prescribed by Marxist-Leninist theory.

Socialist Peoples Republics such as Cuba, China and North Korea are controlled by the Communist Party; although officially atheist they do worship a few things, these being power and the writings of Marx. Pictures of Marx and their communist leaders (Castro in Cuba and Mao in China) are everywhere, from the sides of buildings to the walls of classrooms, and the writings of their idols are more numerous than those of the Bible. The leaders of these nations believe in Marx in the same way that Christians believe in Jesus Christ, and Muslims believe in Allah.

Because socialism and communism are often used interchangeably and there is some confusion as to what precisely these terms represent, the definition of these terms and the elements that make a system either socialistic or communistic will be given.

Communism is defined as the final stage in Marxist theory in which all economic goods are distributed equally, thereby resulting in the communal ownership of property. The state withers away, which means that eventually, political organizations and operations dry up and disappear and a dictatorship of the Proletariat takes its place. Communism is not an economic theory as such, but more closely related to a political theory in the sense that it is a utopian philosophy that could never exist. There are many reasons behind the improbability of such a system being implemented. A few of the many faults of communism are given below.

First of all, the ideas of the state withering away and the dictatorship of the Proletariat taking over are ridiculous. If the massive state bureaucracy that now exists in Socialist countries were eliminated, there would be no one left to implement the various plans and programs designed for the people. In fact, the state organizations and institutions that make up the bureaucracies of the Socialist countries have been getting consistently larger. What this farfetched scheme really amounts to is that instead of a massive bureaucracy running things, a small elite class will run everything; so much for Marx's classless society. Second, the idea that you can implement a system in which all goods and services are distributed equally among the populace is inconceivable. There is no known system that could even come close to carrying out this objective. There would always be someone, somewhere, that managed to get more. Even if you could change human nature, the logistical problems involved would be exceedingly difficult. The growth of the black market in the former Soviet Union and other socialist countries is a prime example of how unrealistic this goal is.

Socialism is more of an economic system than a political system, and like communism, it is a stage in Marx's theory of social development. The economic system of socialism seeks to accomplish three major goals. The first of these goals is the abolishment of capitalistic economic structures including the dispossession of private owners of economic institutions and facilities. This means that the government would take over and manage these institutions and facilities instead of the private sector. The second goal is the nationalization and collectivization of agriculture. The third goal is the inauguration of centralized national economic planning. The flaws inherent in socialism are far too numerous to be covered in this book, which is not meant to be a book on comparative economics. The important fact here is that only when the rest of the world becomes socialist will the true state of communism be possible.

Socialist systems inevitably lead to totalitarian systems. Totalitarianism is a political regime based on subordination of the individual to the state; characterized by strict and total control over all phases of society, such as communications and the economy; accompanied by an official ideology and a system of terrorist police control. Two of the greatest tyrannies of the 20th century arose out of socialism. The death toll from statism and totalitarianism shows what happens when there is unreasonable government control over the lives and liberties of the citizens.

China (communist)	35 million dead
Germany (20th century)	21 million dead
The Holocaust (1938-1945)	6 million dead
Stalinist Purges (1930-1938)	20 - 60 million dead
Cambodia (1975-1979)	1-2 million dead

There are still numerous totalitarian regimes around the world including China, Cuba, and North Korea. All of these countries are communist. What is life like under a socialist totalitarian regime? Below are some examples of events that occurred in the former Soviet Union:

1. People were sent into exile for their beliefs and thoughts.
2. People were put away in psychiatric prison wards because they disagreed with the state not because they were mentally ill.
3. Government goons used snowplows to remove people from the streets.
4. Government goons beat and imprisoned protesters and staged their own pro-government marches. There was no freedom of association or expression. There was no freedom of speech or freedom of the press.
5. People were shot and killed when trying to escape to freedom, their only crime - wanting to be free from a totalitarian police state.
6. The military was used to maintain internal control. The Soviet military deliberately shot down and killed 269 innocent civilians that were on board a Korean Airlines flight.
7. The KGB continuously spied on every country on the planet. This was especially true in the United States where they were continuously stealing technology like common criminals.
8. Starved millions of its own people (4-5 million Ukrainians between the years 1932-33) as a means of maintaining control of the masses.
9. Used slave labor (estimated to be 5% of the population) and forced child labor.
10. In an attempt to conceal the disaster at Chernobyl, the military was given orders which resulted in the death of a dozen soldiers from radioactivity received while

116

fighting fires at the Chernobyl nuclear power plant. Their only alternative was to be shot.

Although anarchism is not a political economic system due to the rise of anarchists involvement in the anti-globalization effort it is worth mentioning. Anarchy means absence of rule. It is a system of social thought, which believes in fundamental changes in the structure of society in the form of replacement of the authoritarian state by some form of non-governmental cooperation between free individuals. Anarchism is based on the idea of extreme individual liberty. The anarchist favors a society in which the lives of its members are directly controlled only by their own decisions. In this way anarchism opposes authority in all its forms including; governmental rule, social constraint, religious domination, and moral compulsion. They believe that individuals must voluntarily select their own norms of conduct. Further they believe that any collective action, no matter how democratically arrived at is not an individual action and that democracy only exists to thwart the individual.

The most famous anarchist was Mikhail Bakunin (1814–1876) whose criticism of bourgeois society was very similar to Marx. The new ideal society that both Marx and Bakunin looked forward to was based on collective ownership and the elimination of the state. Today, anarchists and socialists march together on May Day, which is an occasion for celebrating the solidarity and achievements of labor and demonstrating against the rule of law and free markets. The anarchists are the most dedicated and resolute elements of the working classes and have been called the left wing of socialism.

It is hard to imagine that people still believe in anarchism, socialism and communism. It is even harder to believe that when in 1999 the BBC conducted a poll asking people to name the greatest men and women of the millennium that the people's choice for "greatest thinker" was Karl Marx. How can anyone with any intelligence call a person who was a fanatic and who was wrong on almost every idea a great thinker? It is just another case of ignorance and people not facing up to facts and reality, another case of blind faith, hoping that the future will somehow, for some unknown reason, dramatically change and show that they were right after all. *The Truth About Karl Marx* by the political scientist Ralph Wing is given below:

Even Karl Marx's friend Friedrich Engels, concluded that Marx was a radical revolutionary whose great aim in life was the overthrow of capitalist society and the state institutions, which it had created. Marx was the son of a prosperous lawyer. Engels was the son of a wealthy cotton manufacturer. Marx fathered six children, only three survived to grow up and of the three, two committed suicide. Marx was unable to hold a job, and with a family to support he lived a life of poverty, privation, and misfortune, which contributed heavily to his hatred and bitterness towards the capitalist system. Only handouts from the wealthy Engels saved the Marx family from starvation. Marx's claim to fame is the 1848 pamphlet The Communist Manifesto which is nothing more than revolutionary propaganda calling for the violent overthrow of the whole contemporary social order.

From this miserable existence Marx became delusional and filled with hate as he spent 18 years working on the mostly incoherent Das Capital. Marx believed that his work was scientific, although it had no basis in science. Marx falsely claimed that Das Capital followed scientific method, which contributed immensely to his wide acceptance. He used such tricks as tying his class struggle theory of history to Darwin's theory of evolution in a feeble attempt to give his ideas respectability.

Marx's theory was based on dialectical materialism, which maintains that everything in the world is in a constant state of change. Progress is achieved by the reaction of opposing forces on each other. This led Marx to his invalid theory of historical materialism. Marx believed that the history of mankind is primarily the story of the exploitation of one class by another. Applying his ridiculous idea of dialectical materialism he believed that the

117

dictatorship of the proletariat followed by communal ownership and return to a classless society was inevitable.

In addition to dialectical materialism, Marx came up with additional ridiculous theories such as the theory of labor value, the theory of surplus value, and the inevitable destruction of the middle class. The theory of labor value asserted that labor is the source of all value. Value is derived from demand and utility, not from labor. As has been suggested "Men dive for pearls because they are valuable, pearls are not valuable because men dive for them." The theory of surplus value assumes that the actual value of labor was invariably in excess of wages paid. This nonsensical argument follows the idea that a workingman paid a wage of forty dollars a day actually earned that sum in six hours, but was required to work ten hours. The extra four hours, therefore, were stolen from the worker by the capitalist, proving that the capitalist system is nothing more than an evil scheme set up to exploit and to rob the working class. Although factually invalid, this concept does have value for the purposes of propaganda and agitation. Finally, the destruction of the middle class has not occurred, and the size of the middle class in most developed capitalist societies continues to increase. Capitalism is actually the creator of the middle class, not its destroyer.

Ultimately Marx was a failure in life and a failure at economics. His works have become the bible of radicals who follow it as a faith based religion devoid of facts and evidence. Marx's neurotic ramblings on the plight of the workingman and the rise of the machines as a tool to further enslave the working class have found a small niche of believers who blindly accept the dogma of their religion and the prophet Marx. These mindless believers still dream of a Marxian utopia that will never appear.

With his insane envy of anyone with more than him, and his jealousy of power, Marx has caused more death, misery, degradation and despair than any other prophet who has ever lived. Marxian prophecy is dead; it is time for his followers to awaken to the bliss of reality.

Most of Marx's work was written in a fog of unreality and much of his published works including the *Communist Manifesto* and *Das Capital* were ghost written by Frederick Engels. Marx claimed that his system was predictive. It was, after all, in his feeble mind science. But all of his main predictions were hopeless failures. These include the demise of capitalism; that the Bolshevik Revolution in Russia would be the starting point for a proletarian revolution and communist development in the West; that class warfare would lead to revolution, class warfare is now only a political tool of the left; that the growing polarization of classes would lead to the disappearance of the middle class, when in fact there has been an increase in the middle class in almost all industrialized democracies; that the proletarian revolution was inevitable, even though it has never occurred; that there would be an inevitable decline of profits and the hampering of technical progress under capitalism, obviously just the opposite has occurred. Then there is the idea that the right to private property exists only because it serves the bourgeois, which is again another fallacy. In reality, the lack of property rights is a primary generator of poverty. One only has to look at countries where there is no right to private property to see the failure of this idea.

Beyond the fact that communism is a utopian ideal that could never exist in reality, Marx never actually took the trouble to describe how the communism he predicted and advocated would actually work. Today's anti-capitalists and militant critics of globalization proceed much the same way. They have no concrete or even theoretical alternative to the capitalist economic system. They are simply dissatisfied with a system they don't understand and because of personal, family, or social frustrations, and political idealism, they long for what in their minds is a more just form of social organization. Instead, they invoke a utopian world free of environmental stress, social injustice, and low paying jobs, harking back to a pre-industrial golden age that never actually existed. The anti-capitalists and the anti-globalists have inherited more from Marx including the self-righteous anger, the violent rhetoric, the resort to actual violence, the support of anarchism and revolution and a disdain for democracy, the demonization of big business, and the division of the world into exploiters and victims. Marx was not a scientist, he founded a faith and his secular religion lives on despite the fact that the political economic systems he inspired are dead.

People have to get over the fact that egalitarianism like communism is a utopian myth. Egalitarianism is the belief in the equality of all people especially in political, economic, or social life. These people feel that gross inequality in wealth is a social evil, which poisons life for millions and that people who don't work or who are unproductive deserve just as much as people who work hard and are productive. The fact is that people are not equal. People have varying intellectual and physical capabilities. These variances cannot be changed because someone thinks it would be nice. Most men would like to be able to play basketball and have money like Michael Jordan but all the social engineering in the world is not going to make that happen. There are others who would like to be as smart as Albert Einstein. Again, social engineering is not going to make that happen. Perhaps the socialists can find a way to redistribute Michael Jordan's basketball skills so that everyone can play basketball as well as he does. Redistribution of wealth is no different than the redistribution of skills or intellect. It is utopian thinking that can never be achieved and simply does not work.

The egalitarians believe that family incomes and individual incomes should be identical. Incomes cannot be equal. There will always be differences. Reasons for these differences include the element of good or bad luck. For instance, you could have finished your degree in typewriter repair when the personal computer and word processing software came to market. Markets reward results. Incomes also differ because people are of different ages. Typically, young people and the elderly have lower incomes than those in their prime earning years. Incomes vary with the skills of the individual. Does anyone really believe that a janitor should make as much as a neurosurgeon? Incomes differ with continuity of experience in a certain type of job and with full-time rather than part-time employment. Incomes differ due to the existence of created rents based on monopoly control. An example of these rents is union membership and dues, which are devices to increase the incomes of some workers at the expense of other workers.

The idea that the rich are not working people and that they are undeserving of their wealth is derived from stupidity and envy. Just as everyone cannot play basketball like Michael Jordan, not everybody can be wealthy. Wealth is created by innovation and hard work. Many of the wealthy started off poor and many of the wealthy have become poor. Instead of wasting their time looking for ways to redistribute wealth the socialists should be looking for ways to improve innovation, reduce the regulatory burden on business, get rid of the monopolistic power of labor unions, reduce the size and cost of government, and implement an equitable flat income tax or national sales tax. If these people really cared about the poor and equality this is what they would be doing instead of bellyaching about the rich and the unfairness of life.

Socialism also leads to larger government, which naturally leads to more inefficiencies and corruption. Just a few examples will show the truth that the larger government becomes and the higher taxes are raised to pay for this larger government the more corruption and mismanagement will occur. No government agency could stand up under the level of financial scrutiny that private enterprise is subjected to.

As far back as 1982 President Reagan directed the Grace Commission to root out government inefficiency and waste of tax dollars. The project was funded entirely by voluntary contributions of $76 million from the private sector (after tax money). It cost taxpayers nothing. The Grace Commission made 2,478 recommendations which, if implemented, would save $424.4 billion over three years, an average of $141.5 billion a year - all without eliminating essential services. Citizens Against Government Waste has worked to make this vision of an efficient, well-managed government that is accountable to taxpayers a reality. In a little over a decade CAGW has helped taxpayers save $687 billion. There is still a long way to go. There are countless cases of corruption, mismanagement and frivolous use of funds still occurring every day.

The White House Office of Management and Budget reported on May 31, 2002 that the federal government has doled out nearly $20 billion in erroneous payments in health, housing, food stamps and social security to people and companies that were not entitled to them. This does not include unnecessary and poorly performing assets of $90 billion in farm credits and $72 billion in bad loans. This is your money that is just being flushed down the toilet, while the socialists (Democrats) want to raise your taxes even more.

Elected officials are not responsive to public opinion when an issue concerns a well-financed and well-organized special interest group. Budgets are not approved, expanded or cut based on market forces but instead are based on getting votes for the next election. Bureaucracies have a tendency to take on a life of their own and can seldom be dismantled. Bureaucrats spend most of their time inventing new programs to expand their budgets and power and the remainder of their time justifying past failures as examples of insufficient funding. As a rule, the worse the government bureaucracy performs the more money it gets. Of course in the real world the worse you perform the less you get.

There are many examples of this. Government poverty relief had been around for decades before Lyndon Johnson's Great Society programs and there was no evidence that it worked. Proponents claimed that it was just a lack of funding. Hundreds of billions of dollars later welfare still doesn't work. The bureaucrat's answer, the program needs more funding.

The government's drug czar admitted that the government's multimillion-dollar anti-drug advertising campaign may have backfired and instead of stopping kids from trying drugs might have actually enticed a new generation of youth to try them out. His solution: expand the program with even more funding.

According to the Department of Education from 1972 to 1995 education spending has increased from $200 billion to almost $400 billion while SAT scores have declined from around 530 to 500. From 1980 to 1999 the price tag for a public school education adjusted for inflation rose from roughly $5,000 to $8,000 per pupil, an increase of 60 percent.

ACT and SAT scores are still significantly lower than they were 10 years before the massive bureaucracy known as the Department of Education was established, when spending was only $4,200 per pupil. The U.S. spends more per student on K-12 education than almost all other modern democracies, yet our students perform near the bottom on international tests. Although the trend is that the more you spend the worse the ACT and SAT scores become, the response of the bureaucrats and the teachers union is "we need to spend more money on education."

The people who want a larger government, and the people who want more rather than less government intervention, are the politicians, the bureaucrats and the special interest groups who benefit directly from government actions regardless of whether or not the rest of the country suffers. Whenever you have an increase in the size and power of government you have a decrease in freedom, liberty, productivity and the generation of wealth.

Democratic Political Systems

Political parties are organizations that wish to achieve control of the process of government. They differ from special interest groups that only want to have an influence on government policy through lobbying or education of the public. A party gains control of government by getting more of its candidates elected to office than its opposition parties do. Political parties are the products of representative democracy. During the centuries when laws were made by kings and their advisers, parties could not exist because there were no elected officials. Parties began to emerge in Europe and North America in the late 18th and early 19th centuries, when elected legislatures became a dominant force in government. The number of political parties a nation has depends upon historical circumstances. Some countries have several parties, all of which may be represented in the government. France, for example, has 17 political parties. Other countries function effectively with only two major parties. In some countries, most notably China, Cuba, and several African states, there are one-party systems.

Although the United States, Canada and Britain have multi-party systems only two parties have been consistently strong enough to gain control of the government. In the United States for example, there are the two main parties the Democratic Party and the Republican Party, and there are several other third parties such as the Libertarian Party and the Socialist Party. In Germany, Belgium, Italy, and some other countries, there are several parties large enough to contend for office. But the number of parties usually makes it impossible for any one of them to win decisively. It is often necessary, therefore, for the biggest winners to form coalitions in order to govern. When these coalitions break down it is often necessary to hold elections again until there is a large enough coalition to govern effectively. There have been many debates over which form of government is the most effective. Again, you have to base it on the freedom and prosperity of the people and the relative strength of the nation as compared to others. Here again, the United States with its Constitution, representative democracy and free market capitalism has proven to be the leader of the free world with the largest economy, the most powerful military, the most advanced technology, and the global leader in almost all measures.

Some multiparty countries have adopted proportional representation in their legislatures. This is a device by which seats in the legislature are awarded to members of political parties based on the number of ballots cast for the parties within electoral districts. Various mathematical formulas are used to achieve the representation, but the results are the same: members of minority parties are able to get one or more candidates seated in a legislature. Proportional representation has been adopted by Belgium, Norway, Denmark, Sweden, Greece, Italy, Switzerland, Germany, Israel, and a few other nations. The chief reason for the existence of a large number of parties in a single nation is ideology. These parties typically adhere to narrow fixed economic or political doctrines, such as Marxism or socialism, but such parties seldom are ever able to attract broad enough support to win elections.

Great Britain and the United States both have, in general, two-party systems of government. They do not operate in the same way, however. In Britain elections are held for members of Parliament. After the election the leader of the winning party is named prime minister. This individual thus serves both in Parliament as a legislator and in the Cabinet as an executive and policymaker.

This cannot happen in the United States because of the constitutional separation of powers. A president cannot serve in Congress while in office. It is therefore possible for the presidency and the Congress to be controlled by different parties, a situation that cannot occur in Britain. This control of the Congress by one party and the presidency by another has generally been the rule instead of the exception since World War II. The disadvantage of the American system is the deadlock that can develop between the president and the Congress over policy when each is in the control of a different party. The advantage is that U.S. constitutional concept of separation of powers and checks and balances provides the balance necessary for long-term stability and reduces the likelihood of extremism and radical change.

Federalism is the system of government whereby states or entities unite under a centralized (federal) government, while retaining a measure of autonomy. Each member state agrees to subordinate its governmental power to that of the central authority in certain specified common affairs. The federalist system established by the U.S. Constitution (1789) placed foreign affairs, common defense, and interstate commerce, under the federal government. Existing autonomous state and local governments in the various states that joined the federal union continued to function, though with reduced powers. A republic is a state or nation in which the supreme power rests in all the citizens entitled to vote (the electorate) and is exercised by representatives elected, directly or indirectly, by them and responsible to them. In being a representative of the people, their job is to act in behalf of the people, not for their own agenda. They are to serve the people who elected them, not themselves.

The word democracy is derived from two Greek words: *demos*, meaning "the people," and *kratos*, meaning "rule". A democracy is a way of governing in which the whole body of citizens takes charge of its own affairs. As citizens of towns, cities, counties, states or provinces, and nations, the people are the sovereigns, the source of power. Democracy means that they can freely make the decisions about what is best for them: what policies to adopt and what taxes to pay. A true democracy, as Lincoln was defining it, means a society in which all the people are citizens with the same rights to participate in its government.

In a representative democracy, such as the United States, the citizens exercise their political rights indirectly, through elected representatives not through a direct democracy. In most cases such democracies operate under legal limitations imposed by a constitution, though it is possible to have a representative democracy without a constitution. When a state or nation has a constitution, these governments are called republics or constitutional monarchies. Greece is a republic, for example, while Denmark and Norway are constitutional monarchies because they have a king or queen.

In a small ancient Greek city-state or a colonial New England township, direct democracy was possible. It was not inconvenient for all the voting citizens to gather in one place to debate public issues. In large nation-states, such as Canada or the United States, direct democracy is impossible. There is no way for all the citizens to gather in one place for decision-making purposes. Representative, or indirect, democracy became a necessity. The most common type of government in the 20th century, representative democracy prevails in Western Europe, North and South America, Australia, New Zealand, Egypt, and Japan.

Within nations, there may be only one level of representation, or there may be several. American citizens elect representatives to the national government, state governments, some county governments, and local governments in cities and towns. The nature of representation itself may vary. The president of the United States is considered the representative of all the people. Members of the United States Senate represent the people of their states, and members of the House of Representatives represent the people (constituents) within their Congressional districts.

The American Declaration of Independence states: "We hold these truths to be self-evident, that all men are created equal, that they are endowed by their creator with certain inalienable rights that among these are life, liberty, and the pursuit of happiness." This does not mean that all people are equal in every respect. It only asserts that all individuals are equally human. This being true, all people have the same natural rights to life, liberty, and the pursuit of happiness. This means that people have a right to the pursuit of happiness, not an implicit right to happiness. A person has the right to take the legal actions they feel are necessary to achieve happiness, it does not mean that others must make him or her happy, or that it is the government's job to make everyone happy. These rights are guaranteed under the constitution. The most important of these individual rights are defined in the Bill of Rights.

Governments derive their just powers from the consent of the governed. There is no innate or implied government power. In a real democracy all laws apply to all individuals in the same way at the same time. This is the basis of equal justice under the law. Constitutional governments are governments under law, not the whims of elected officials or judges. All citizens, from the president down to the homeless, are subject to the same laws.

As Ayn Rand points out in her book *The Virtue of Selfishness* "all previous systems had regarded man as a sacrificial means to the ends of others, and society as an end in itself. The United States regarded man as an end in himself, and society as a means to the peaceful, orderly, voluntary coexistence of individuals. All previous systems held that man's life belongs to society, that society can dispose of him in any way it pleases, and that any freedom he enjoys is his only by favor, by the permission of society, which may be revoked at any time. The United States held that man's life is his by right, that a right is the property of an individual, that society as such has no rights and that the only moral purpose of a government is the protection of individual rights." From this it follows that "the right to life is the source of all rights – and the right to property is their only implementation. Without property rights, no other rights are possible. Since man has to sustain his life by his own effort, the man who has no right to the product of his effort has no means to sustain his life. The man who produces while others dispose of his product is a slave."

Capitalism

Capitalism can be traced back to the 16th century, when mercantilism rose to replace feudalism. However, it wasn't until the Industrial Revolution in the 18th century that capitalism really began to flourish. Capitalism is derived from nature and the natural order of the interactions of man. These include self-interest (survival), private property (the right of ownership or in nature territorial control), competition (the struggle for finite resources and constant improvement), supply and demand (scarcity and the pricing mechanism – species numbers decrease or increase based on the food supply), freedom (the absence of coercion, or constraint in choice or action), division of labor (specialization – in nature the social insects), survival of the fittest (some individuals and companies are more fit than others by virtue of their particular traits). The use of natural language and reciprocity, or as Adam Smith put it "the propensity to truck, barter and exchange one thing for another" are an evolutionary link between culture and biology going back over 2 million years. Before there was money and economic systems, all transactions were through the means of the direct exchange of one good for another in a process called barter. An exchange is the acceptance of one thing for another. When the volume of exchanged goods became larger and more complex it was gradually realized that exchange would be easier if there were some single commodity that everyone would accept as valuable. Initially this single commodity was precious metals such as gold and silver. Since gold was the scarcest it was usually more highly valued than other metals.

There were many advantages of using gold as an exchange mechanism. Gold has universal purchasing power, it can be processed into different sizes representing different values, it is durable and will not rust or decay, even small amounts are valuable so it is easy to carry around, and gold has never lost its value as an exchange commodity. Even after 4000 years, gold is still acceptable in any civilized society as money.

The use of gold in exchange has generally been abandoned in favor of paper bills and coins made of cheaper metals. Paper money is not hard money. There is no limit to the amount of paper money that can be printed. Paper money is called fiat money. Fiat money is inconvertible and derives its quality of full legal tender from the government that issues it. Governments print currency and declare it to be money and its use is mandated as both legal and necessary as the proper medium of exchange within a nation. Paper money has no value in itself. It has only the value that a government says it has. Money is no longer tied to gold by law (the gold standard), and the amount of it in circulation can vary greatly. The gold standard used gold as the basis of the monetary system and as a standard of value for currency.

The U.S. money supply consists of currency, such as dollar bills and coins issued by the Federal Reserve System and the Treasury, and various kinds of deposits held by the public at commercial banks and other depository institutions such as savings and loans and credit unions. Different measures of money have different technical definitions. Typically a measure has a name consisting of the letter M followed by a number, where the higher the number, the broader the measure.

In the United States a measure of paper cash, the amount in checking or demand deposit accounts in circulation is called M1. M2 is a broader measure including M1 plus savings accounts, money market accounts and certificate of deposit accounts (CDs) under $100,000. The broadest measure in use in the U.S. is M3, which includes M2 plus all other CDs and Eurodollars held by the US.

If a government's central bank allows the money supply to increase greatly, prices will rise steeply. This happens because money decreases in value in relation to other goods. When the money supply increases, people prefer holding other goods, because they fear that prices will keep going up. An oversupply of money in relation to other goods is called inflation, and it has been a persistent problem for many centuries, ever since governments took command of issuing money. Inflation is a general rise in the prices of goods and services. Inflation is not the rise in price of one particular commodity it is the rise in all prices simultaneously. Inflation is generally not a problem until the price increase is large and sustained over a large period of time. For sustained increases in the prices of all goods and services there must be an increase in the amount of money paid for each and every good and service. If there is a constant supply of money, then more of it paid for a particular good implies less of it paid for all other goods. Therefore, sustained inflation is impossible with a constant supply of money and conversely an increase in the supply of money is a necessary condition for inflation. The only entity that benefits from high inflation is the government.

Inflation often leads to calls by the uninformed to implement price controls. Price controls merely transform inflation into shortages and create black markets. With price controls you have a choice, paying a higher price to obtain goods or having lower stated prices for goods that cannot be obtained at all. Under market conditions prices tend towards equilibrium. Price controls destroy private ownership of the means of production. The right to set buy and sell prices is a fundamental, indispensable right of ownership. Price controls are fully as destructive of the rights of ownership as socialism itself.

An excessive increase in the money supply, called hyperinflation, completely destroys the value of a currency, and has often destroyed governments as well. This happened in the late Roman Empire, in Hungary and Germany after World War I, in China after World War II, and in Russia and Ukraine after the collapse of the Soviet Union in 1991. Inflation decreases the value of money, and hyperinflation destroys it because it destroys purchasing power.

All money has two values, nominal and real. The nominal (or named) value is what is stamped on it by a government mint or printing press; "five dollars," for example. The real value of money is its purchasing power or what it will buy at a given moment. This idea applies to wages as well. The real wage is what money received as wages will buy. As the general price level advances the money wage will buy less, and as the price level declines, a money wage will buy more.

The early experiments with paper money in Europe and the United States were not successful because the money was over issued. Because governments needed money, mostly for war, they resorted to printing it. Because it was not tied to a gold standard, the paper quickly became worthless. Creditors and merchants would not accept it, and it drove good money out of circulation into private hoarding.

In a hard-money or gold-based economy, without government interference, the money supply tends to regulate itself, based on economic necessities. The supply of money being fairly constant, it tends to bear a stable relationship to the production of goods. Attempts are made to locate new gold mines. If the supplies of gold do not increase, however, prices will tend to fall because the demand for money will be greater than the demand for goods. This is a typical deflationary situation. It derives from an absence of liquidity, or cash in hand. The most liquid of all assets is cash. Assets that can be quickly turned into money, such as stocks or bonds, also have a high degree of liquidity.

In a paper-money economy, a different situation emerges. The money supply is easily variable. If money is poured into an economy by the central bank, producers may be fooled into believing that the economy is expanding rapidly and that demand for products and service will rise. Producers will double their efforts to increase productivity. They do this by building new plants, buying more machinery and materials, increasing their inventories, and hiring more workers. After a while they learn, to their dismay that markets have not expanded, consumer demand has not increased, and new investment was unnecessary. Large inventories of goods have been built up that no one is buying. Soon, the whole economy grinds to a halt, or a drastic slowdown such as a recession or depression occurs, until the excesses of production and bad investment have been eliminated from the economy.

Capitalism is a social-economic system based on the recognition of individual rights, including property rights, in which all property is privately owned. Capitalism also provides for the freedom of the individual to contract with others and to engage in economic activities of his or her choice for his or her own profit and well-being. In a capitalist society government should play a limited role with its main functions being the maintenance of law and order and the national defense. Regulations and other barriers to entry for small businesses should be minimized. All one has to do is look at impoverished countries to see what legal and regulatory barriers to entry do to increase and sustain poverty. As Hernando De Soto points out in his book *The Mystery of Capital: Why Capitalism Triumphs in the West and Fails Everywhere Else* as much as 90 percent of the population in such nations operates extra-legally, that is, outside the formal economy. His solution is to restructure the legal system to enable proper, streamlined titling of properties and businesses, which can then be leveraged and traded; thereby unlocking the value of the working poor's assets. These assets or so-called "dead capital" are estimated to be worth $9.3 trillion. Countries that are poor are poor because they are corrupt, do not have stable governments, have too many rules and regulations, and do not have legal protection of private property. It is not capitalism that makes countries and people poor it is governments.

The rule of law and absence of corruption are essential to the proper functioning of the capitalist economic system. Corruption reduces competition, distorts market mechanisms resulting in market inefficiencies, and perpetuates poor performance. The legal system must protect the right to own private property, including intellectual property, enforceable contracts, and title to land. Intellectual property rights include patents, trademarks, and copyrights. Without legal rights and the possibility of reward for owning and protecting property rights, innovation would come to a halt.

The word capital refers to what are called factors of production. These factors of production include the money, land, buildings, and machinery that it takes to operate a factory or farm. The capitalist is the individual, or group of individuals, who supplies the money to get the enterprise going. With free enterprise people have the right to do what they wish with their property, as long as it does not harm anyone else. These freedoms set capitalism apart from all other kinds of economic arrangements. All other economic systems are top-down, command-and-control political systems in which personal freedom and the rights of property are sacrificed for the good of the state. The heart of capitalism is the producer's right to make what they want and the consumer's right to choose what they wish to buy. Central to the economic system of capitalism is the idea that markets set a price for goods and services that matches the supply and demand. At the equilibrium price, producers are willing to sell precisely as much of a good or service as consumers are willing to buy at that price.

Capitalist society is a division-of-labor society, which is dependent on the operation of a price system, which in turn depends on private ownership of the means of production. Division of labor is a means of production whereby each worker performs a limited number of specialized operations. Specialization increases efficiency and the system of exchange creates wealth for society as a whole. Private ownership of the means of production is the foundation of both the profit motive and freedom of competition, which are respectively the driving force and regulator of the price system. Capitalism is the essential framework for economic progress and the rising productivity of labor, and is characterized by a harmony of the rational self-interests of all people under freedom. Capitalists make it possible for people to live as wage earners and to live ever more prosperously. Capitalists not only supply the wages they continuously drive prices down thereby raising the standard of living for everyone. Part of the beauty of capitalism is that like science, nothing is permanent or sacred; change and improvement are continuous. Past achievements do not count if they are obstacles to further improvement. A society depends on the continued creation of wealth for its prosperity and survival.

Without human action economic systems would be dormant. The economist Ludwig von Mises defines the prerequisites of human action as follows:

We shall call contentment or satisfaction that state of a human being, which does not and cannot result in any action. Acting man is eager to substitute a more satisfactory state of affairs for a less satisfactory. His mind imagines conditions, which suit him better, and his action aims at bringing about this desired state. The incentive that implies a man to act is always some uneasiness. A man perfectly content with the state of his affairs would have no incentive to change things. He would have neither wishes nor desires; he would be perfectly happy. He would not act; he would simply live free from care. But to make a man act, uneasiness and the image of a more satisfactory state alone are not sufficient. A third condition is required: the expectation that purposeful behavior has the power to remove or at least to alleviate the felt uneasiness. In the absence of this condition no action is feasible.

Economics is the study of how people make choices. Choice is necessary because of scarcity. It is not possible for each one of us to have everything we want. Therefore, we must choose some things and forego others. The cost of choosing one thing over another is the enjoyment, which the foregone alternative could have provided. These decisions come down to individual choice not societal choice. Different individuals will have different preferences with respect to their willingness to sacrifice current for future consumption. Self-interest exists due to human nature it is not derived from a political economic system.

A market is any arrangement that individuals devise that permits voluntary exchange for the mutual benefit of those engaged in trade. A market must transmit information about relative scarcities and provide incentives to react to this information. It is important to note that for a socialist central planning organization to work it would have to have information on all goods and services, including the quantities, prices and locations of all resources, the wants, desires, tastes, locations and preferences of all consumers, the production and distribution schedules of all manufacturers, all the legal actions that could impact the delivery of goods, and the availability and cost of all workers. Obviously, the acquisition and management of all this information would be impossible by one organization. Even if you could somehow gather all of this information, by the time you entered and updated the information into a central database it would be obsolete.

To solve the allocation problem to the best advantage of society, an enormous amount of information is required, but no single individual has access to more than a minute portion of that information. The remarkable thing about the market system is that it enables each individual to make optimal decisions with very little information. The individual does not need to know anything about the structure of the economic system. All the individual has to do is observe the market prices for goods and services and act accordingly. A social system based on liberty is very complex. In a free society, the activities of millions of people are in a state of constant flux and interaction. The efficient coordination of millions of plans, the global and orderly flow of millions of goods, and the execution of millions of individual decisions, all without any central control or direction is the beauty of market economics.

There have now been hundreds of experimental demonstrations of the power of markets. What Nobel Prize winning economist Vernon Smith and others have learned from such experiments is that any group of people can walk into a room, be given incentives with a well defined private economic environment, have the market rules explained to them for the first time, and they can make a market that usually converges to a competitive equilibrium and is 100 percent efficient within two or three repetitions of a trading period. This is true even when the participants don't understand what market supply and demand is. This demonstrates Ludwig Von Mises' assertion that "everybody acts on his own behalf; but everybody's actions aim at the satisfaction of other people's needs as well as the satisfaction of his own. Everybody in acting serves his fellow citizens." Under true capitalism there is no economic exploitation.

There has been additional experimental evidence that most people in relatively stable societies find it pays, in the long term, to show a cooperative, accommodating face to their fellow humans. Experimental market research strongly corroborates the Smith-Hayek-Mises theme of cooperation through market institutions in which property rights harness self-interest to create wealth.

Scarcity, choice, utility, and cost are the ideas that underlie supply and demand. In a market system, scarce goods are rationed by prices. Sellers want to get as high a price as they can for their goods, and so they sell to the buyers who are willing to pay the most. On the other hand, buyers want to purchase at as low a price as they can, so they buy from sellers who are willing to sell for the least amount. Those sellers who are willing to take a lower price bid customers away from those who are willing to take a higher price. The market price also coordinates the plans of buyers and sellers. The competitive bidding of the market channels resources into their highest valued uses. Without this bidding process, it is impossible to know what the most highly valued uses for resources are. No one person, or small group of persons, can know and evaluate all the possible alternative uses for all the resources in a market economy. This is one of the reasons why free markets are so much more productive than regulated economies.

Economics is a complex field of study. It is obvious that unless you are a true believer there is no need for further study of socialism except from a purely historical view. For a complete understanding of capitalism there are three main books that should be read. The first is *Capitalism: The Unknown Ideal* by Ayn Rand, the second is *Human Action: A Treatise on Economics* by Ludwig Von Mises and the third is *Capitalism: A Treatise on Economics* by George Reisman.

There are many schools of thought in the field of economics. Since socialism and other systems are not even an alternative, the two remaining competing schools of thought are the Keynesians and the Classical / Austrian School. The Classical / Austrian economists include the Classical economists such as Adam Smith (1723-1790), David Ricardo (1772-1823), John Stuart Mill (1806-1873), and Frederic Bastiat (1801-1850) and the Austrian economists Carl Menger (1840-1921), Ludwig Von Mises (1881-1973) and Frederic Hayek (1899-1992).

The Keynesians believe that the market is inherently unstable, but government can achieve economic stability by printing and spending money on a discretionary basis. Keynes was an interventionist and believed that the government should enact fiscal and monetary policies to counter the negative effects of the business cycle. Gwartney and Stroup provide the answer to why politicians have embraced Keynesian economics. The gains from printing and spending money are immediate, highly visible, and can be concentrated on individuals who make up powerful voting blocks. The costs of this policy are incurred at a later date, are difficult to perceive, and can be spread thinly across the population. From a political point of view, advocating and implementing Keynesian policy is the surest way to election and re-election.

As Mises points out, today the majority of the citizens look upon government as an agency dispensing benefits. The wage earners and farmers expect to receive from the treasury more than they contribute to its revenues. The state is in their eyes a spender, not a taker. These popular tenants were rationalized and elevated to the rank of a quasi-economic doctrine by Keynes and his disciples. Spending and unbalanced budgets are merely synonyms for capital consumption.

The failed and broken dogmas of Keynesian economics have been discredited. After decades of misinformation, biased economic textbooks, and a lack of understanding of economics by the media and politicians, the ideas of higher taxes, increased regulation and government intervention, and income redistribution have been shown to lead to higher interest rates, inflation, high unemployment, low productivity, slower growth and exaggerated boom bust cycles. The idea that government can take care of every problem that arises from the free market is dangerous. Government can make many problems worse rather than better. One has to look no further than Argentina to see the results of the failures of Keynesian policies. Argentina was one of the world's ten richest countries having grown at an average rate of 5% over the past three decades. Recently, the country was on the verge of financial collapse. How could this have happened? By retreating into protectionism, financing generous benefits to workers by printing money, corruption and political instability, too much government debt, rigidity (non-market mechanisms) in managing their currency relative to other countries, increase in the share of public spending at the expense of private investment, and mismanagement by the central bank which triggered a run on the banks. All due to government actions, not as some would lead you to believe due to capitalism and globalization.

The problems associated with central planning and government intervention are related to the fact that there are too many variables to allow for accurate predictions. When predicting the weather, wind speed and direction, pressure gradients, and temperature variations are used. When predicting future economic activity variables such as inflation, employment, interest rates, currency fluctuations, stock prices, and personal income are used. Economics and weather are stochastic (random) non-linear systems. The behavior of non-linear systems that are essentially equivalent to random behavior is ultimately unpredictable. There is an element of chance in all forms of predictions. Statisticians attempt to use trends to establish direction and movement of variables. A trend is a statistically significant change in performance measure data, which is unlikely to be due to random variation in the process. There are situations where the best decision is to take no action. Taking action, which is not necessary and actually degrades a process is referred to as process tampering.

In all processes, including nature and economics, there is some variation. The two types of variation are special cause variation and common cause variation. Special cause variations occur when there are significant changes in the data and are assumed to change the mean or variation of the normal distribution. It is special cause variations that put a process out of control. Special cause variations are generally transient in nature and influence predictability. Common cause variations are ongoing, apparently random fluctuations in the data and are considered to be a natural part of a process. Any unknown random cause of variation is common cause variation. Generally, there is little to be gained from determining the exact sources of this random variation.

Statistical process control techniques can be used to identify the existence of special causes of variation in a process. The basic rule of statistical process control is: variation from common cause systems should be left to chance, but special causes of variation should be identified and eliminated.

When the Central Bank attempts to forecast the economy and determine monetary policy it has a tendency to overcompensate. A large part of this overcompensation is due to the fact that a determination cannot be made as to whether fluctuations in economic activity are due to special causes or common causes. If control limits are arbitrarily established as variation from the common cause system any variability beyond these fixed limits will be assumed to have come from special causes of variation. Control limits are calculated from actual process data using valid statistical methods. Without accurate statistical guidance there is no way to determine whether special or common causes were to blame for variability.

When adjustments in monetary policy are made in the form an interest rate increase or reduction there is no way to know if the change is in reaction to special or common causes. If the change is made in reaction to a common cause it more than likely means that the change was unnecessary since the reason for the change could have been based on what was just a random fluctuation. If the change is made in reaction to a special cause the special cause could be misidentified and could lead to unintended consequences. This means that the economy and interest rates should be directed my market forces not government intervention. Man cannot control the weather nor should he try to control the natural market forces of the economy. All attempts to try to control the economy have failed. Capitalist economies without government intervention are self-adjusting. When the government intervenes in the economy it creates special causes.

A perfect example of the benefits of less government regulation and more competition is the deregulation of the airline industry. When Alfred Kahn (a liberal Democrat) under President Jimmy Carter was brought in to deregulate the airline industry, air travel was only for the wealthy. Under deregulation millions of people who could not afford to travel by air can now travel. They can visit their families and afford vacations. Not only have prices decreased dramatically, safety has increased with airline accident rates down more than 50 percent. Other benefits from airline deregulation include increased load factors on planes, and an increase of over 70 percent in the number of jobs in the airline industry. The market has to be the mechanism to conserve scarce resources by charging people the real cost of the resource. Consolidation reduces costs and competition protects the public.

Even though the socialist idea of central planning is a proven failure, there are still those who cling to the belief that the government can save the economy by properly managing fiscal and monetary policy. They cling to the belief that an activist government, guided by a so-called intellectual elite of utopian democrats can get things right. They can't get things right. The markets do not need protection from themselves they need protection from government intervention. Exaggerated boom and bust cycles are created by failed monetary and fiscal policies not by capitalism.

The more the government taxes people to finance its higher spending the poorer people become. When you have to give up a third or half of your income to the government in the form of taxes it robs people of any incentive to save and invest, and to work hard and take risks. Most of the existing government regulations are geared towards one goal, the redistribution of income. Income redistribution can never be equal or fair, only the market can determine what is equitable.

Government actions, in the form of printing and spending money, taxes, and regulations cause distortions in the economy and interfere with the efficient allocation of resources. Government actions often end up protecting and aiding the very industries they were originally designed to regulate and have turned into mechanisms for preventing competition that would have benefited consumers. The government is a vehicle by which organized groups can secure advantages for themselves, not by efficiently providing for the desires of the general public, but by imposing costs on the general public. The government is responsible for creating and maintaining monopoly power in areas such as education, electric power generation, and the United States Post Office.

The government is also responsible for anti-business laws such as the Clayton Act and the Sherman Act. These were acts passed by politicians who did not understand economics but were eager to gain the support of labor special interest groups. They mistakenly believed that market forces do not influence human labor and that there was no such thing as a labor market in which supply and demand governed the price of labor. It also meant that unions, unlike businesses were exempt from antitrust laws and could not be prosecuted as illegal combinations or conspiracies in restraint of trade. Unionism means high wages and more jobs for union members, and lower wages and fewer jobs for everyone else. Antitrust immunity for unions has lead to higher unemployment, higher prices for consumers, decreased productivity, and less economic growth.

The fact is that these outdated laws impose arbitrary government limitations on competition, keep consumer prices high, and weaken American industries in the face of increased global competition. When many of these antitrust laws were passed the companies that were accused of being monopolies were actually increasing their output faster than the overall economy and decreasing their prices faster than the general price level. Mergers, acquisitions, divestures, and bankruptcies, are all part of making the economic system more efficient.

Problems of Capitalism

As with all systems there were some problems with capitalism. Most of these are related to the ignorance of the capitalists not the capitalist system. Mistakes were made in the early days of capitalism. Probably the biggest of these mistakes was labor relations and environmental damage. Many of the capitalists of the day did not understand the importance of the relationship between healthy and happy workers and productivity and in many cases showed a total disregard for worker safety and health. Andrew Carnegie for example, was notorious for fatalities at his steel plants. The early capitalists were not as smart as they were ruthless. They were not smart enough to know that treating workers with respect and dignity was in their own self-interest.

Along with the lack of management knowledge, there was virtually no understanding of the environmental impact of fossil fuels and chemicals. The science for the impact of air and water pollution and chemicals on the environment did not exist. Compounding these problems was widespread corruption both in business and government.

These problems have to be put in the context of the day. In the late 19th century and during the depression, competition was ruthless. There was a lack of compassion between the capitalists and the workers, and between the workers themselves. In addition, there were no laws protecting workers against intentional negligence and abuse. Modern management practices in the late 1800's did not exist. The enterprises and systems that were being developed were new. Even the concept of the corporation had to be invented. Limited liability corporations paved the way for risk, and risk allowed for speculation and invention. There was no blueprint on how to run a company. It wasn't until 1911 that Frederick Taylor published his first book on scientific management, *Principles of Scientific Management* that a blueprint started to take shape. Taylor's book was the start of what was to become modern management theory. Today companies understand that a happy, healthy employee is a productive employee. They also know the benefit of being a good corporate citizen and protecting the environment.

The critics of capitalism denounce the fact that there is unemployment and that companies and even whole industries disappear. The market economy is dynamic, flexible, and in constant flux, because it depends to a great extent on technological change, new information, and innovation. Just as farmers have declined to about 3 percent of the American population, now the number of blue-collar manufacturing jobs is shrinking worldwide. Such dislocations are inevitable, as the economy continually corrects and readjusts itself. Attempts to halt or reverse change would, if successful, lead to stagnation and a decline in the standard of living. Success in a free market depends in large part on individual effort and ability. Effort and ability are unevenly distributed among human beings. Firms are born from the ideas of the entrepreneur. Firms die due to the competition of others and the will of the consumer. It is all part of the natural process of capitalism. Just as in Darwinian natural selection, firms best fitted for the conditions in which they are placed to survive propagate and spread, while the less fitted die out and disappear.

Capitalism has been denounced for having business cycles, periods of "boom and bust." But a free market system does not of itself suffer exaggerated business cycles or high unemployment. These are the result of government intervention, regulations, high taxes, and fiscal and monetary intervention in the economy.

There are also those who are blinded by their prejudices and still believe that wage earners toil for the benefit of other people. As Mises points out, the outstanding fact about the Industrial Revolution and capitalism is that they opened an age of mass production for the needs of the masses. The wage earners are no longer people toiling merely for other people's well-being. They themselves are the main consumers of the products the factories turn out. Business depends upon mass consumption. The very principle of capitalist entrepreneurship is to provide for the common man. There is in the market economy no other means of acquiring and preserving wealth than by supplying the masses in the best and cheapest way with all the goods they ask for.

The socialists complain that the human costs of capitalism are too high and that capitalism creates low paying jobs and insecurity. Without entrepreneurs and capitalism, there would be no job or wealth creation. Perhaps they would prefer to return to feudalism or the socialist states that are collectively responsible for the enslavement and deaths of millions of people.

The Benefits of Capitalism

Capitalism is the only economic system that fully allows and encourages the virtues necessary for human life. It is the only system that safeguards the freedom of the independent mind and recognizes the sanctity of the individual. It is the capitalist who takes the achievements of scientists and scholars out of the realm of the laboratory and theory and turns them into reality. It is the capitalist that takes the risks and builds the dream. It is the capitalist that creates the enterprise and provides the jobs. It is not the government or the workers.

Thanks to democratic free market capitalism more human progress has been achieved in the last 100 years than has been achieved in all the previous centuries combined. Listed below are just a few of the ways the human condition has improved dramatically over the last 100 years. For a complete listing please refer to the book *It's Getting Better all the Time: 100 Greatest Trends of the Last 100 Years* by Stephen Moore and Julian Simon.

- The average life expectancy in 1900 was 47 years. Today it is 77 years and increasing every year. People are living longer because they escape many of the illnesses and events that plagued our ancestors, death during childbirth, tuberculosis, typhoid fever, and cholera, largely because of better sanitation, cleaner water supplies, and medical advances such as immunizations and antibiotics.
- The infant-mortality rate has dropped from 1 in 10 to 1 in 150 and the number of women who die giving childbirth has fallen from 1 in 100 in the 19th century to 1 in 10,000 in 1980.
- In 1900 per capita GDP was about $4,000 compared with $32,000 in real dollars at the end of the century. The so called "poor" Americans today have routine access to better quality housing, food, health care, consumer products, entertainment, communications and transportation than the Carnegies, Rockefellers, and Vanderbilts.
- A farmer a century ago could produce only one-hundredth of what his counterpart is capable of growing and harvesting today while at the same time the price of food relative to wages has plummeted. In the early part of this century the average American had to work two hours to earn enough to

purchase a chicken, compared to 20 minutes today. A dozen eggs required an hour and twenty minutes of work in 1919 versus 5 minutes today.

- In the 19th century, almost all teenagers toiled in factories or fields. Today, 9 in 10 attend high school and may work part-time.
- Despite the doomsday scenarios of the radical environmentalists, the lakes, rivers, and streams are cleaner, smog has decreased (over the 25-year period 1962-1987 smog levels fell by more than half), and air quality has improved while emissions per unit GDP have decreased.
- Worker safety has improved. The accidental death rate at work has plummeted from about 38 workers per 100,000 in 1930 to about 4 per 100,000 today.

As with most things there is room for improvement, but the trends are positive and heading in the right direction. As the authors point out most of this progress was made possible by America. They site the fact that "the unique American formula of individual liberty and free enterprise has cultivated risk taking, experimentation, innovation, and scientific exploration on a grand scale that has never occurred anywhere before."

Capitalism and Innovation

If people are left free they will try to improve the quality of their lives. Therefore, most individuals will seek to do or make something that others will benefit from and pay for, or they will work for an organization that makes products or provides services. In pursuit of their own advantage, people in a free society use their imaginations; they innovate. They find new ways to do old tasks. They discover new processes and new resources. Innovation is the foundation of continued wealth creation. Free people in a free market economy provide the dynamism for consistently higher standards of living. The result has been a significantly improved standard of living for whole societies, not just for the rulers or an elite few.

Another reason that capitalism is the best economic system for generating growth is the ability to produce a continuous stream of successful innovations. Under capitalism innovation is mandatory for the survival of the firm. Competition is brutal. Those firms that don't innovate and compete don't last. New technology is shared and disseminated through the economy much faster than in other economic systems. This is a result of the incentives for developing innovations that add to economic growth. Without the market forces of capitalism the small amount of innovation that may occur in non-capitalist systems does not contribute to growth. This is especially true in countries that have a high percentage of state owned firms.

America is the greatest success story of all time. It has the most wealth, the most Nobel Prize winners, the most powerful military, the most immigrants per year of any country, and a culture that has spread around the world. A liberal immigration policy has allowed some of the greatest minds in the world to come to the United States. People are fleeing from stifling and hostile environments, persecution and lack of freedom to come to America. They don't call America the land of opportunity for nothing. Economic freedom has allowed millions of poor people to become middle class.

There are many reasons for this success. One of the most important is that historically (although the U.S. is now going in the wrong direction) American has had the most economic freedom and the least amount of government regulation and intervention in the economy. When you leave things alone people just get on with it. It is very simple. You cannot protect everyone from everything. This is what is happening today. People don't look out for themselves they rely on the government to look out for them. When you don't have a crutch to support you, it changes your attitude. The remarkable success of welfare reform clearly demonstrates this to be true. Without a government crutch people are inspired to create things. When the government intervenes by trying to decide for people how they should live their lives it upsets the harmony and natural rhythms of society. People have to learn to be responsible for themselves. Self-reliance is required for success in a capitalist economy.

Almost all of the modern conveniences that people take for granted today were invented in America. What has American capitalism delivered? A short list of the major inventions and innovations is given below:

Air conditioning (1902) - Willis Havilland Carrier (1876–1950)
Frozen foods (1924) - Clarence Birdseye (1886–1956)
Rocket engine (1926) - Robert Goddard (1882–1945)
Television (1927) - Philo Farnsworth (1906–1971)
Penicillin (1928) - Alexander Flemming (1881–1955)
Nylon (1934) – Wallace Carothers (1896–1937)
Xerography (copy machine) (1938) - Chester Carlson (1906–1968)
Helicopter (1939) – Igor Sikorsky (1889–1972)
Electronic digital computer (1942) – John Atanasoff (1903–1995)
Cellular phone (1947) - D. H. Ring
Transistor (1947) – William Shockley, John Bardeen, Walter Bratain at Bell Labs
Polaroid instant photos (1947) – Edwin Land (1909–1991)
Microwave oven (1947) – Percy Spencer (1894–1970)
Tupperware (1947) – Earl Tupper (1907–1983)
Containerized shipping (1956) – Malcolm McLean (1913–2001)
Disk drive (1956) – Reynold Johnson at IBM
Laser (1958) – Gordon Gould
Integrated circuit (1959) – Robert Noyce (Fairchild Corp.) and Jack Kilby (Texas Instruments)
The computer mouse and onscreen windows (1968) – Douglas Englebart (Stanford Research Institute)
Relational database (1970) – Edgar Codd
Microprocessor (1971) Robert Noyce and Marcian Hoff (Intel Corporation)
Personal computer revolution (1976) – Steven Jobs and Stephen Wozniak (Apple Computers) / Bill Gates (Microsoft) and IBM
The Internet (1960-1985) - Paul Baran, Bob Kahn, Vincent Cerf, and Tim Berners-Lee (United Kingdom)
Ethernet (1973) – Bob Metcalfe (Xerox PARC)
Multi-protocol Router (c. 1983) – William Yeager (Stanford University)

What made America great, and the world a better place, was the efforts and hard work of capitalists like those above and the titans of industry and progress Andrew Carnegie, Henry Ford, George Eastman, Thomas Edison, and the Wright brothers.

Andrew Carnegie (1835-1919) was born in Dunfermline, Scotland. He went to the U.S. in 1848 and soon began work as a bobbin boy in a cotton mill in Allegheny, Pennsylvania, for $1.20 per week. By 1899, when he consolidated his interests in the Carnegie Steel Company, he controlled about 25 percent of the American iron and steel production. In 1901 he sold his company to the United States Steel Corp. for $250 million and retired. Carnegie did not have a formal education, but as a youth working in Pennsylvania he developed a life-long interest in books and education. During his lifetime he gave more than $350 million (90 percent of his wealth) to various educational, cultural, and peace institutions, many of which bear his name. He was a benefactor of Tuskegee Institute (now Tuskegee University). He also endowed nearly 1700 libraries in the United States and Great Britain, and he donated funds for the construction of the Peace Palace at The Hague, Netherlands, for what is now the International Court of Justice of the United Nations.

George Eastman (1854-1932) played a leading role in transforming photography from an expensive hobby of a few wealthy devotees into a relatively inexpensive and immensely popular pastime for the masses. He was also one of the outstanding philanthropists of his time, donating more than $75 million to various projects. Notable among his contributions were a gift to the Massachusetts Institute of Technology and endowments for the establishment of the Eastman School of Music in 1918, and a school of medicine and dentistry in 1921 at the University of Rochester.

Cornelius Vanderbilt (1794-1877) entered the transportation business at the age of 16 when he established a freight-and-passenger ferry service between Staten Island and Manhattan. He owned a fleet of schooners during the War of 1812, entered the steamer business in 1818, and bought his first steamship in 1829. Rapidly expanding his operations, he became a vigorous competitor, reducing his rates and simultaneously improving his ships. Vanderbilt sold his steamboats in 1862 and began to buy railroad stock; within five years he controlled the New York Central Railroad. He continued his policy of improving service and reducing rates and greatly expanded his railroad holdings. Late in life Vanderbilt became a philanthropist; his endowments included $1 million to Vanderbilt University.

John D. Rockefeller (1839-1937) was educated in the public schools of Cleveland, Ohio. He became a bookkeeper in Cleveland at the age of 16. In 1862, he went into business with Samuel Andrews, the inventor of an inexpensive process for the refinement of crude petroleum. After rapid expansion, the firm became the Standard Oil Company, organized by Rockefeller, his brother William, and several associates. At its peak, Rockefeller's personal fortune was estimated at almost $1 billion. The total amount of his philanthropic contributions was about $550 million. Some 80 percent of these funds were given to four charitable organizations founded by Rockefeller. These were the Rockefeller Foundation; the General Education Board; the Rockefeller Institute for Medical Research (now Rockefeller University); and the Laura Spelman Rockefeller Memorial, established in 1918 and incorporated into the Rockefeller Foundation in 1929.

Thomas Edison (1847-1931) developed the first practical electric light bulb; electric generating system, sound-recording device, and motion picture projector all of which had a profound effect on the shaping of modern society. Edison eventually patented more than 1000 inventions.

Henry Ford (1863-1947) was born on a farm near Dearborn, Michigan, on July 30, 1863, and educated in district schools. He became a machinist's apprentice in Detroit at the age of 16. From 1888 to 1899 he was a mechanical engineer, and later chief engineer, with the Edison Illuminating Company. In 1893, after experimenting for several years in his leisure hours, he completed the construction of his first automobile, and in 1903 he founded the Ford Motor Company. In 1913, Ford began using standardized interchangeable parts and assembly-line techniques in his plant. Ford brought the price of a car down from a luxury affordable only by the rich to a necessity affordable to everyone.

Wilbur Wright (1867-1912) was born in Millville, Indiana, on April 16, 1867. As boys, he and his younger brother, Orville, made simple mechanical toys, and in 1888 they built a large printing press. The following year they began to publish the Dayton, Ohio, West Side News, which Wilbur edited. Already successful printers, the brothers opened a bicycle repair shop and showroom in 1892, and three years later they began assembling bicycles with tools of their own invention. On December 17, 1903, at Kitty Hawk, they made the first powered airplane flight in history. Despite public indifference, they dedicated themselves to the development of better engines and planes.

Orville Wright (1871-1948) was born in Dayton on August 19, 1871. His individual contributions to the improvement of aircraft include the development of the first wind tunnel in 1901. In 1902 he discovered that substituting a movable vertical tail for the stationary one that was then in use could eliminate tailspins in airplanes. After the death of Wilbur in 1912, Orville Wright became president of the American Wright Company. Three years later he sold his stock in the company for over $500,000.

One hundred years later we have the Lockheed Martin F-22 Joint Strike Fighter, the most advanced fighter aircraft in the world, and the Northrop Grumman Global Hawk. The Kitty Hawk used a gasoline-powered engine that delivered 12 horsepower. It was a propeller driven aircraft constructed of wood and fabric. The Kitty Hawk's first flight covered a distance of 540 feet at a speed of 45 feet per second. The flight lasted only 12 seconds. The F-22 can fly at speeds of up to Mach 2.0, which is twice the speed of sound, or at 30,000 feet, 1991 feet per second. The F-22 can take off and land both vertically and horizontally, is made of advanced stealth fiber composites, has a combat range of 600 nautical miles, and its Pratt & Whitney F119 jet engine delivers 40,000 pounds of thrust.

The Global Hawk is a high-altitude, long-endurance unmanned aerial reconnaissance system designed to provide military field commanders with high resolution, near-real-time imagery of large geographic areas. The aircraft's 13,500 nautical mile range and 36 hours of endurance, combined with satellite and line-of-sight communication links to the ground segment, permit worldwide operation of the system. The aircraft can be flown from a ground based station located anywhere in the world. High-resolution sensors, which can look through adverse weather (day or night), from an altitude of 65,000 feet, can conduct surveillance over an area the size of Illinois in just 24 hours. Like the Kitty Hawk, the Global Hawk and the Joint Strike Fighter are the products of American capitalism.

Contrary to the robber Barron image created by the left, and the demonization by the press and the socialists, these are the kind of people who built this country. Capitalists are the foundation of many of the most important discoveries and advances of man. Their philanthropic efforts have benefited untold numbers of people. Philanthropists are wealthy people who give the bulk of their money to support charitable, educational, or cultural institutions or activities. Philanthropists have given hundreds of billions of dollars to numerous charities and organization in an effort to make the world a better place. Many museums, foundations, and educational institutions of today were established through the donations of 19th- and 20th-century philanthropists.

The Ford Foundation, established in 1936, has worked to strengthen democratic values, reduce poverty and injustice, promote international cooperation and advance human achievement. The foundation has provided more than $11 billion in grants and loans worldwide. The W. K. Kellogg Foundation, established in 1930 by Will Keith Kellogg the inventor of corn flakes, made grants to improve the quality of life of over $224 million in 2002 alone.

Modern capitalists are equally as generous with their wealth. The Walton Family Foundation established by Sam Walton, the founder of Wal-Mart, in 2001 awarded almost $100 million dollars to youth programs, education and the United Way. The Bill and Melinda Gates Foundation, established by Bill Gates the founder of Microsoft Corporation, has awarded over $5 billion dollars in grants since its inception, including $3 billion to improve global health.

The socialist glorifies the downtrodden, the destitute, the poor, the miserable, and the negative aspects of existence. The capitalist glorifies the inventor, the innovator, the risk taker, the resourceful and successful, and the positive aspects of existence. Who deserves to be glorified the lazy, the criminal, the pessimist, and the beggar, or the hard worker, the philanthropist, the optimist, and the creator of wealth and jobs?

The socialists glorify the poor and despise and demonize the rich as greedy and self-centered, yet most capitalists and entrepreneurs were themselves once poor. The capitalists continue to do more for the good of society and the planet than any other group of people. Their work supports libraries, education and the arts, scientific research, poverty eradication, conservation and environmental research, and global healthcare. Billions of dollars are given away every year by hundreds of foundations, corporations and wealthy individuals. The fact is that the more money people make the better the world becomes.

Without the foresight, ingenuity, inventiveness, hard work and generosity of these men, the world would still be living in the dark ages. The one thing that the early capitalists had in common was they lived in a time when the government stayed out of peoples business, and there were no income taxes. Innovation, competition, and free enterprise used to be things that people admired. Today free enterprise and capitalism are demonized and success is punished. It is time to discard socialist utopian ideals and embrace capitalist market directed performance based reality.

Comparative economics is made easy when you contrast Vietnam (communist/socialists) and Hong Kong (capitalist) and North Korea (communist/socialists) and South Korea (capitalist). For the comparisons below, all Gross Domestic Product (GDP) figures are based on purchasing power parity (PPP) numbers. A purchasing power parity (PPP) exchange rate equalizes the purchasing power of different currencies in their home countries for a given basket of goods. These special exchange rates are often used to compare the standards of living of two or more countries. The adjustments are meant to give a better picture than comparing gross domestic products (GDP) using market exchange rates. Hong Kong has few regulations, low taxes (flat tax rate of 15%), and an entrepreneurial culture. Per capita GDP of $25,000 compares with the level in the four big economies of Western Europe and the United States. GDP was $180 billion in 2001 and GDP growth averaged a strong 5% in 1989-97. Hong Kong has accomplished this with limited resources (food and raw materials must be imported), limited land area 1,092 sq km, and a population density of over 6000 people per square kilometer. The current population is 7,303,334.

Compare these numbers to those of Vietnam. Vietnam is poor and suffering from the consequences of the rigidities of a centrally planned economy. Vietnam began its long transition from a planned economy in 1986. Faced with mass starvation, the government disbanded the Soviet-style agricultural collectives, freeing farmers to grow and sell their own crops. Vietnam is now the world's biggest exporter of rice after Thailand. The communist party still cannot come to grips with capitalism and corruption is rampant. Transparency International ranks Vietnam as the second most corrupt country in Southeast Asia after Indonesia. Per capita GDP is a dismal $2,100. GDP was $168.1 billion in 2001. Population was 81,098,416 in 2002.

Since South Korea became a democracy and implemented economic reforms the country has achieved an incredible record of growth. GDP was $865 billion in 2001 and per capita GDP was $18,000. North Korea is one of the world's most centrally planned and isolated economies. As a result, the country faces desperate economic conditions. GDP was $21.8 billion in 2002 and per capita GDP was a dismal $1,000. While South Korea is prospering, North Korea faces shortages in almost every industrial sector including power output, spare parts, fertilizer and fuel. North Korea's Soviet-style collective farming produced the famine of 1995-98 that killed up to 1 million people, or over 4% of the population. Massive international food aid deliveries are the only thing that has prevented mass starvation but the population is still suffering from prolonged malnutrition, and deteriorating living conditions. Life expectancy in North Korea is only 67.3 years compared to 78.6 years in South Korea.

Even the Chinese communists are smart enough to know that without capitalism they would remain a third world country forever. When the communists came to power under Mao Zedong strict controls over everyday life were implemented which cost the lives of tens of millions of people. After 1978, the Chinese leadership began moving the economy away from the sluggish unproductive Soviet-style centrally planned economy to a more market oriented system with decentralized economic decision making. Because of these changes by the year 2000 output had quadrupled. The Chinese economy (2001 GDP $5.56 trillion) is now one of the fastest growing economies in the world and is second only to the United States (based on PPP GDP). The Chinese leaders are continuing to relax economic controls and implement economic reforms.

Finally, one should not forget Japan. Japan was totally destroyed after World War II with very little natural resources, no infrastructure, and a new constitution and democratic form of government. Today, thanks to the system of democratic free market capitalism it is the second largest economy (based on nominal GDP) in the world after the United States.

There should be absolutely no dispute about which economic system works the best, or what is required to make the capitalist system work to its fullest potential. It is obvious that socialism is a terrible failure and doesn't work. It is also obvious that capitalism is the most efficient economic system and is by any measure the only economic system that actually works. There is no denying the numbers given above. It is also obvious that the countries with the least amount of corruption, government intervention, regulations and spending, the lowest taxes, and the greatest amount of freedom and liberty perform the best. Additional evidence comes from the World Bank report *Doing Business in 2007*, which ranks the best places to do business in the world. The two primary measures of the ease of doing business are the number of days needed to start a business and the cost of starting a business. Other factors include dealing with licenses, employing and terminating workers, getting credit, protecting investors, tax rates, trade, contract enforcement, and closing a business. The smaller the number of days to start a business, the lower the cost required starting a business, and the lower the tax rate, the better the economy performs. It should not be a surprise that Singapore, the United States, and Hong Kong are consistently ranked as the top countries for doing business.

The United States has followed the global trend of larger government. Government outlays have grown from 28.4 percent of GDP in 1960 to 34.6 percent in 1996 while during the same period GDP growth rate has fallen from an average 4.4 percent in the 1960s to an average of 1.9 percent during the 1990s. The evidence points to the fact that larger government and higher taxes mean slower economic growth.

The only way a government can be of service to national prosperity is keeping its hands off. These are facts and should not be subject to debate. Why do the socialists keep insisting that socialism will work and the bigger government and higher taxes are the way to go? The reason is simple; they choose to ignore reality in favor of their own utopian worldview. Evidence and facts are meaningless to these people.

President Calvin Coolidge was right when he said, "the business of America is business." Business is the foundation of America's success. It is the businessman who creates the jobs and builds the wealth of nations, not the government and the labor unions. For the government, the media, and the labor unions, to continuously demonize business is irresponsible and dangerous.

The attributes that lead the U.S. to its preeminent position in the world are badly needed today. These attributes include self-reliance and individualism, imagination and innovation, determination and drive, and persistence and perseverance. As a country America has to return to the belief that there is no obstacle or hardship to great for the American people to grasp and master. That anything is possible if the country stays on a common path towards glory.

As Stephen Ambrose stated in his book on the transcontinental railroad *Nothing Like it in the World: The Men Who Built the Transcontinental Railroad 1863-1869*; "Americans were a people such as the world had never before known. No one before them, no matter where or how they lived, had had such optimism or determination. It was thanks to those two qualities that the Americans set out to build what had never before been done."

One of the most striking features of American history between the end of the Civil War and 1914 was the staggering growth of industry. By the time the United States entered World War I in 1917, the U.S. had outstripped every other industrial nation in terms of manufacturing output, and had the highest per capita income in the world.

Today, America leads the world in almost all categories including the highest GDP per person of OECD countries after Luxembourg. With just 5 percent of the world's population the U.S. produced more than one-fifth of total world output. But if the United States is not to be eclipsed by China or the European Union and become just another has been country blindly following the edicts of the United Nations there must be a return to the ideals formulated by the constitution and by the tenants of capitalism that made this country what it is today. The United States combination of democracy and free enterprise are the key components that make the system of democratic free market capitalism the best political economic system the world has ever known.

Managing Your Life

What does it take to lead a life of happiness and fulfillment? Everyone has their own idea of what brings happiness and meaning to life. But many people do not have the tools and understanding to lead a virtuous life, or a productive life, or a successful life. The definition of happiness and success has to be determined by the individual. This section provides information and tools that affect your daily life and are an integral part in developing a life plan and worldview. Part of being happy is reducing stress, staying out of trouble, and getting along with others. Leading a moral and ethical life will provide a strong foundation for success in all other areas of life. Therefore, ethics and morals will be the first topic discussed.

Ethics and Morals

Ethics, from the Greek *ethika* or character, or moral philosophy, are principles or standards of human conduct. Morals, from the Latin word *mores* or customs, are the principles or rules of right conduct or the distinction between right and wrong. Morals and ethics are often used in the same context. Ethics and morals have evolved from the concepts of good and evil and right and wrong. Many philosophers have come up with various explanations for how good and evil came about. Of course, proponents of the goodness and perfection of God have a difficult time explaining the existence in the universe of death, suffering, and hate. As mentioned earlier, good and evil are man made concepts, and are not physical entities or forces that are transmitted from person to person. The Apologists taught that God created man good but he turned from God to flesh and from this act sin came into the world. Hence, man being the descendent of this first man is harassed by evil and must seek salvation through the divine grace of God. This of course is nonsense. Part of the problem is that good and evil are generally learned as part of religious education, which portrays them as a force and an innate part of man. This leads to the mistaken belief that some people are destined to be bad or evil.

The history of ethics begins with laws handed down from tribal chieftains to prevent disharmony in their tribes, and evolved to maxims and precepts handed down by secular leaders. In ancient China, the maxims of Confucius were accepted as the moral code. Pre-Christian religions, such as Judaism presented moral standards as commandments from God, to which the individual was expected to submit without question.

Ethical systems were being developed long before the birth of Christ. Confucius (551-479 B.C.) taught that each human being must cultivate personal virtues such as honesty and love through the study of the models provided in the ancient literature and that this would bring harmony to the graded hierarchy of family, society and state. Confucianism developed from the teachings of Confucius and his disciples into a major system of thought in China, and is concerned with the principles of good conduct, practical wisdom, and proper social relationships.

The central idea of Confucian ethics is jen, variously translated as "love," "goodness," "humanity," and "human-heartedness." Jen is a supreme virtue representing human qualities at their best. In human relations, construed as those between one person and another, jen is manifested in chung, or faithfulness to oneself and others, and shu, or altruism, best expressed in the Confucian golden rule, "Do not do to others what you do not want done to yourself." Other important Confucian virtues include righteousness, propriety, and integrity. One who possesses all these virtues becomes a chün-tzu (perfect gentleman).

Politically, Confucius advocated a paternalistic government in which the sovereign is benevolent and honorable and the subjects are respectful and obedient. The ruler should cultivate moral perfection in order to set a good example to the people. In education, Confucius upheld the theory, remarkable for the feudal period, in which he lived, that "in education, there is no class distinction." Additional words of wisdom from Confucius include the following:

- 'The superior man thinks of virtue; the small man thinks of comfort. The superior man thinks of the sanctions of law; the small man thinks of favors which he may receive.'
- 'Hold faithfulness and sincerity as first principles. Have no friends not equal to yourself. When you have faults, do not fear to abandon them."
- 'Let the superior man never fail reverentially to order his own conduct, and let him be respectful to others and observant of propriety: Then all with the four seas will be his brothers."
- 'Hold faithfulness and sincerity as first principles, and be moving continually to what is right; this is the way to exalt one's virtue."
- 'To be able to practice five things everywhere constitutes perfect virtue. Gravity, generosity, sincerity, earnestness, and kindness. If you are grave (having a serious and dignified quality or demeanor), you will not be treated with disrespect. If you are generous, you will win all. If you are sincere, people will repose trust in you. If you are earnest, you will accomplish much. If you are kind, this will enable you to employ the services of others."

The ancient Greek scholars contributed greatly to the field of ethics. Aristotle is considered the founder of modern ethics. His major ethical treatise was the *Nicomachean Ethics*. According to Aristotle, happiness is the chief good and everything man does is directed towards its attainment. Happiness implies the absence of suffering, and the possession of goods in addition to the virtuous activity of the soul. Aristotle believed that goodness of character is developed by habit. That we become good by doing good acts and the truly virtuous person consciously and consistently elects the proper action because he has the motive and disposition to make the right choice.

Aristotle introduced his famous principle of the golden mean, the middle way, as a guide to excellence. By recognizing what is too little or too much, we come to an understanding of what is right. Between cowardice and rashness is courage; between stinginess and extravagance, liberality; between laziness and greed, ambition; between humility and vanity, self-respect; between shyness and shamelessness, modesty; between boastfulness and self-deprecation, truthfulness; between buffoonery and boorishness, good humor; and between indecisiveness and impulsiveness, self-control; with the ideal being nothing in excess.

Another Greek scholar who contributed to the field of ethics was Socrates (469-399 B.C.) who believed that knowledge was the highest good. According to Socrates knowledge and virtue are one, in the sense that the wise man that knows what is right will do what is right. This is based on the belief that man is rational. It is the irrational mind and moral weakness, which leads man to do what he knows to be wrong. According to Socrates that action is right which serves man's true utility, in the sense of promoting his true happiness. Everyone seeks his own good as a matter of course (self-interest). But it is not every kind of action, however pleasant it may appear at the time, which promotes man's true happiness. For example, being continuously drunk is not to the true good of man. It is injurious to his health, enslaves him to a habit, and disables reason.

The wise man knows that it is more advantageous to be self-controlled, than to have no self-control; to be just, rather than to be unjust; courageous, rather than cowardly - advantageous meaning what is conducive to true health and happiness. Socrates considered that pleasure was good, but he thought that true pleasure and lasting happiness attend the moral rather than the immoral man, and that happiness does not consist in having a great abundance of external goods. Like many great thinkers Socrates ran afoul of the authorities. The leaders of the restored democracy brought Socrates to trial. The indictment before the court of the King Archon is recorded as follows:

> Socrates is guilty of (1) not worshipping the gods whom the state worships, but introducing new and unfamiliar religious practices; (2) and, further, of corrupting the young. The prosecutor demands the death penalty.

Another Greek scholar with similar views to Socrates was Plato (427-347 B.C.). To Plato reason was the highest good. The good life for man must be a mixed life, neither exclusively the life of the mind, nor exclusively the life of sense-pleasure. This includes pleasures, which consist in the satisfaction of desire, provided they are innocent and are enjoyed in moderation. Just as honey and water must be mixed in due proportion in order to make a pleasing drink, so pleasant feeling and intellectual activity must be mixed in due proportion in order to make the good life of man.

Happiness must be attained by the pursuit of virtue. To become righteous requires wisdom and understanding. The pursuit of virtue and leading of a virtuous life is the means of attaining happiness, virtue itself is not external to happiness, but is integral to it. It is only the truly virtuous man who is a truly good man and a truly happy man.

The intemperate man is one who pursues what is really harmful to man while the temperate man pursues what is truly good and beneficial. To pursue what is truly good and beneficial is wise, while to pursue what is harmful is foolish. In *The Republic,* Plato considers the four cardinal virtues to be wisdom, courage or fortitude, temperance, and justice.

Cicero (106-43 B.C.) the Roman writer, statesman and orator, in his last book *On Duties*, provided a simple solution to what can be a complex problem. Always do the right thing, because a wrong action, although perhaps apparently advantageous, can never be really advantageous because it is wrong. What is the right thing? The right thing is what is legal and required by law. The right thing is what is honest, open and fair. The right thing is keeping your word, no matter what the consequences, and telling the truth, even if you have not taken an oath. The right thing is to treat everyone alike because they are all human beings. Being human gives them the right to be treated with dignity and respect.

Christian ethics was the beginning of the demise of reasoned thought that had been formulated by Confucius and the Greek scholars. Christianity introduced a religious conception of good into Western thought. In the Christian worldview a person is totally dependent upon God and cannot achieve goodness by means of will or intelligence but only through the grace of God. The primary Christian ethical belief is stated in the golden rule, "so whatever you wish that men would do to you, do so to them" (Mathew

7:12), in the injunctions to love one's neighbor as oneself (Leviticus 19:18), and to love one's enemies (Mathew 5:44). The Ten Commandments of the ancient Hebrews are believed by many to be handed down from divine authority yet even with the fear of God's wrath many people violate their tenants. There are some useful examples of moral behavior in the Bible including some of the Ten Commandments.

1. Respect your father and mother
2. You must not kill
3. You must not commit adultery
4. You must not steal
5. You must not give false evidence against your neighbor
6. You must not be envious of your neighbor's goods. You shall not be envious of his house nor his wife, nor anything that belongs to your neighbor.

You would think that Christians and Jews who both believe in the Ten Commandments would adhere to their advice. Obviously religion, worship, and the belief in God do nothing to help people lead an ethical and moral life. Church membership in America, which is around 60 percent of the population, is higher than any other secular Western country; yet the United States has the highest rates of crime, violence, and people in prison. Most criminals have read the Bible and believe in God, but it did not deter or stop them from committing some of the most heinous and brutal acts imaginable. So-called good Christians or Jews cheat on their wives, are dishonest, steal when they think they can get away with it, and in general violate most of the Ten Commandments. Homosexuality and pedophilia in the Catholic Church are additional examples of how ridiculous the idea that religion contributes to the moral fiber of individuals. Over the last 30 years almost 1000 U.S. priests have been accused of sexual misconduct with minors. As of June 2002 the Catholic Church has removed 218 priests from their positions because of sexual abuse allegations. This is another example of the hypocrisy and mendacity of established religion. Over the centuries some of the most pious have committed the greatest atrocities.

The dualism of good and evil, happiness and misery, and right and wrong, were put forth long before Judaism and Christianity. A formal system of ethics and morals was put forth during the Confucian period in China. This was well before the development of any of the new religious sects. Confucian ethics and morals were developed without the need for a supernatural force or God. This proves that there is no need for a religious belief system or a supreme moral authority for the development of ethics and morals. The major religions have derived contradictory moral commandments. This again shows that there is no universality of morals based on religion. None of the religions can agree on even the most basic moral and ethical issues. These issues range from marriage and contraception, to murder and the death penalty. Ethics and morals are learned behaviors, an internalized sense of right and wrong. They need not be based on the fear of God's wrath, or the commandments of religious dogma.

There have been numerous other philosophers who have tried to define a system of ethics. The problem is not trying to define the nature of good and evil, the Greeks scholars had it pretty well figured out back in the 4th century, but how to have a system of ethics that people will actually adhere to. A belief system in and of itself will not make anyone an ethical and moral person. You have to be committed to doing the right thing. You have to believe that being virtuous is best way to live your life. A morally developed person understands that he should not lie. Not because God or society opposes lying, but because trust is essential in human relations. If everyone lied about everything there would be chaos.

Virtue is a learned behavior. People need to learn the difference between right and wrong, good and evil, misery and happiness and they need to learn the consequences of making bad or incorrect decisions. Errors result from a lack of knowledge. Action without knowledge will produce results, which are not desired, and pain will follow. The problem is that ethics and morals, and the consequences of not leading a moral and ethical life are not taught as subjects in elementary and high school education. The solution is to make ethics and morals a mandatory part of elementary and high school education. In a complex and morally ambiguous world this is a job that cannot be left to the parents. Unfortunately, many parents are unfit for this duty and set a poor example. Some are in prison and can do nothing, others are alcoholics, drug addicts, gambling addicts, or abusive to their spouse or children. Obviously, parents have a tremendous impact on their children and should be the ones to instill high standards of ethics and moral behavior. Extensive research has shown that parents who are more accepting and affectionate, supportive of their child's individuality, and firmer about rules and discipline produce healthier and happier children. An over emphasis on self-esteem is damaging and can lead to weakness. Guilt and shame are important factors in shaping fundamental moral emotions.

To be capable of ethical behavior one must first have dignity, self-respect, self-discipline, and care about oneself and about others. If a person has no self-respect and doesn't care about his or her own life, they are certainly not going to care about someone else's life. Without dignity and honor a person has nothing. What is a good person? A good person is disciplined, gentle, fair, equitable, truthful, honorable, faithful, trustworthy, sincere, virtuous, honest, kind, benevolent, polite, and helpful. If you are missing any of these traits you have some work to do.

How do you lead a moral and ethical life? Just think about how you would like to be treated. Would you like it if someone killed your mother? Would you like it if someone stole your car? Would you like it if someone robbed your house? Would you like it if someone raped your sister? Would you like it if someone were seducing your wife? Do you like it when people lie to you? Unless you are a sick individual the answer to all these questions is definitely no.

Empathy is the intellectual identification with, or the experiencing of, the feelings, thoughts or attitudes of another. It is the imaginative projection into another person's situation. Empathy is essential for the emergence of the moral emotions of pride and guilt. Empathy develops naturally in the first years of life and is the foundation of human morality. Put yourself in the other person's shoes and ask yourself; would I want someone to do this to me? If the answer is no, then don't do it. Treat others, as you would like to be treated.

A growing problem that is related to ethics and occurs both on an individual and national basis is envy. Envy is a feeling of discontent or covetousness with regard to another's advantages, success or possessions. To feel resentful, jealous, or unhappy because someone else has something you don't is the highest form of ignorance and weakness. Envy can lead to very bad decisions. Envy is a poison whether it is person or a nation. If someone is doing better than you are you should respect it, not hate it. You should use the fact that you do not have all you want, while someone else does, as motivation to do better, not to feel sorry for yourself. Get over it and get to work.

Happiness

Happiness is a state of well being characterized by emotions ranging from contentment to intense joy. To be happy is to experience a pleasurable or satisfying experience. Other characteristics of happiness include freedom from want and distress, and inner peace or assurance of one's place in society or in the universe.

Hedonism is the view that pleasure is the sole intrinsic good in life. Pure hedonism rarely provides long-term happiness. Many of the most pleasurable aspects of life, such as love, friendship, work, the quest for knowledge, and child rearing, come most often to those who are engaging in an activity for other reasons than pleasure seeking. It is doubtful that humans in fact only seek pleasure, and it is equally doubtful that seeking pleasure to the exclusion of everything else is the best way to achieve happiness.

As with most aspects of life, there has to be a balance between the extremes of pure hedonism and denial of pleasure. As Aristotle has said, pleasure is not a good in itself, since it is by its nature incomplete. Genuine happiness lies in action that leads to virtue, since this alone provides true value and not just amusement. Cardinal John Henry Newman would agree, from his *Sermons on Subjects of the Day*, "Virtue is its own reward, and brings with it the truest and highest pleasure; but if we cultivate it only for pleasure's sake, we are selfish, not religious, and will never gain the pleasure, because we can never have the virtue."

Perhaps John Stuart Mill said it best, "Those only are happy, who have their minds fixed on some object other than their own happiness; on the happiness of others, on the improvement of mankind, even on some art or pursuit, followed not as a means, but as itself an ideal end. Aiming thus at something else, they find happiness by the way."

Although it is very difficult to make someone happy who does not wish to be happy, there are certain things that have been shown to lead to a happier life. These include marriage, creating and valuing friendship, doing something good for someone, being optimistic, ridding your self of envy and jealousy, and not worrying about growing old. Aging is a natural process that cannot be halted or reversed. Finally, be a minimalist, less is more, have the attitude that material things are meaningless. Relying on material possessions for happiness is a recipe for misery. The more things you possess, the more problems you have.

Being happy is more than a state of mind it also keeps you healthy. Researchers at University College London, UK, have linked everyday happiness with healthier levels of important hormones, such as the stress hormone cortisol. The happier you are, the lower your cortisol levels during the day, and for men, but not for women, the happier you are the lower your average heart rate. Lower heart rates are associated with good cardiovascular health. High levels of cortisol are linked to conditions such as Type II diabetes, hypertension, and damage to the hippocampus portion of the brain.

Self-Discipline

The self is a person's nature or character. Self-concept is a person's perception of his or her own personality and ability. This is important in understanding self-discipline because life changes are initiated and controlled by the individual. Self-discipline depends on self-praise and self-criticism, which are responses people make after perceiving their behavior and its consequences. Self-control refers to people's ability to withhold a response normally elicited by a particular situation. An example of self-control is the delay of gratification in which a person waits patiently for a larger reward rather than immediately taking a smaller one.

Self-discipline is defined as correction or regulation of oneself for the sake of improvement. Discipline in the context of self-improvement is training that develops self-control, character, orderliness, and efficiency. Self-discipline is not easy and it is harder for some people than for others, but what it boils down to is this, if you do not discipline yourself, nobody else can or will. Everything eventually comes down to the individual. It is the individual that makes the final decision. Nobody can make you do anything unless you want to do it. You have to determine for yourself whether or not a certain action is what you really want to do. If you want to truly be in control of your own life, you cannot allow others to influence you and turn you away from your goals.

To be well disciplined, you must develop the mental attitude whereby you can endure pain, misery, unhappiness, frustration, and rejection. That is not to say that in every endeavor you will encounter these emotions, but you should be prepared for them. If you give up on your goals every time you run into a problem or experience discomfort you will never become disciplined and you will never accomplish anything.

Self-confidence and self-discipline go hand in hand. Without self-confidence good self-discipline is very difficult. It is only when you feel inferior that you will allow life to defeat you. There is no such thing as an inferior person. There are only varying levels of skills.

The words of the 19th century educator William Edward Hickson (1803-1870) are still true today "If at first you don't succeed, try, try again." You cannot let defeat and humiliation detour you from your goal. Many of the best, brightest, and most successful people in history failed many times before obtaining success. You cannot be afraid to take risks, just make sure they are calculated risks. Taking foolish and dangerous risks is generally not a good idea. You have to set personal goals and be a risk taker. If you are afraid of failure, you will never know what you can achieve in life. Fear is a distressing emotion aroused by impending danger, evil, or pain. Whether real or imagined it is the feeling or condition of being afraid. Fear of failure, fear of embarrassment and criticism, or fear of rejection, can block you from attempting or completing what you want to accomplish. As Franklin Roosevelt said "There is nothing to fear but fear itself."

Taking risks and succeeding develops confidence. You take a chance, you learn something from your attempt, even if it's only what not to do next time, and you use that knowledge in your next trial. This is not failure. It is gradual success that is impossible without an attempt or taking a risk. Reinforcement is crucial for learning; without it learning does not occur. From the act of doing we learn what works or what doesn't work. No one is perfect on his or her first attempt. It is inevitable that we do things badly when we first begin. It is part of the learning curve. Remember learning to ride a bicycle? For most of us, who crashed after the training wheels came off, this was a painful experience. As Poor Richard says "little strokes fell great oaks." You only fail when you stop trying.

These rules apply to raising children as well. Parents, who refuse to allow their children to learn the hard way because they are so worried about their self-esteem, end up with kids who have little or no self-confidence and poor self-discipline. You should never discourage them from trying anything that it is not foolishly dangerous. Unless people suffer the consequences of their actions, they will never act more wisely. If a child is spoiled their whole life, getting everything they want when they want it, they will not know what it means not to get their way. They will not have learned that to achieve success requires hard work and the ability to handle frustration and failure.

Repetition and practice are the only way to get good at any endeavor. Scientific studies have consistently shown that there is no evidence of high-level performance without experience and practice. Even the most accomplished people need around ten years of hard work (the ten year rule) before they reach world-class levels. The best people in any field are those who devote the most hours to consistent constant deliberate practice. Deliberate practice is an activity that is explicitly intended to improve performance and involves high levels of repetition, constantly working for objectives just beyond one's level of competence, measuring performance, and providing feedback for further improvement.

Studies by Ericsson and Lehmann (1996) found that (1) measures of general basic capacities such has natural abilities and Intelligence Quotient (IQ) do not predict success in a domain (sphere of knowledge), (2) the superior performance of experts is often very domain specific and transfer outside their narrow area of expertise is surprisingly limited and (3) systematic differences between experts and less proficient individuals nearly always reflect attributes acquired by the experts during their lengthy training.

For example, the critical difference between expert musicians differing in the level of attained solo performance concerned the amounts of time they had spent in solitary practice during their music development, which totaled around 10,000 hours by age 20 for the best experts, around 5,000 hours for the least accomplished expert musicians, and only 2,000 hours for serious amateur pianists.

Everyone has to know his or her limitations. No one can be an expert at everything. You have to determine what is most important, what you enjoy doing, and what your strengths are. Time, money, and physical abilities limit everyone. There is simply not enough time to do everything at once. For instance, it takes about 5 years to learn to play the piano respectably; it takes 4 to 7 years to get a black belt in Tae Kwon Do. Not everyone can play the violin like Itzhak Perlman, or play basketball like Michael Jordan. Most people will never achieve greatness in their fields for the simple reason that it is demanding. The extra practice and work required to achieve greatness is just too difficult and painful. If superior performance were easy, it would not be so rare.

Most of us are not the best in the world at anything, yet life can still be fulfilling, happy and meaningful. Therefore, you need to limit yourself to the most important tasks and try to finish one task before going on to the next. Once you determine what your goals are and what is most important you need to focus on these alone. Do not let other things or counter influences distract you. The steps to achieve self-discipline are as follows:

1. Define your purpose and what it is that you want to achieve.
2. Determine if it is a reasonable and achievable goal.
3. Instill the determination to succeed in your mind. Make up your mind that you are going to do it no matter what it takes.
4. Define a plan on how you will achieve your goal.
5. Acquire the knowledge you need to make it happen.
6. Implement the plan and do not deviate from the goal. You have made the decision to do it, so just do it.

Self-discipline requires persistence and perseverance. If you begin to feel that you cannot complete your task remember that you can accomplish anything if you set your mind to it. No matter how painful and difficult it may seem you have to keep going. Nothing is easy, you are going to encounter difficult times but you must have the strength and courage to continue. In many cases, there are no gains without pains.

Self-discipline and procrastination are inter-related in that they both arise from the behavior of the individual and, therefore, the individual can control them. Procrastination is defined as putting off something intentionally and habitually that should be done. This can range from something as minor as not calling someone back because you really did not feel like it, to putting off quitting smoking because you think you really enjoy it or you want to wait until next year. Many people follow the theory "why do something today I can put off until tomorrow." If you use delaying tactics, and look for and find ways to put off doing something because it is unpleasant, then you are procrastinating.

Perfectionism and procrastination are interrelated. Perfectionism is a personality style in which a person is overly critical of his or her own performance. Perfectionist traits include extreme negative reactions to mistakes and the tendency to view mistakes as personal failures. Perfectionists also tend to have an excessive need for approval and are overly concerned about making mistakes. They differ from high achievers who are driven by a goal to achieve, whereas perfectionists are driven by a fear of failure.

It simply does not make sense to define success as perfection. There are very few things that can reach the stage of 100 percent perfection. Think of success as an improvement over what you were able to do before. You have to face up to the fact that you are human and cannot achieve total perfection in everything you do. People who think they are failures and feel dejected or depressed have many times defined success as perfection. Perfectionism leads to procrastination because people believe that if they cannot do it perfectly they will not do it all. In this way, many things just don't get done. People who are optimistic and who feel good about themselves have defined success as reaching reasonable achievable goals. They have rejected the notion of all or nothing. You have to forget about perfection and think about diminishing returns.

Beating procrastination is not easy because no one enjoys doing things that they find unpleasant. Sometime in your life you are going to have to do things that are unpleasant, so you may as well face up to it, get it over with, and move on to the next task. Listed below are a few ways that may help you beat procrastination.

1. Subdivide large jobs into smaller parts that can be done one at a time. Doing this can help make what appears to be an overwhelming job seem easier to handle.
2. Start on tough jobs or tasks when you feel rested, energetic, and ambitious.
3. Get the work done first then you can enjoy yourself. Business before pleasure should be the rule.
4. Make a commitment to yourself or someone else and set a deadline.
5. If interruptions in the form of phone calls or unexpected visitors add to your procrastination, find a place where you can get peace and quiet, and be free from interruptions.
6. Reward yourself after you have accomplished difficult tasks, you deserve it.
7. If something needs to be done, don't just sit around in a stupor, just do it!

Self-discipline also means that you don't rely on false hopes. You have to be a realist. Stay away from con artists such as astrologers, faith healers, fortunetellers, and psychics. These are all shams designed to fleece the weak of mind and the vulnerable. Astrology is the belief that the movements of the stars determine human's life and all of nature. Of course, this is absurd. The movements of the stars and planets are due to gravity. Gravity has no effect on the outcome of human destiny. How people can believe in such trash is beyond belief. Psychics are even worse. A psychic is someone who claims to have a heightened sensitivity to psychic influences or forces. There is no such thing as telepathic powers, psychic phenomena, or spirits. Only you can determine your future. If you want to know how the world works and what the future holds get an education. There have been many cases where these con artists have embezzled a persons life savings under the guise of be able to predict their future or ward off evil spirits. Use your head. Stay away from these people. Remember, if you do stupid things you will get stupid results.

Self-reliance and Personal Responsibility

The foundation of self-reliance is knowledge. Once you have completed this book you will have the foundation. It is up to you to continue to gain knowledge and build on that foundation to become truly independent and self-reliant. You must rely on yourself to achieve your goals. You cannot, nor should you have to, rely on anyone else for your security, welfare, and success. You have to face up to you own problems. If you have problems try to figure out how to solve them yourself. That is not to say that everyone doesn't need help in some areas occasionally. But assistance is not dependence. Dependence leads to weakness. You never want to have to be dependent on someone else for anything. You should not expect others to be responsible for your happiness.

You must take responsibility for your own emotions and actions, and never think of yourself as a defenseless victim. These days everyone is a victim. People blame everyone and everything else but themselves for their problems. You have to accept personal responsibility. People claim to be a victim of big business, or a victim of the system, or a victim of their upbringing, or a victim of circumstances. You are only a victim if you allow yourself to be one. You have to acknowledge the fact that you are solely responsible for the choices in your life. The individual chooses the direction of their life. You cannot blame others for the choices you have made. You can't sit around feeling sorry for yourself, wallowing in self-pity because life is sometimes unfair. If you do not accept personal responsibility, you run the risk of becoming overly dependent on others for recognition, approval or acceptance. You may also become fearful about ever taking a risk or making a decision.

There are many things you can do to become self-reliant and accept personal responsibility. You have to be optimistic about the future; you can't live in the past. You have to determine what your strengths are and then focus on your strengths not your weaknesses. You have to make up your mind that your happiness is not dependent on others. You have to get over the fact that trying to make everyone else happy at the expense of your own happiness is destructive behavior and will surely lead to misery. Hindsight is 20/20. You can't relive the past, so get over it, put it behind you and move forward. You cannot be fearful of taking a risk or making a decision. Without risks you do not learn. Without making decisions you do not move forward. Remember, make quick informed decisions and never look back.

Peer Pressure

Peer pressure is social pressure by members of one's peer group to take a certain action, adopt certain values, or otherwise conform in order to be accepted. Peer pressure can be either negative or positive. For example, pressure to be a good student or active in sports is certainly positive peer pressure. Pressure to do drugs, drink alcohol, participate in delinquent behavior, or commit criminal acts is obviously negative peer pressure.

In many cases it may seem easier to go along with the crowd than to stand up for what you believe in or what you know is right. Don't take the easy way out. Think about the consequences of your actions. Have an answer when someone asks you to do something that you either don't want to do or know is wrong. Learn how to say no. You can't please all the people all the time you can only please some of the people some of the time. You have to position yourself wisely; you cannot be all things to all people. Stay out of situations that can lead to social pressures. For example, don't go to a party if you know that there is going to be people there doing drugs. Stay away from temptation.

If you run with the wrong crowd you will absolutely regret it. You may not regret it right away but 10 to 20 years from now you will regret it. You can't live your life over again that is why it is so important to make the right decisions when you are young.

For those in high school, you have to know that although you want to try to be cool and fit in now, chances are you will never see most of the people in your graduating class again. If you do, it will probably only be at your 10 or 20-year class reunion, and they will not recognize you anyway. So don't let the temptation to run with the wrong crowd take control just because it seems like the thing to do or it is cool. It could be a big mistake that could ruin your life, or quite possibly even end it. Don't follow the herd. You are not a sheep you are a freethinking individual. If you follow the herd you are a sheep. Then it becomes the blind leading the blind. Don't let fear of being ridiculed lead you down a path to destruction. As long as you are virtuous, what do you care what other people think anyway?

Adolescents like to spend time with their peers. Peers replace the family as the center of a young person's social and leisure activities. Many teenagers rebel against their parents because they think their parents just don't get it. They are embarrassed even to be seen with their parents. They want to establish their own identity and have autonomy independent from their parents. Family stress often follows, and an increase in parent-adolescent conflict and disagreement occurs. For the young people, this again is something you will regret. Once you are no longer a teenager and realize how much your parents have done for you and how much they love you, you will feel bad about all the problems and distress that you caused. As your parents get older, and you don't have time to spend with them, you will understand that you should have spent more time with them and tried to make their life easier. They have worked hard their whole life just to make your life better. Respect your parents, try to make their life better just as they are trying to do for you. You will be happy that you did. Save yourself a lot of grief and regret, live your life right the first time when you are young. You can't go back and relive your life.

Health and Longevity

Part of developing a worldview and a plan for a successful life includes being healthy so you can execute your plan and enjoy yourself. The goals for this part of the plan are to live a long healthy life free from sickness and disease. Being healthy is a prerequisite for success, if you are sick or incapacitated you will be unable to perform the daily tasks necessary to succeed. In some cases health problems are genetic and for those cases there is not much a person can do to improve their situation except adapt and enjoy the time that you have.

As far back as 420 B.C. Hippocrates taught that the most valuable tools for good health are diet and exercise. The best guarantee of health is a moderate amount of nourishment with a moderate amount of exercise. To prevent disease Hippocrates also recommended moderation in working, eating, drinking, exercising, and sleeping. All things, which over two thousand years later, studies have validated and people still don't seem to understand. Its simple, you don't need fad exercises, fad diets, and other nonsense, all you have to do is to follow Hippocrates advice, everything in moderation.

There are many things that can be done to improve your health and increase your longevity and conversely there are equally as many things that you can do to degrade your health and decrease your life span. The scientific research to date establishes the fact that bad habits such as smoking, drugs and alcohol, stress and destructive behavior, poor nutrition and diet, and lack of exercise will certainly lead to poor health and a shortened life span. Most health problems today are self-induced and are the result of life style decisions. For example, people smoke, they drink too much alcohol, they eat too much, or they are sedentary and never exercise. These are things that people can control and can make a huge difference in your longevity and health. For instance, being overweight or obese are known risk factors for diabetes, heart disease, stroke, hypertension, gallbladder disease, osteoarthritis, sleep apnea, and some forms of cancer including colorectal, gallbladder, kidney, uterine and breast cancer. The leading causes of death in 1997 were as follows:

1. Heart disease
2. Cancer
3. Stroke and brain lesions
4. Lung disease
5. Accidents
6. Pneumonia and flu
7. Diabetes
8. Suicide
9. Kidney inflammation
10. Liver disease

Health and longevity apply to mental health as well as physical health. Without a healthy mind, the quality of life can diminish greatly as humans' age. The old saying, "use it or lose it," turns out to be a scientific fact. Unless neural connections are constantly challenged with new information, they will gradually weaken with age. In neuroscience, synaptic plasticity is the ability of the connection, or synapse, between two neurons to change in strength. There are several underlying mechanisms that cooperate to achieve synaptic plasticity, including changes in the amount of neurotransmitter released into a synapse and changes in how effectively cells respond to those neurotransmitters. Since memories are postulated to be stored in synapses of the brain, synaptic plasticity is one of the important neurochemical foundations of learning and memory. Learning occurs by adding new synapses, strengthening existing synapses, or adding neurons. Little used neurons tend to die.

Unless neural connections are constantly challenged with new information, they will generally weaken with age. As humans age they produce less chemical neuromodulators. A neuromodulator is a substance other than a neurotransmitter, released by a neuron at a synapse and conveying information to adjacent or distant neurons, either enhancing (excitatory) or damping (inhibitory) their activities. An 80-year-old person produces one-fifth of the dopamine, a neurotransmitter related to motor activity, attentiveness and memory, than a 20 year old does. Reading, working, and staying busy can help, but to produce enough chemicals to make synapses stronger you have to challenge your brain with greater complexity. The best activities for mental conditioning are learning a new language, learning to play a musical instrument, and studying mathematics.

Studies have shown that higher levels of physical activity are correlated with better brain aging. Regular exercise helps your brain by improving concentration and attention. Exercise promotes neurogenesis, which is the production of new nerve cells as a result of neuronal cell division. Laboratory animals that are allowed to voluntarily run on an exercise wheel show increases in the generation and survival of new neurons (brain cells) in the hippocampus (the area of the brain involved in short term memory). This increased neurogenesis is associated with improved learning. In animals, running also increases the strength of synaptic connections. This occurs through the same molecular mechanism that is believed to underlie long-term memory formation.

Exercise increases the production of nerve growth factors (neurotrophins), which play vital roles in nourishing and supporting nerve cells. BDNF (brain-derived neurotrophic factor) increases significantly in the brains of animals that run. Laboratory tests with mice showed that the runners had about twice as many new brain neurons as the sedentary mice. Carl Cotman, a neuroscientist at the University of California, refers to BDNF as "brain fertilizer" because of its effects on nerve cell growth.

Exercise also increases the density and size of brain capillaries, which has the effect of increasing blood flow and oxygen to the brain. This may in turn help support the survival of new neurons and facilitate faster "firing" by neurons. Exercise and diet have emerged as key factors that may prevent (or at least delay) the onset of Alzheimer's and Parkinson's disease.

Another old saying, "Fish is good brain food," appears to have a basis in scientific fact as well. Recent studies have show that fish oil (omega-3 fatty acids) increased the amount of BDNF, improved the performance of brain-damaged rats, and dramatically slowed neurodegenerative symptoms in mice bred to develop an Alzheimer's like disease. For top mental and physical conditioning the only three things you have to remember are, exercise regularly, adhere to a healthy diet, and train your brain with mental exercises.

Diet and Nutrition

The only intervention ever shown to extend maximum life span reliably, at least in laboratory animals, is calorie restriction. Caloric restriction appears to work because the more calories animals consume, the more the body generates free radicals: negatively charged particles that cause oxidation damage in cells. Extreme caloric restriction is not easy; to put yourself on a specialized diet of only 1,500 calories a day for the rest of your life would be quite difficult.

As of this writing, there is no conclusive evidence that taking antioxidant vitamins such as beta-carotene and vitamin E produce anti-aging effects or increase longevity. The same is true of hormone supplements such as melatonin, testosterone, estrogen and dehydroepiandrosterone (DHEA). Some of these supplements can even be bad for your health. DHEA, for instance has been associated with increased risks of breast and prostate cancers and liver problems. Until there is conclusive scientific evidence on what works and what doesn't work, you are better off just eating a balanced diet with large amounts of fruits and vegetables. For a good healthy diet, reduce your consumption of red meat, eggs, butter and processed foods, and increase your consumption of fish, whole grain foods and fiber, and of course fruits and vegetables. Since fruits and vegetables contain hundreds of compounds that are not in antioxidant vitamins, your best bet for preventing cellular damage from free radicals is by eating foods rich in antioxidants. The fruits with the most antioxidants are blueberries, cherries, pink grapefruit, oranges, raspberries, strawberries, and red grapes. The vegetables with the most antioxidants include broccoli, red bell peppers, spinach, onions, and corn.

The genetics of exceptional longevity is likely a combination of having certain protective genes and not having certain risk-producing genes. Although lifestyle may be less important than genetics in determining who will live a long life it is still an important factor. The older you get the healthier you have been so it still is very important to take care of yourself while you are young. The healthier you are now the better your chance of living to significantly older age in better health.

While the effectiveness of taking antioxidant vitamins and supplements is still being tested there are some recent studies that seem to show that minerals such as calcium can produce beneficial results. In a recent report in the Journal of the American College of Nutrition people who consumed less calcium tended to be overweight and have greater midlife weight gain. At least two studies have reported that weight reduction diets that included higher calcium produced greater weight loss. A Purdue University study found that calorie consumption being equal, people consuming 1000 mg of calcium (the adult recommendation) lost more weight and fat than those consuming only 600 mg (the average for women). Calcium is not a magic fat burner. People who consumed more calories than they burned still stored the excess as fat, regardless of calcium intake. Other studies suggest that calcium may lower the risk of colon cancer. In studies of cancer risk, calcium was protective at levels of 700 to 900 mg per day. Studies of weight control found benefits from 1000 to 1500 mg per day. The National Academy of Sciences currently recommends 1000 mg per day for adults to age 50 and 1200 mg per day for older adults. A diet with sufficient calcium and vitamin D can also help in the prevention and treatment of osteoporosis.

Vitamin D has additional health benefits. The major biologic function of vitamin D is to maintain normal blood levels of calcium and phosphorus. Vitamin D aids in the absorption of calcium, helping to form and maintain strong bones. Recently, research also suggests vitamin D may provide protection from hypertension (high blood pressure), cancer, cold and flu viruses, and several autoimmune diseases.

Vitamin D is found in many dietary sources such as fish, eggs, fortified milk, and cod liver oil. The sun also contributes significantly to the daily production of vitamin D, and as little as 10 minutes of exposure is thought to be enough to prevent deficiencies.

Studies have shown that healthy cognitive functioning is a better predictor of independence in old age than is physical health. In an article by Jessie Evert in the *Journal of Gerontology and Biological Science,* twenty percent of centenarians have completely escaped any particular lethal disease, like heart disease, stroke, diabetes, and cancer until at least the age of 100. About 40 percent have markedly delayed such illnesses until after the age of 85 and the remaining 40 percent are survivors who develop these diseases before the age of 65 but survive their illnesses for a long time. The results indicate that children and siblings of centenarians have a lower mortality rate than children in the control group suggesting a familial component to exceptional longevity. Also, members of this group tend to weigh less and have a lower body mass index, suggesting that fat metabolism may play an important role in reaching very old age.

Findings of the Georgia Centenarian Study, led by Leonard Poon showed that few centenarians smoked, were obese, or drank heavily. They remained active throughout life, ate breakfast regularly, and consumed plenty of Vitamin A and carotenoids (organic pigments such as carotene, which is found in carrots) by eating fruits and vegetables.

The Problem of Obesity

Obesity is defined as the excessively high amount of body fat in relation to lean body mass. Overweight refers to an excess of body weight compared to set standards. Recent figures from the Center for Disease Control (CDC) indicates that an estimated 61 percent of U.S. adults are either overweight or obese, defined as having a Body Mass Index (BMI) of 25 or more. The percentage of children and adolescents who are defined as overweight has more than doubled since the early 1970s. About 13 percent of children and adolescents are now seriously overweight. In fact, due to these alarming new figures the CDC has declared obesity to be an epidemic and the incidence of obesity is rising to the point where there are as many obese people in the world as there are people suffering from hunger.

Body Mass Index (BMI) is found by dividing your weight in kilograms by height in meters squared (weight (kg) / height (m^2). To determine BMI using pounds and inches, multiply your weight in pounds by the National Institutes of Health multiplier 704.5 then divide the result by your height in inches and divide that result by your height in inches a second time. For additional information refer to the Center for Disease Control Web site at http://www.cdc.gov and the National Institutes of Health Web site at http://www.nih.gov.

Being overweight robs you of your energy. It turns you into a sluggard. It makes life in general more difficult and it costs both the individual and the country a tremendous amount of money. The National Institutes of Health estimates the total cost of obesity and being overweight at $99.2 billion with $51.6 billion (5.7 percent of the total U.S. health care expenditure) being direct costs and $47.6 billion being indirect costs, which is comparable to the economic costs of smoking.

Americans spend $33 billion annually on weight-loss products and services. This figure includes spending on low calorie foods, artificial sweeteners and related products such as diet sodas, and memberships to commercial weight-loss centers. Unfortunately, most of this money is wasted. The only way to loose weight and keep it off is to eat less and exercise more. So save your money. The majority of the weight loss diets, pills, drinks, devices, etc., are a scam. Instead of wasting time and money on diet scams it is better to remember the following words of wisdom, "you dig your grave with your teeth" and "it's the lean horse for the long race."

What does this all mean? It means that the majority of Americans is fat and lazy and need to do something about it. What is the solution? There are two reasons people are overweight and obese. One is they eat too much and the other is they don't exercise enough or at all. Only 22 percent of U.S. adults get the recommended physical activity of vigorous activity 5 times a week for at least 30 minutes. About 25 percent of U.S. adults get no vigorous physical activity. In addition to helping to control weight, physical activity decreases the risk of dying from coronary heart disease, and reduces the risk of developing diabetes, hypertension, and cancer.

There are many weight loss programs available. One of the most simple and effective is the DEW diet. Where *D* is Don't eat out, *E* is Exercise, and *W* is Weigh everyday. Eating out on a regular basis is a sure way to gain weight. Restaurants generally use more fats when preparing meals and portion sizes are larger than you would generally serve at home. Exercise is the key to burning calories. Weighing everyday provides input on whether or not you are gaining weight, losing weight, or your weight is stable. It gives you immediate feedback so you can keep your weight in a narrow range. It is much easier to lose five pounds than twenty five.

There are also many diet programs available one of the best based on scientific evidence is the Mediterranean Diet. The Mediterranean diet is thought to reduce your risk of heart disease. In fact, a 2007 study conducted in the United States found that both men and women who consumed a Mediterranean diet lowered their risk of death from both heart disease and cancer. The key components of the Mediterranean diet include:

Eating a generous amount of fruits and vegetables
Consuming healthy fats such as olive oil and canola oil
Eating small portions of nuts
Drinking red wine, in moderation, for some
Consuming very little red meat
Eating fish on a regular basis

The Mediterranean diet is similar to the American Heart Association's Step I diet, but it contains less cholesterol and has more fats. However, the fats are healthy, including monounsaturated fats, such as olive oil, and polyunsaturated fats, which contain the beneficial linolenic acid (a type of omega-3 fatty acid). These fat sources include canola oil and nuts, particularly walnuts. Fish, another source of omega-3 fatty acids, is eaten on a regular basis in the Mediterranean diet.

Exercise and Fitness

Although many more Americans are now walking, running, playing tennis, and engaging in other active sports than in the past, most still do not get sufficient exercise. People drive to and from work and to the shopping malls, use elevators instead of stairs, are a spectator rather than participant in sports, and do little heavy labor on the job. Inactivity is common among all age groups. Even those who do exercise often don't exercise vigorously enough. The most common reason people don't exercise is because they are just too damn lazy. People are great at making excuses. You have probably heard many of them yourself; with work and everything I don't have time to exercise, exercise is too boring, by the time I get home from work I am too tired to exercise, I don't have any money to join a fitness club, the list goes on and on. The fact is, there is no excuse for not exercising. So get off your ass and just do it!

You can start being more active by using the stairs instead of the elevator, park further away from the store entrance instead of circling around hoping to find a closer spot that might save you a few steps, instead of stuffing a donut in your face for a snack get up and stretch and walk around, mow your own lawn and get rid of the riding lawnmower, instead of sitting around in a stupor watching the idiot box (television) get out and take a walk.

There are many benefits to exercise. Exercises helps lower blood pressure and control diabetes, control body weight and reduce body fat, increase levels of high-density lipoproteins (the "good" cholesterol) in the blood, and it helps lower stress. In addition to benefiting the cardiovascular system, regular exercise enhances a person's sense of well-being and confidence and has been shown to help people with depression. Exercise also improves muscle tone and flexibility, and gives you more stamina and energy. Exercise can even help people quit smoking. Exercise increases longevity and allows the elderly to lead a more active life. There is a decidedly lower death rate among the elderly who exercise. In addition to all these wonderful things being active and exercise just makes you feel better. Consider the benefits of a well-conditioned heart, in 1 minute with 45 to 50 beats; the heart of a well-conditioned person pumps the same amount of blood as an inactive person's heart pumps in 70 to 75 beats. Compared to the well-conditioned heart, the average heart pumps up to 36,000 more times per day, 13 million more times per year.

Various studies have shown that physical inactivity is a risk factor for heart disease. Overall, the results show heart disease is almost twice as likely to develop in inactive people as in those who are more active. Regular physical activity (even mild to moderate exercise) can help reduce your risk of heart disease. In fact, burning calories through physical activity will help you lose weight or stay at your desirable weight - which also helps lower your risk of heart disease. The best exercises to strengthen your heart and lungs are the aerobic exercises such as brisk walking, jogging, cycling, and swimming.

Just because you are old doesn't mean you should not exercise. Research has shown that strength training is vital to maintaining strong bones and preventing osteoporosis, which can lead to bone fractures. Strength training can also help control cholesterol and blood sugar levels, reduce arthritis pain, and reduce the risk of disabling falls.

Exercise and fitness does not have to cost a lot of money. Walking is obviously free; you can walk pretty much anywhere at anytime you wish. Running or jogging is free as well, whether you run on the sidewalk (it is not a good idea to run on the street because cars hit people all the time) or you run on a track at your local high school or college. Other inexpensive ways to get into shape include handball and basketball. There are many outdoor handball and basketball courts at public parks and community centers and there is generally no usage charge. A pair of handball gloves is about $25.00 and a can of two handballs costs about $3.00. A basketball costs about $50.00. Handball is great aerobic exercise and a great way to improve your eye-hand coordination. A game of singles usually takes 30 minutes.

Stepping up in cost is tennis. With tennis there are plenty of courts available at parks, high schools and colleges and again there is generally no charge for usage. A good tennis racquet is relatively expensive at about $100.00 but tennis balls can be found for under $3.00 a can. For a larger investment you can purchase your own gym. For a full gym you will need the following:

> Olympic weight set, which includes the bar and 310 lbs. of weights; Cost $250.00 - $350.00
> Free weight bench system which includes a bench, a lat pull-down attachment and leg extension / curl attachment; Cost: $489.00 - $899.00
> A set of solid one piece cast iron hexagonal dumbbells 5 to 50 lbs; Cost: $299.95

The total cost for a full gym would range from $1038.95 to $1448.95. For those who do not have the money for a full gym a 110 lb barbell set can be purchased for around $140.00 and individual dumbbells can be purchased for about 10 cents per pound.

For those who cannot afford, or do not have room for a set of weights and a bench, there are community centers that offer weight training programs, or you can join an organization like the YMCA, which generally offers weights, aerobics, and swimming. Membership fees can range from $100 membership fee and $44.00 per month and up. These fees generally include full facility access and other benefits as well such as nursery service. For additional information contact your local YMCA. To find a YMCA near you go to the national YMCA Web site at http://www.ymca.net. There are also fitness clubs that usually have weights, aerobics and handball / racquetball courts. Prices range from a $500.00 annual fee to clubs that charge $100.00 membership fee and up to $250.00 per month.

One of the best fitness programs is the martial arts form of Tae Kwon Do. Tae Kwon Do is the art of kicking and punching. There are other martial art forms such as Karate, which means "empty hand" and is the Okinawan-Japanese style of fighting. Karate uses abrupt movements along straight lines. Kung Fu, which means "tasks", is a Chinese style, which uses flowing, circular movements. Tae Kwon Do incorporates the abrupt linear movements of Karate and the flowing, circular patterns of Kung Fu with its own kicking techniques to form a unique integrated system.

Tae Kwon Do is also a state of mind. The ability to control one's mind, have self-restraint, kindness, and humility must accompany speed, power and balance, and the ability to seriously injury a person using Tae Kwon Do techniques. The five tenants of Tae Kwon Do are principles that everyone should follow, courtesy, integrity, perseverance, self-control, and indomitable spirit.

Tae Kwon Do is not easy; it requires dedication, practice, patience, self-discipline, and conditioning. But the rewards are well worth the effort. The physical benefits include improved speed and coordination, balance, muscle tone, flexibility, and energy. The mental benefits include self-confidence, self-discipline, patience, and humility. Along with these benefits Tae Kwon Do provides you with the ability to defend yourself. Prices for Tae Kwon Do instruction vary from 25.00 per month up to 95.00 per month for advanced training. Many Tae Kwon Do schools have introductory programs that allow you to sign up for a month to see if it is right for you. Classes are usually 1 hour long two to three times a week.

These are just a few of the cheapest ways you can get exercise for little or no money. Now you have no excuse. You cannot say fitness programs are too expensive. What is the best way to stay in shape? This depends on your existing physical condition and how much time and money you have. Based on available evidence it appears that a combination of strength training and aerobic exercise is the best way to stay in shape and to prevent diseases such as heart disease and osteoporosis. The best way to accomplish this is through a weight lifting program and an aerobic program such as jogging, cycling, or aerobic dancing.

Approximate Energy Expenditures during 30 Minutes of Exercise*

Aerobic dancing: 210 cal
Basketball: 300 cal
Carpentry: 120 cal
Cleaning: 130 cal
Cycling: 190 cal
Gardening: 160 cal
Golf: 180 cal
Running: 360 cal
Swimming: 300 cal
Walking: 180 cal

*Note: Values vary based on body weight and the vigor with which activities are performed. You need to burn 3,500 calories more than you take in to lose 1 pound.

It is extremely important that you always warm up and stretch out before you begin your workout. Do a few warm-up exercises first to stretch the muscles, tendons, and ligaments, to flex joints, and to increase the blood flow. Start slowly and increase speed, distance, and duration gradually. Avoid exercise on days when the wind-chill factor is below 20°F (6.6°C), or when the temperature is above 90°F (32.2°C) and the humidity is above 80 percent.

Being out in cold and wet conditions can cause hypothermia. Hypothermia is a dangerous condition in which the body temperature falls below 95°F (35°C). Symptoms of hypothermia include a pale, puffy face, a slow heart rate, and the patient is often drowsy and confused. Areas of the body that are normally warm (such as the armpits) are cold. In severe hypothermia breathing becomes shallow and slow, the patient may become unconscious, and the heart may beat only faintly and irregularly or it may stop beating altogether. Immediate medical attention is required for severe hypothermia.

Conversely, strenuous exercise in high heat and humidity can lead to hyperthermia (heat stroke), which can cause serious injury or death. Hyperthermia occurs when body temperature is elevated above the normal range. In some cases body temperature can reach 107°F (41.5°C) or more. Without emergency treatment the patient could lapse into a coma and death can follow. Hyperthermia is often preceded by heat exhaustion with fatigue, weakness and profuse sweating. With the onset of heat stroke, sweating diminishes and the skin becomes hot, dry and flushed. Breathing is shallow, and the pulse is rapid and weak. As the condition progresses, the body temperature rises dramatically and without treatment the patient may quickly lose consciousness and die.

Stop exercising if you feel dizzy, breathless, or nauseated, or if you feel pain in a joint or muscle. Seek medical help at once if you have pain in the center of your chest that lasts more than 2 minutes and that may be accompanied by pain in the arm, shoulders, neck, or jaw. Wait at least 2 hours after a heavy meal before exercising, and at least 4 hours after consuming alcohol. Drinking alcohol before exercise can cause irregularities of the heartbeat and dehydration. Drink water before, during, and after exercising, especially on a hot or humid day. Before beginning any exercise program, it is imperative that you consult your doctor. It is also recommended that you get the following tests. No test is perfect but these tests may show whether you have a genetic heart condition that could lead to heart failure.

- Electrocardiograph (ECG or EKG from the German Elektrokardiogramm) - an ECG is a device that is used for recording the electric activity of the myocardium to detect transmission of the cardiac impulse through the conductive tissues of the muscle. The ECG allows diagnosis of specific cardiac abnormalities.
- Holter Monitor - the patient wears a device that makes prolonged electrocardiograph recordings on a portable monitor while conducting normal daily activities.
- Ultrasonography - the process of imaging deep structures of the body by measuring and recording the reflection of pulsed or continuous high-frequency sound waves. Ultrasonography is used to detect structural abnormalities in the heart.
- Stress Test - a test that measures body functions such as cardiopulmonary and respiratory function when subjected to controlled amounts of physiological stress.

Getting in shape and staying in shape can be very difficult for some people. If you follow the advice from the self-discipline section you will be able to start and continue an exercise routine. Once you get started it will become a habit. Most experts agree that it takes twenty-one days to either adopt a new habit or to break an old one. Once you start feeling better you will not want to miss your workout because you will actually feel worse. Schedule your workouts when you feel the best and most energetic. Some people are more energetic in the morning before work others prefer afternoon workouts. Consider moving other activities around. Schedule your workout as a regular part of your routine. By choosing activities you like, you will be more likely to keep doing them regularly and enjoying the many benefits of physical activity.

One of the biggest problems facing people who want to be more physically active is that they get bored with all the lonely and repetitious rituals. Group workouts may be one way to counteract boredom partly because wavering participants can see that some of the other participants are in worse shape than they are. Either way, you have to perform your workout on a regular basis. The hardest part is getting started. If you are not consistent and don't make it habitual you will crumble. Missing even two weeks is like starting all over again. So keep it up. You will be happy that you did.

The *Advanced Human Thought* preferred method of getting into shape and staying in shape is the combination of weight training and running. This program uses weight training for muscle tone and strength and to help prevent osteoporosis, combined with aerobic training for your cardiovascular system and endurance. To be in superior condition requires work and dedication. The program below is not easy. If you follow the program consistently you will be in superior condition and be prepared for almost any other physical activity.

The weight-training regime consists of the workout given below, where 1 set is equivalent to executing the weight movement a defined number of repetitions. The set / repetitions format is 1 x 10 which is equivalent to 1 set 10 repetitions. Three sets of ten would be 3 x 10 for a total of 30 repetitions. Many of the movements use the idea of a superset. A superset is when you alternate one exercise or movement with 1 or more different exercises or movements. For more body mass increase weight and decrease the number of repetitions. For more muscle definition decrease weight and increase the number of repetitions. If you are unfamiliar with these weight lifting techniques please refer to any good weightlifting book or consult a physical fitness instructor. Caution: The *Advanced Human Thought* workout is very demanding and rigorous and should not be attempted without a physical checkup and cardiac examination. A lifting belt is recommended.

Chest
> Progressive flat bench press beginning with your warm up weight - 1 x 15
> Second set add 5-20 pounds - 1 x 10
> Third set add 5-20 pounds - 1 x 8
> Fourth set add 5-20 pounds - 1 x 5
> Fifth set maximum weight as many repetitions as you can (spotter or safety rack recommended)

Arms
> Super set one
>> Seated dumbbell curls 3 x 15
>> Alternate with barbell triceps extensions (lying or standing) 3 x 15
> Super set two
>> Triceps press downs on lat attachment 3 x 15
>> Alternate with standing barbell curls 3 x 15
> Super set three
>> Standing dumbbell hammer curls 3 x 15
>> Alternate with wrist curls 3 x 15

Shoulders and Back
> Super set one
>> Lat pull downs 3 x 15
>> Alternate with barbell bent over rowing 3 x 15
>> Alternate with barbell cleans 3 x 15
>> Military Press 3 x 15 (optional)

Legs
> Super set one
>> Super set leg extensions 3 x 15
>> Super set (alternate with) leg curls 3 x 15
>> Squats 3 x 15 (optional)

If you do not have any restrictions on your back, knees or shoulders you can add or substitute dead lifts, squats, and military or behind the neck presses with the above. These exercises are considered the basic three of weightlifting but can be hard on your back, knees, and shoulders respectively. The weight-training workout takes between 1.5 and 2.0 hours and should be done 3 times per week.

Why running and jogging? Jogging and running burns calories faster than any other activity. The average calories spent per hour by a 150-pound person are given below. A lighter person burns fewer calories; a heavier person burns more.

Jogging 7 mph	920 calories / hour
Running 10 mph	1280 calories / hour

The *Advanced Human Thought* running program, otherwise known as the "Three Tens" for 10 laps, 10 wind sprints, and 10 hills or stairs, takes about 45 minutes to 1 hour depending on running speed. The running regime consists of the following activities three times per week:

> Jogging - 2.5 to 3 miles (depending on track size 10-12 laps with a standard track being 400 meters)
> Wind sprints - 50 yard sprints up (regular forward sprint) 5 times and back (running backwards) 5 times
> Hills or stairs - 10 repetitions (up to the top and back down is one repetition)

The running and weight regimes are done on alternating days. For example, you would lift weights Monday, run Tuesday, lift weights Wednesday, run Thursday, and lift weights Friday, run Saturday, and run or rest Sunday.

When it comes to losing weight and staying in shape forget about all the diet pills, fad diets, diet supplements, fat burners, fat dissolving devices, expensive exercise equipment, and other gimmicks claiming that you can get into shape and lose weight fast with little or no effort, they are all a bunch of scams. There is no easy way to get in shape and stay in shape. All you need to do is eat less and exercise more. Standard barbells and dumbbells, aerobic exercises like jogging or cycling, and a sensible nutritious diet with no snacks or deserts are all that you need, so save your money.

Bad Habits - How to Ruin Your Life

Illegal drugs are bad. Why do you think they call it dope? If you want to find the quickest way to ruin your life start using drugs. What is the other quickest way to ruin your life? Commit a crime. Of course possessing and distributing drugs is also a crime and alcohol and drugs are the leading contributors to criminal acts. If you like prison, drugs are for you. According to the Federal Bureau of Prisons 55 percent of the people doing time are in for drug offenses.

According to the National Institute on Alcohol Abuse and Alcoholism the economic costs to U.S. society of drug abuse was an estimated $97.7 billion in 1992. The parallel cost to society for alcohol abuse was estimated at $148 billion, bringing the total cost for substance abuse in 1992 to $246 billion. This total represents a cost of $965 for every person in the United States in 1992. The per-person cost for drug abuse alone was $383. Who pays for these costs? Everyone pays. Many of the costs fall on the alcohol or drug abuser. Drug abusers and their family's bear $42.9 billion of the total including costs related to health problems, early death, or lost earnings. The government (the taxpayers) bears the largest share for services such as welfare, health coverage, treatment programs, unemployment, disability insurance, and criminal justice.

According to the August 1998 article *Preventive Intervention Cost-Effectiveness and Cost Benefit Literature Review* by Lisa Werthamer, M.S.W., Sc.D. of The University of Tennessee, Knoxville and Pinka Chatterji, M.A. of Johns Hopkins University School of Public Health almost one-third of all deaths in the United States are attributed to drug use. Drug use is linked to increases in the user's health-related risk behaviors such as failure to use condoms, failure to use birth control, and sharing of intravenous needles (Cahalan, 1991). It is also linked to an increase in the risk for a number of health conditions including cancer, chronic liver disease, pancreatitis, peptic ulcers, and tuberculosis (Rice, Kelman, Miller, & Dunmeyer, 1990). Drug use has a psychological and economic impact on the user's family (Brook, Brook, Gordon, Whiteman, & Cohen, 1990) and increases the risk of infant mortality and morbidity for the childbearing user's offspring (Chasnoff, 1988; Kleinman, Pierre, Madaus, Land, & Schwann, 1988; Little, Snell, Klein, & Gilstrap, 1989). Community impacts stem from the association of drug use with motor vehicle crashes, suicide, homicide, drowning, boating deaths, rape, assault, and robbery (Grossman, Chaloupka, Saffer, & Laixuthai, 1994; Inciardi & Pottieger, 1991; Perrine, Peck, & Fell, 1988). A current analysis of the costs generated by drug use problems in the U.S. population estimate that the U.S. economy absorbed $70.3 billion in alcohol costs and $44.1 billion in drug abuse costs (Rice et al., 1990). Most of the costs of drug abuse are due to crime, including the costs associated with police protection, private legal defense, property destruction, and productivity losses for those who engage in drug-related crime or for people incarcerated in prison as a result of a drug-related crime (Rice, Kelman, & Miller, 1991). Additionally, researchers have linked substance use during high school and young adulthood to lower educational attainment and lower earnings (Cook & Moore, 1993; Kenkel & Ribar, 1994; Yamada, Kendix, & Yamada, 1996).

There are other reasons not to use drugs. Drugs are bad for you physically as well. Cocaine can lead to heart attacks, doing drugs and driving can lead to fatal accidents, you can die from overdoses of heroin or other drugs, and marijuana use can result in short term memory loss and cause cancer. In addition, you will be dazed and confused, and life will pass you by while you are in a drug-induced fog.

Drugs can adversely effect your education in many ways. Your brain will not function properly so you will forget things and do badly on tests. It will also affect your ability to get into college. Due to a new federal law, students with drug related convictions could be ruled ineligible for federal grants and loans. Congress imposed the drug conviction restriction when it renewed the Higher Education Act in 1998. The provision denies aid to students who have been convicted in state or federal court of possessing or selling drugs. As of October 2002, 1,311 applicants were ruled ineligible and an additional 5,617 students must complete a waiting period before they become eligible. If you are a student without the money to go to college drugs can prevent you from getting the money you need to get an education.

Smoking is bad. The fact that cigarettes cause cancer and heart problems has been known since the 1960's but people continue to smoke and continue to try to blame tobacco companies for their own weakness. According to the Department of Health and Human Services' Substance Abuse and Mental Health Administration (SAMHSA), more than 57 million individuals currently smoke, putting themselves at risk for serious health consequences such as cancer, heart disease and high blood pressure. In addition, data from HHS' Centers for Disease Control and Prevention (CDC) indicates that more than 430,000 deaths in the United States are attributable to tobacco use, making tobacco the leading preventable cause of death and disease in the country. Adolescents and young teens are particularly at high risk for smoking. Every day, 3,000 young people become regular tobacco users, and one third of them will die from smoking-related diseases. The CDC estimates that smoking related deaths worldwide will reach 10 million per year by 2030, with 70 percent of deaths in developing countries.

Commit a crime ruin your life. It is as simple as that. If freedom and the prospect of making a decent living are important to you, don't get involved in any criminal activities. Crime is now epidemic in America. According to FBI crime statistics in 1999 there were over 15,000 murders. This is 12,000 more people than were killed in the Islamic extremist's terrorist attack on September 11, 2001. Although down from over 23,000 murders in 1990 this is a staggering number. As of 1999 there were over 6 million people or 3.1 percent of the adult population on probation, in jail or prison, or on parole. The prison population is almost 2 million people. One person in 142 is behind bars. The U.S. now spends almost $40 billion a year, roughly $20,000 per prisoner, keeping offenders behind bars.

In the most comprehensive study of its type, "The Aggregate Burden of Crime" in the October 1999 issue of the *Journal of Law and Economics* (University of Chicago Press) stated that crime costs $4,100 per person, or $1.7 trillion in 1997 dollars. The report, researched and written by David Anderson, an economist at Davidson College in North Carolina, covered such details as police and private security expenses, corrections costs, expense of crime-related injuries, and amount of theft. Anderson states that criminals annually steal $603 billion in assets while also creating an additional $1.1 trillion worth of lost productivity.

This is just insanity. The solutions to the crime problem are complex and would require another book. Suffice it to say that crime is ruining the country and every effort must be made to educate young people in ethics and morals and the dangers of bad habits, and improve the economic and educational opportunities for people.

What else can be said of gambling that has not already been said before? How about an analogy? Gambling is no different than standing over your toilet throwing dollar bills in the toilet bowl, flushing and hoping that eventually more dollar bills than you put in will come back up. The odds are about the same as winning the big money on the lottery or at a casino.

More than $50 billion was spent on legalized gambling in 1997. Where did all that money go? The money went into the pockets of the casino owners and state tax collectors. In addition to the direct cost to the individual, there are additional costs to society that arise from pathological, or addicted gamblers. These costs run into the billions and include crime to support the gamblers habit, employment costs which include lost work days, productivity and theft, suicide and social service costs, and family costs such as bankruptcy, counseling and divorce.

John Kindt, professor of commerce and legal policy at the University of Illinois and a leading authority on the economics of gambling, calculates that for every $1 a state receives in gambling revenues, it costs that state at least $3 in increased criminal justice, social welfare, and other costs. Save your time, sanity, and money, and don't gamble. Gambling makes people poorer. Typically, the people who can least afford to gamble are the ones that gamble the most.

Wealth and Poverty

Poverty is the state of one who lacks a normal or socially acceptable amount of money or material possessions. Poverty may cover a range of conditions from extreme want of necessities, such as food and shelter, to an absence of material comforts. Poverty is a relative state of wealth. To be poor is to be lacking a normal or adequate supply of something. The state of being poor is the condition whereby one person or state, has less relative to another.

When it is stated that poverty is a relative state of wealth this means that the concept of wealth varies between people, societies, regions, and nations. The state of being poor itself is subjective. What one person may view as being poor, another may view as having everything they need. A good example of the relative measures of poverty was given in an Economist article titled "The Mountain Man and the Surgeon." The article describes a man who lives in a trailer in Eastern Kentucky, in the Appalachian Mountains, and a prominent surgeon who is the head of the emergency department at the main public hospital in Kinshasa, the capital of the Democratic Republic of Congo.

The article shows the juxtaposition between a poor man in a rich country and a relatively well-off man in a poor one. This is useful for two reasons. First, it puts the rich world's wealth into context. A Congolese doctor, a man most other Congolese would consider wealthy, is worse off materially than most poor people in America. Second, the mountain man makes $521 a month in a country where median male earnings are $3,400 a month. The surgeon earns $600 a month in a country where most people grow their own food and hardly ever see a bank note. Despite their differences, the article's author found it difficult to measure the relative happiness of the two men. This leads to the fact that being poor is a state of mind as well as a state of material wealth. Once people gain a modest sufficiency in goods, further increases in income don't result in rising happiness. Some people are perfectly content not having a great deal of wealth, while others are miserable even with great wealth.

Poverty describes two quite different phenomena: destitution of the sort experienced by the billion or so people who subsist on $1 a day or less; and the situation of people in rich countries who are less well off than their compatriots. For the first group, finding enough to eat is a daily struggle, and a $2-a-day job hand-washing mineral ore in a river is considered a lucky break. Congolese ore-washers were delighted to have found such lucrative work. In America, people complain about only making the minimum wage of $5.15 per hour or $41.20 a day. If poor Americans were to compare their standard of living with what is normal elsewhere in the world, let alone in Congo, they would see they have little cause for discontent.

According to the U.S. Census Bureau there were 32.9 million people or 11.7 percent of the population living at or below the poverty level in 2001. The poverty thresholds are updated each year for inflation. In 2001, the average threshold for a family of four was $18,104; for a family of three, $14,128. The National Average Wage Index in 2001 was $32,922.

Because of the economic system of capitalism, by all measures material wealth is rising for all of society. A greater number of people are living a more comfortable life. According to the Census Bureau, as of 1998, more than 92 percent of Americans below the poverty line said they had enough food, while 86 percent said they had no unmet need for a doctor, 89 percent said they had no roof leaks, and 87 percent said they had no unpaid rent or mortgage payments.

Almost everyone living in poverty in America have the standard appliances, 95 percent own a color television, 99 percent have a refrigerator, 98 percent have a stove, 66 percent of those in poverty had air conditioning in 1998, up from 50 percent in 1992, and personal computer ownership has risen from 20 percent in 1992 to nearly 60 percent in 2002 (so much for the "digital divide" nonsense from the left).

There are many reasons for poverty including, catastrophic events such as fires, floods, and health problems, drugs and alcohol, mental illness, gambling, having children at a young age, loss of a wage earner through death or divorce, large unexpected expenses, a lack of desire to work, and making bad decisions. By far the two biggest causes of poverty are having children too young and out of wedlock, and drug and alcohol addiction. The greatest percentage (over 70 percent of female headed households are poor) of poverty is found in female-headed households. This is a household with a single mother, no father, and children. For the most part female-headed households are the result of shortsighted, self-destructive behavior of one or two people.

How do you stay out of poverty? Simple, don't do drugs, and don't have children before you have an education, a good income, and some savings. According to an NPR / Kaiser Family Foundation / Kennedy School of Government Poll, the leading cause of poverty identified by both the poor (75%) and the non-poor (65%) was drug abuse. This same survey shows that even the poor know that one of the biggest reasons people are poor is because of drugs, yet they still continue to use them. Drug use leads to criminal activities beyond the illegality of drug possession including burglary and theft, the inability to get and hold a job, and increased school dropout rates. Drug addicts have no future and will always be poor.

If you are poor and you have children, chances are you will always be poor and so will your children. The main reason people are poor and stay poor is because they have too many children at too young of an age. Therefore, the easiest way to stay out of poverty is to delay having children until you are financially ready to have them. With abstinence, proper precautions, and the general availability of birth control pills and condoms, there is no excuse for getting pregnant before you are married and financially ready to have a child. If you do have children, don't have them out of wedlock. Being a single parent compounds the burden of raising children and making a decent living. The children of single parents are more likely to be abused, become sick, use drugs, commit crimes, be imprisoned, and have out-of-wedlock children thereby, perpetuating the vicious cycle of maladjusted and poor children. Abstinence or poverty it's your choice.

Since the New Deal and the Great Society eras, the federal government has established approximately 80 assistance programs targeted to low-income individuals and families. Federal expenditures in 1993 for these programs total $223 billion or $1000.00 for every man, woman and child in America. By 2000 this number had grown to $290 billion or 13.5 percent of the entire federal budget. Under President Bush, federal spending on low-income families has increased 42 percent with total spending reaching $400 billion for the fiscal year 2005. Still poverty rates are no lower today than before the War on Poverty started.

After having spent over $7 trillion since the "War on Poverty" began in 1965 the poverty rate remains about the same as when the "war" began, around 11-12 percent. This is because at any given time, for the reasons mentioned above, roughly 10 percent of the population will be at the poverty level. Those who are in poverty today don't stay there long: The data shows that for the period 1996-1999 the majority of poverty episodes last less than one year.

Some people are just destined to be poor. There are many cases where children of wealthy people have inherited substantial fortunes only to loose it all. There are also many cases of poor people wining millions of dollars in the lottery only to end up bankrupt a few short years later. In one case, a New Jersey woman actually one the lottery twice, for a total of $5.4 million, today the money is a distant memory and she is living out her days impoverished in a trailer.

Anyone can be a critic. So what is the solution? The solution in the United States is to get rid of the central welfare bureaucracy in Washington and allocate money directly to the states based on poverty levels. The states have local people who can see who really needs help and who doesn't. The huge amounts of fraud and abuse in the current system could be eliminated. This alone would save billions of dollars per year. The money saved from the elimination of fraud and the huge bureaucracy in Washington could help millions of people who need assistance, most of which only need temporary assistance until they can back on their feet.

The money would go directly to the people in need and could cover education and job training, temporary housing assistance, temporary childcare assistance, money for food and clothing, and temporary health care assistance. Once the individual or family was self-sufficient the temporary assistance would end.

The solution for the world's poorest nations is to change governments and political-economic systems. Countries that are poor will always remain poor regardless of how much aid they receive until they change their system of government. Until they do, all foreign aid should be terminated. If these countries really wanted to eliminate poverty, all they would need to do is to duplicate the US constitution and allow laissez-faire capitalism. Two hundred years ago America was a poor nation, made poorer by fighting a war of liberation and independence against the British. Today, thanks to the constitution and democratic free market capitalism, the United States is the most powerful nation on earth. The formula is simple more freedom equals more prosperity.

Today, instead of promoting self-discipline, self-reliance, and personal responsibility, many organizations that claim they are helping the poor are directing most of their efforts and money to lobbying the government for more handouts for the poor and fighting against work oriented welfare reforms. Many charities are dependent on government grants and contracts leading them to adopt the non-judgmental politically correct party line that the poor are merely victims of discrimination or the system. They focus on political and social change rather than on the people they are supposedly trying to help.

The only real solution to poverty is the teaching of self-discipline, self-reliance, and personal responsibility at an early age. Bad decisions made early in life are what leads to poverty, not discrimination or capitalism. Due to the self-interest of the poverty merchants and the bureaucrats who make a living of perpetuating poverty, the situation is unlikely to change. If you are poor and you have children, chances are you will always be poor and so will your children. The main reason people are poor and stay poor is because they have too many children at too young of an age. Therefore, the easiest way to stay out of poverty is to delay having children until you are financially ready to have them. With abstinence, proper precautions, and birth control pills and condoms, there is no excuse for getting pregnant before you are married and financially ready to have a child. If you do have children, don't have them out of wedlock. Being a single parent compounds the burden of raising children and making a decent living. The children of single parents are more likely to be abused, become sick, use drugs, commit crimes, be imprisoned, and have out-of-wedlock children, thereby perpetuating the vicious cycle of maladjusted and poor children.

Raising children has never been easy. Once you have made the decision to have children you should do your best to raise them in an optimal way. Mihaly Csikszentmihalyi describes five characteristics for raising children in the book *Flow: The Psychology of Optimal Experience*. "The family context promoting optimal experience could be described as having five characteristics. The first one is clarity; the teenagers feel that they know what their parents expect from them - goals and feedback in the family interaction are unambiguous. The second is centering, or the children's perception that their parents are interested in what they are doing in the present, in their concrete feelings and experiences, rather than being preoccupied with whether they will be getting into a good college or obtaining a well-paying job. Next is the issue of choice; children feel that they have a variety of possibilities from which to choose, including that of breaking parental rules - as long as they are prepared to face the consequences. The fourth differentiating characteristic is commitment; or the trust that allows the child to feel comfortable enough to set aside the shield of his defenses and become unselfconsciously involved in whatever he is interested in. And finally there is challenge, or the parent's dedication to provide increasingly complex opportunities for action to their children. Children who grow up in family situations that facilitate clarity of goals, feedback, and feeling of control, concentration on the task at hand, intrinsic motivation, and challenge will generally have a better chance to order their lives so as to make flow possible."

According to the US Department of Agriculture (USDA) a family with a child born in 1999 can expect to spend about $160,140 ($237,000 when adjusted for inflation) for food, shelter, and other necessities to raise that child over the next seventeen years. The report by USDA's Center for Nutrition Policy and Promotion notes that family income affects child rearing costs, with low-income families projected to spend $117,390; middle-income families $160,140; and upper-income families $233,850 over a seventeen year period. Housing costs are the single largest expenditure on a child, averaging $53,310 or 33 percent of the total costs over seventeen years. Food was the second largest expense, averaging $27,990 or 18 percent of the total.

These costs do not reflect the costs of childcare. For a single working parent it gets even worse. According to the Children's Defense Fund childcare for a 4-year-old in a childcare center averages $4,000 to $6,000 per year in cities and states around the country. Some centers charge $10,000 or more per year. Families with younger children or with more than one child in care face even greater costs. In some cities, childcare costs twice as much as college tuition. Even if a two-parent family with both parents working full time at minimum wage ($21,424 per year before taxes without any vacation) managed to budget 10 percent of their income for child care ($2,140 per year) they would be left several thousand dollars short of what they would need to afford average priced child care. As you can see children are expensive. If you can't afford children, don't have them!

Where does the money go? If you earn $30,000 per year the allocations typically look like the following:

Housing	9600.00	32%
Food	4800.00	16%

Federal Income Tax	4500.00	15%
Transportation	3900.00	13%
Child Care and Education	2700.00	9%
Health Care	2100.00	7%
Clothing	1350.00	4.5%
Miscellaneous	1050.00	3.5%

How do you get out of poverty? In a two-parent family one parent will have to work a day shift and the other person will have to work the night shift. Even at minimum wage, currently $5.15 per hour, two people working day and night can earn $21,424 per year. This is based on a 40-hour workweek 52 weeks per year with no vacation.

Follow the money. If there are no jobs where you live move to a larger town where there are jobs. This can be difficult, especially if your parents or other family members cannot or will not move with you, but being poor means that you have to make tough choices and sacrifice. Start saving money as soon as possible. In order to break the cycle of debt you have to save money. In order to continue your education or start your own business you need capital. Even if the amount saved is small to begin with you have to get started saving. You can always increase the amount as you reduce expenses and increase income. If you do drugs, gamble, drink, smoke or own a pet stop immediately! These actions not only sap your will, they sap your wallet.

Get an education. There is no better way to get ahead and lead a prosperous and productive life than by getting an education. You absolutely have to finish high school. Without a high school diploma there is little hope for future success. If you didn't finish high school, get your General Educational Development (GED) certificate. GED tests measure the outcome of a high school education. The GED tests consist of five tests, one in each of these subjects: mathematics, science, social studies, writing skills, and interpreting literature and the arts. In many locations, adult education and literacy classes are provided for free, with a minimal fee for testing. The majority of U.S. employers consider GED graduates the same as traditional high school graduates with regard to hiring, salary, and opportunities for advancement.

To get a good high paying job and have the most career options, you really need at a minimum an associate's degree, or better yet, a bachelor's degree. If you are poor and cannot afford college what do you do? There are two solutions. Get a job that provides tuition reimbursement. Most companies offer tuition reimbursement but few people take advantage of it. If you can't find a job that provides tuition reimbursement, join the military. The different services have a variety of programs that assist you in getting your degree. For instance, the Army offers the Montgomery GI Bill (MGIB) and Army College Fund (ACF) to help pay for college.

Investing in an education it is one the best investments you can make. The more education you have, in the form of more advanced degrees (Associates, Bachelors, Masters, and Doctorate), the more money you will earn over your lifetime. Recent figures released by the Organization for Economic Cooperation and Development (OECD) show returns from an investment in education that range from 6.5 percent in Italy to 17.3 percent in Britain. Returns in the U.S. were 14 percent. The calculation treats the costs of study, including earnings forgone, as the investment; and the gains in post-tax earnings above those of people who do not graduate college as the payoff. Shorter university courses are one reason why returns are so high in Britain. According to U.S. Census Bureau figures, average annual earnings in 1999 for levels of educational attainment were as follows:

High school dropouts	$18,999
High school graduate	$25,900
Associates degree	$33,000
Bachelors degree	$45,400

Masters degree	$54,400
Doctoral degree	$81,400
Professional degree	$99,300

Success in education is never guaranteed, but parental educational attainment and household structure have a major impact on academic performance. The USA Today Academic All-stars are students that have been honored by USA Today for their high school achievement. A survey of 378 of the winning students revealed that 94 percent said they grew up in homes with both a mother and a father. In these households 100 percent of the parents had at least a high school diploma. More than 95 percent of the fathers and 92 percent of the mothers had at least a bachelor's degree, while 52 percent of the fathers had a doctorate degree, and 58 percent of the mothers had masters or doctorate degree. Families that value education, and instill the value of education in their children, can have a significant impact on future academic success.

Smoking cigarettes is one of the worst things you can do for your health, and it is also one of the most expensive habits one can have. Second hand smoke is also unhealthy for your friends and family. The average price for a pack of cigarettes purchased by the carton can vary widely from state to state based on the tax rates that a particular state charges. Using a typical average price of $4.25 per pack and a light smoker who smokes 1 pack per day the cost is $29.75 per week or $1551.25 per year based on a 365-day year. Do yourself and your family a favor, and quit smoking! How do you quit? Read the section on self-discipline, and you will know how to quit. You make up your mind that you are going to do it, and you just do it. Smoking, drinking, and drugs are all habitual and addictive activities. Addiction is not a disease it is a choice. The only way to quit these vices is immediate cessation ("cold turkey"). Stop today and never do it again. You will be glad that you did.

There are only four reasons to own a pet. The first is to own a dog for hunting. The second is if you are a professional and make money off the animals. The third is to own a dog for security. And the fourth is to own a pet for companionship. The only two reasons that owning a pet is essential and beneficial is for hunting and to make money. The other two reasons are unnecessary. A home security system and a can of mace are cheaper and more effective than a guard dog, and humans should find companionship with other humans not animals.

Owning a pet is expensive. To own a medium sized dog for an average life span of 14 years can cost more than $11,000. First year costs for a puppy which includes veterinary care, immunizations, parasite treatment and control, spay / neuter, food, and accessories can range from $700 to $1325. This is in addition to the adoption or purchase price which can cost anywhere from $50 to $100 for adoption to $500 to $2500 to purchase a dog from a breeder. Annual costs for a dog which would include veterinary care, immunizations, parasite treatment and control, spay / neuter, food, and accessories can range from $500 to $1000 per year.

First year costs for a kitten which includes veterinary care, immunizations, parasite treatment and control, spay / neuter, food, and accessories can range from $385 to $900. This is in addition to the adoption or purchase price which can cost anywhere from $25 to $50 for adoption to $500 to $2500 to purchase a cat from a breeder. Annual costs for a cat which includes veterinary care, immunizations, parasite treatment and control, spay / neuter, food, and accessories can range from $325 to $600 per year.

According to the American Veterinary Medical Association dogs bite more than 4.7 million people each year and approximately 60% of those bitten are children. Of these, almost a million people seek medical treatment, and at least 20 people die each year as a result of dog bites. Dog bites can result in serious life-threatening injury to victims, and can leave survivors scarred and disfigured for life.

The cost of dog bit injuries is staggering. According to the National Center for Injury Prevention and Control direct medical care charges for dog bites are estimated at

$164.9 million. Moreover, direct costs represent only 65% to 70% of the total costs of injury. Total costs are actually much higher at an estimated $235.6 million. The human suffering related to the 17 deaths, nearly 6,000 hospitalizations, and more than 333,000 emergency room visits in 1998 alone should be enough to convince anyone that pets are bad for society, and bad for your wallet.

Pet overpopulation has reached crisis proportions. According to the Humane Society, in six short years one female dog and her offspring can give birth to 67,000 puppies. In seven years, one cat and her young can produce 420,000 kittens. Every year between 8 and 10 million dogs and cats enter U.S. shelters; some 4 to 5 million of these animals are euphemized (put to death) because there are not enough homes for them. Stray animals are a menace to society, and pose a health threat to humans and other animals. These strays get into trash containers, defecate in public areas and on private lawns, prey upon wildlife such as birds and attack and sometimes kill small children. Each year communities are forced to spend millions of taxpayer dollars trying to cope with the consequences of pet overpopulation.

Television, movies, computer games, and the Internet have helped turn America into a mindless wasteland. Quit watching television and if you have cable or satellite television get rid of it. Cable TV can cost up to $75.00 per month or $900.00 per year. Put this money into your savings account. For the most part television is a total waste of time. It turns people into mindless zombies. Instead of watching television, improve your mind by reading books, or improve your body by exercising.

As can be seen from the figures above, by just quitting smoking and not owning a pet, you can save up to $6.98 per day, $48.86 per week, and $2551.25 per year. If you don't own a pet you not only save a substantial amount of money you save time by not having to clean up after the pet, not having to go to the store to buy pet food and accessories, and not having to go to the veterinarian. Instead of wasting your time playing with a pet, read a book and improve your mind or read to your children.

Additional tips for successful living:

1. Stay out of debt and if you have any debt pay it off as soon as possible. If you use credit cards pay off the full amount every month.
2. Do not buy things on impulse without taking the time to consider their usefulness. Most of these types of items will end up in the basement, garage or junk drawer never to be used. As Ben Franklin (Poor Richard) would say "beware of little expenses, a small leak will sink a great ship."
3. Start saving early in life. Put away 10 percent of you earnings as savings whether you think you can afford it or not. Always have enough money to live for 1 year without an income in case you are terminated from work or you are injured and can't work.
4. If you are on welfare do yourself and your country a favor, get off it and get a job. In the long run you will be happier, you will make more money, and you will improve your chances for better opportunities.
5. As Ben Franklin would say "sloth, like rust, consumes faster than labor wears" and "the sleeping fox catches no poultry, there will sleeping enough in the grave."
6. As Ben Franklin would say "early to bed and early to rise makes a man healthy, wealthy and wise."
7. Chance favors the prepared mind. Have a plan, be prepared for any eventuality, and always have a Plan B in case things don't go according to plan.
8. Always live below your means. If you come into a large amount of money invest it, don't spend it.
9. Due to the excessive tax burden in the U.S. the average American in 2001 worked 117 days (one third of the year) just to pay their federal, state, and local taxes. Taxes have a huge impact on your budget make sure you account for them.

10. Never make the same mistake twice. If you keep on making the same mistake you are not learning and therefore not evolving.

In America there is no reason everyone cannot succeed and get out of poverty. The following true examples should provide you with both the motivation and knowledge to help you and your children succeed.

Chris Gardner started out his career as a homeless person living in a bathroom at a Bay Area Rapid Transit station in Oakland California and cheap hotels when he could afford it. His mother raised him and he never knew his father. He enlisted in the Navy and after his military service he took a job as a medical supply salesman. Mr. Gardner married and had a son but when he was jailed for $1200 in parking violations that he could not pay his wife left him alone with his son.

One day in a parking lot he met a man driving a Ferrari and he asked the man what he did for a living. The man was a stockbroker making $80,000 per month. Mr. Gardner then began knocking on doors, and applying for training programs at brokerage firms. Eventually, he found a position as a brokerage trainee but still could not find a place to live. He would stand in a meal line at the Glide Memorial Church with his son just to get a meal. The Rev. Cecil Williams wondered what in the world a man was doing with a baby. With Rev. Williams' help, and a room supplied by Glide Memorial when he needed it, Mr. Gardner made it through the training program and passed his licensing exam on the first try. Although black brokers were rare and he encountered racism, he says he learned a valuable lesson; "that it's not a black thing, it's not a white thing it's a green thing. If you can make me money, I don't care what color you are." Through hard work and diligence he excelled and after saving $10,000 in capital started his own company. Operating at first out of his home, his company is now an institutional brokerage firm with offices in Chicago's financial district.

Ironically, when the Bay Area transit authority issued new bonds to raise money one of the underwriters was Mr. Gardner's company run by a man, who when he was homeless, had bathed his son in the bathroom of one its train stations. He often returns to Glide Memorial to work on the food line where he used to stand. When he speaks at high schools he keeps his message simple, telling students: "No books, no bucks. That's it."

This is the story of how one woman decided to change her life and did. Karen is a black, thirty-year-old, single working mother, with five young children. Dissatisfied with advice not to go to law school and instead become a paralegal she decided that she would pursue her dream of becoming a lawyer. She wanted to prove to herself that she could do whatever she put her heart into. She reached her goal, graduating from the University of Missouri law school twenty years after first graduating from high school. Karen does not consider herself exceptional but most would agree she displayed exceptional hard work, perseverance and a will to succeed. She had to adapt and she did. She had a plan and a goal and she succeeded.

Another great American success story involves the Chavez family. Ray Chavez, a technical illustrator with a high school education and his wife Rose, an office administrator with a high school education raised their five children with the belief that education can make life better. When the Chavez children were young they spent hours nurturing their education and doing everything they could to help their children learn. This included getting all of the children to learn at least one musical instrument. At one point Rose even took a night job so she could be home full-time with her children and spend time teaching them. She taught all of them how to read before they started school. Their hard work and efforts paid off. All five of their children have now graduated from Harvard University. Not bad when you consider that only 1 in 10 applicants are admitted.

How did a middle class family find the money to send 5 children to Harvard University? They worked hard and sacrificed. They only had one car between them. Ray would ride his bicycle to work. They also ate a lot of peanut butter and jelly for lunch;

loans, scholarships, and after school jobs helped, as well as refinancing their mortgage six times. The Chavez's knew what mattered most, a love of learning and knowledge, a first-rate education, hard work and diligence. Ray has a few words of wisdom for keeping your children focused on learning they include:

- Restrict how much and what your children can watch on television. When your children do watch television, encourage them to watch educational shows such as Nova, Frontline, and American Experience on Public Broadcasting System (PBS).
- Play classical music and read to your children. Both of these activities have been shown to improve cognitive abilities in children.
- Give your children a head start. Teach your children math, reading, geography and music at an early age so when they finally do start class they will start at the head of the class.
- You have to be willing to sacrifice. You can't have everything. You have to decide what is important. You can't have a big house, a fancy car, and take expensive vacations if you want to afford the best schools in the country.

As these stories illustrate, you have to determine your priorities in life, you have to have a plan, and you have to work hard and stay focused. Once you do anything is possible.

One of the best books ever written on leading a successful life is Dale Carnegie's *How to Win Friends and Influence People*. Everyone should purchase and read this book. A major part of being successful is getting along with other people. The six ways to win friends as defined in the book are as follows:

1. Become genuinely interested in other people.
2. When meeting and interacting with other people, smile.
3. People love to hear their own name so use it often.
4. Be a good listener. Encourage others to talk about themselves.
5. Talk in terms of the other person's interests not yours. People are more interested in talking about themselves than listening to someone else's life story.
6. Make the other person feel important and do it sincerely.

The other main point from the book that is very beneficial in changing people's attitudes is to start meetings or correspondence off by beginning with praise and honest appreciation. People are much more receptive when the first thing they hear from you is praise for their work or efforts. Just implementing these few simple techniques can have a dramatic impact on your life. You will be amazed at how effective they really are.

Even if you are at the lowest point in your life be thankful for what you have. Remember things could always be worse, and there is always hope as long as you believe in yourself. Think things couldn't get any worse? You could live in Africa, China, Cuba, Iraq, or North Korea. According to the United Nations Conference on Trade and Development (UNCTAD) almost nine out of ten people in Africa's poorest countries live on less than $2 per day and two-thirds survive on less than $1 per day.

You could live in Zimbabwe, which is run by the depraved Robert Mugabe. Zimbabwe is facing its worst food shortage in 60 years. By the government's own estimates 7 million of the country's 13 million people will be without adequate food to survive in a few months. The remaining farmers who were not killed or chased off their farms have been commanded by Mr. Mugabe to park their tractors and stop farming.

Some 2,900 white farmers whose farms were earmarked to be seized by Mr. Mugabe's mobsters and turned over to blacks were legally obligated to cease work. Those who didn't would face jail terms of up to two years. Unbelievably, Mr. Mugabe has called his plan to redistribute wealth form rich whites to poor blacks "a firm launching pad for our fight against poverty and food insecurity." As is true anytime a government attempts

168

the redistribution of wealth, the nation is robbed of its most productive workers and all incentives to produce are removed. Mr. Mugabe's plan doesn't appear to be working very well. Cereal production has fallen by 67% since 1999-2000 according to the World Food Program (WFP). According to the International Monetary Fund, Zimbabwe suffers the highest rate of inflation in the world running above 4,500 percent although analysts believe the figure to be double that. Prices can literally double overnight. Price controls that are being enforced will only exacerbate shortages and ultimately fuel further inflation. With the country on the brink of starvation Mr. Mugabe doesn't seem to care. His chief concern has been to punish those who dared support his opponent for the presidential election.

You could have been born or live in Nigeria. Here is a country that is corrupt beyond belief. Transparency International, an organization that fights worldwide corruption, ranks Nigeria as one of the most corrupt countries in the world. In addition to the corruption, religious fanatics inhabit the country. Where else would 105 people be killed and over 500 injured because a newspaper article suggested the Prophet Mohammed would probably have married one of the Miss World beauty queens? Bloody mayhem is common in this mostly Muslim country. Relations between the Muslim majority and a sizeable Christian minority have always been tense. Apparently, Muslim Friday prayers are often a flashpoint of unrest in this volatile region. Recently, tensions spread after an unexplained stampede among Muslims leaving Mosque prayers. The Miss World contest, which Nigerian officials had hoped would showcase their country and add to its tourist appeal, ran into trouble amid worldwide publicity over a 31 year old woman who was sentenced under Islamic law to death by stoning for bearing a child out of wedlock.

Earlier in the year more than 200 people were killed in two days of religious clashes in the Northern city of Kano. Most of the killings took place overnight as rival Muslim and Christian gangs slaughtered people and left bodies burning in the street. Religious riots over the past two years have claimed hundreds of lives. Nigerian authorities are always keen to downplay the death figures so as not to provoke an escalation in clashes. The authorities are attempting to regain control. The Kano police commissioner issued the order to shoot rioters and other troublemakers on sight. Even if you are dirt poor, homeless, or living in your car, it is still not as bad as living in these countries. At least in America there is still hope and opportunity, in these countries there is none.

Creating a Life Plan and Time Management

In order to get where you are going you first have to define your destination. You would not take a trip by just wandering around aimlessly hoping someday you might reach your destination. The first thing you do when you plan a trip is to figure out exactly where you are going. Since you made the decision to purchase this book, it would appear that you know where you are going and your destination is success. Always remember, people don't plan to fail, they fail to plan!

With the increased complexity and competition of today's modern society, effective time management has become increasingly important. For those people who are serious about getting the most out of life, effective use of time is essential. The effective use of time will not only make life simpler and more enjoyable, but will also give you more free time to pursue the things that are really important to you.

Although there are many fine books available on the subject of time management, many of them are quite long, and implementing the programs or guidelines themselves requires large amounts of time and effort. Since your time is valuable, this section is designed to give you the necessary facts to get started immediately on the task of saving time. All unnecessary information and details have been omitted so that you do not have to spend hours of time developing and implementing an effective time management system.

The first section defines time and related concepts. This section attempts to give you an idea of how short life really is. Since life is short, it is a good idea to make the best of every moment. When you die the fun is over, there are no second chances. The second section describes a time management system that, among other things, will help you determine what it is in life that means the most to you, and how to go about achieving these objectives. The third section gives you a categorized list of things that you can start doing today to save time.

The information in this section contains general guidelines that will work for most people. However, some alterations may be necessary to fit a particular individual. The idea is to implement a system that you feel comfortable with, that works for you, and stick with it. No sense wasting time - let's get started improving your life.

Time Defined

Time is an exceedingly difficult concept to describe. This is especially true if you are trying to describe time in the physical sense, as in Albert Einstein's Special Theory of

Relativity. Fortunately, we need not understand relativity to make effective use of our time.

To get a good idea of what time is about, and how to manage it effectively, the term itself must be defined. Although there are many definitions of time, we will concentrate on only two.

1. Time is the measured or measurable period during which an action, process or condition exists or continues. Generally, time is duration and has a beginning and end.
2. Time is a moment, hour, day or year as indicated by a clock, a calendar or other man-made device that measures intervals.

The first definition of time is the one that we are most interested in because duration is the time during which something exists, and for us, this duration is our lifetime. The objective of most people, and of this book, is to help make this period of human existence a more pleasant and productive one. The second definition lists some of the intervals of time (such as minutes, hours, days, years, etc.) and the tools that are used to measure these intervals. Because time is a measurable period, it can be tracked, and improvements in time utilization can be made.

Time Related Facts

Now that we have defined time, we can look at some facts associated with time. These facts are given for two reasons. First, to give you an idea of the structure and quantity of time and second, because knowing the various quantities of time may be useful in setting up time tables and for calculating other values that may be of interest to you.

The Elements of the Day
      24 hours per day
      1,440 minutes per day
      86,400 seconds per day
The Average Week
      168 hours total
      40 hours per week for work (assuming no overtime)
      48 hours per week for sleep (assuming 8 hours per night)
      80 hours per week for other activities
The Elements of the Year:
      255 work days per year (assuming 2 days off for weekends)
      2000 work hours per year (assuming 2 weeks off for vacation)
      8,760 hours per year
      525,620 minutes per year
      31,536,000 seconds per year

Time is the most precious of all commodities. Time is the one thing money cannot buy. This is due to the fact that time, as far as the individual is concerned, is finite; meaning that once time is elapsed it can never be recovered. From the moment you are born, your time on the planet begins to run out, and although a lifetime may seem like a long time, it is actually a very short period, as a wise philosopher once said, "Life is but a mere second in time." A "second" may sound like an exaggeration, far too short a time to be an accurate analogy, but when you consider the fact that the universe is approximately 13 billion years old, the normal life span of a human seems like a very short period indeed.

For instance, the average life expectancy of males and females in the United States in 1978 was 69.5 and 73 years respectively. Of these years, the average person spends approximately 213,160 hours, or one-third of their life sleeping, 94,000 hours or one-sixth of their life working, and the remaining 332,520 hours on everything from electronic video games to mountain climbing. These figures are based on the following assumptions:

1. A life expectancy of 73 years at 8,760 hours per year, which gives you a total of 639,480 hours of life.
2. It is assumed that you sleep 8 hours per day.
3. It is assumed that you start working at age 18 and retire at age 65, for a total of 47 years of work. It is also assumed that you work an average of 40 hours per week for 50 weeks per year, which comes to approximately 2,000 hours of work per year.

From these facts, you can readily see that there are two activities that take up the major portion of your time, these being sleep and work. From this, it stands to reason that if you cut down on sleep, or are more productive at work, you can begin to increase your time availability immediately.

Developing a Time Management System

Time management, like other forms of management, involves three basic functions. These functions are:

- Planning - planning is the process of deciding what objectives to pursue during a future time period, and what to do in order to achieve those objectives.
- Organizing - to organize is to arrange elements into a whole of inter-dependent parts; it is carried out through the grouping of activities that are necessary to attain objectives.
- Controlling - controlling is the process of insuring that activities are going according to plan. Control is accomplished by comparing actual performance to predetermined standards or objectives and then taking corrective actions to rectify deviations.

There are three things that must be done before you implement a time management system, and become a successful time manager.

1. Determine your values
2. Set your priorities
3. Establish goals

Determine Values

The value of something is its relative worth, utility, or importance. For the purpose of time management you need to define the things in life that are the most important to you. For example, is marriage and raising a family the most important to you, or is making money and having an active social life more important? These are the kinds of questions you must ask yourself when determining values. Once you have determined what values are the most important to you, you are ready to set your priorities.

Setting Priorities

Now that you have determined your values, you must determine the priority that these values should be given. In setting priorities and identifying them on your task sheet and yearly time table, it is easier to recognize high priority items if you have a method for labeling these priority items according to their value. This can be done by assigning labels to the different levels of priorities for example, Priority Level 1 = P-1, Priority

Level 2 = P-2, Priority Level 3 = P-3. These represent the three levels of priorities, which are defined as follows:

- Priority Level 1 - This level is the primary objective, or activities that are of immediate concern. These are the activities that are the most important to you and should be finished before going on to anything else.
- Priority Level 2 - These are activities of secondary importance and should be worked on only after Priority 1 items are complete or if they are a parallel or sub task to a Priority Level 1 task.
- Priority Level 3 - These are activities of lesser importance, or activities that can be completely eliminated or delegated. It should be remembered that if you sincerely wish to achieve your main goals, you should eliminate all activities that are not directly related to the primary objective.

Establish Goals

Goals are statements that are designed to give you organization, or an individual direction and purpose; they are the ends toward which effort is directed. When establishing goals you should:

1. State the goal
2. State the means of achieving the goal
3. State the resources needed to meet the goal
4. Set up some sort of time limit for achieving the goal

In determining your goals, there are three classifications that should be used:

Life Goals - These are things you would like to do before you die. If you were going to die one year from today, what things would you do before your last year came to an end? These things are obviously the most important things to you, and you should make every effort to achieve them before it is too late.

Short Term Goals - These are goals that are obtainable within a relatively short period of time, generally ranging between 6 months to 3 years. Some examples could be getting a job, going to school, finishing a project or quitting smoking.

Long Term Goals - These are goals that you wish to achieve during your lifetime, and generally wish to accomplish in a period of 3 to 20 years. Goals that fit into this category could include, getting married and raising a family, making a million dollars and retiring, or doing something that you have always wanted to do but have not had time to do because of other priorities.

After you have finished the first three steps of determining your values, setting priorities, and establishing goals, the next step is to prepare a written plan. In developing a plan, there are three things that must be done:

1. The plan must be put in writing or it will generally not be adhered to, or it will be totally forgotten.
2. Determine the resources needed to carry out the plan or project. These resources can range from the capital needed to start a business, to items that you are going to take with you to a sporting event.
3. Determine scheduling requirements and set up a timetable. Most people tend to underestimate the time any given activity will take, so when estimating time for schedules or timetables, try to set realistic goals.

Once the written plan is complete, it should be implemented immediately. Remember to work on the highest priority (P-1) items until they are complete before going on to something else, unless the activity is to be done concurrently with the main priority. Also, do not neglect to follow through with your plan once it has been established. If you do not follow through with the plan, you may as well not have even written it down in the first place. While carrying out the plan, stay with the task at hand even though you may find it difficult or boring. Remember, perseverance pays, so do not allow other desires to weaken your pursuit of the primary objective.

When implementing your new time management system, there are a few simple tools that will be very helpful to you, and can be purchased at your local office supply center for a moderate price. The first of these tools is a desk calendar. When purchasing your desk calendar, make sure that it has plenty of room for writing notes. This calendar serves as a scheduling and activity recording device, which gives you a record of what you have already accomplished, and what your future activities will be.

The second item is a pocket calendar that you should use to list your daily tasks such as phone calls, appointments, meetings and other miscellaneous tasks. The pocket calendar provides two functions. First, since you have recorded your daily tasks in writing it serves as a memory aid so you will always know where you are supposed to be and what you are supposed to be doing. Second, it serves as a business tool by giving you added credibility. When you take out your pocket calendar to check your schedule, it will be obvious that you are an active, organized person. This in turn will encourage people to get to the point when you meet with them, and people will generally respect your wishes if you say that you already have a previous engagement. The great thing about having plans and tasks in writing is that, once they are written down, you can forget them and go on to something else without the worry of whether or not you forgot something.

In setting up schedules it is best to make up your daily schedule the night before so that in the morning you will be able to wake up fresh, check your schedule, and know exactly what you are supposed to be doing without giving it a second thought. Every day when you get up - check your schedule. This will let you know exactly how the day will proceed, and if you may have forgotten something during the night it will serve as a daily reminder of where you have to go, and what you have to do.

Time Saving Tips

1. Think before you act. Every activity, no matter how insignificant, takes time.
2. Carry out activities according to a written plan. Define and clarify goals and objectives. Organize and coordinate activities.
3. Set priorities. This reduces needless or unproductive and counterproductive activities.
4. Learn to be able to say no, otherwise you will end up doing things that you really did not want to do in the first place. Even though this can be difficult, especially with persuasive friends, it will save you time and enable you to work on things that are really important to you.
5. Discontinue non-productive or counterproductive activities as quickly as possible.
6. Do two complementary activities at once. This can save you large amounts of time. A few examples include: cook and clean up at the same time, while you are talking on the telephone do the dishes at the same time, and read or work while you eat.
7. Since most people sleep more than they need to, reducing the hours per night that you sleep will increase your time availability. For example, if you were to get up 1 hour earlier than you are now for a month, you will have an average of 30 extra hours of free time; if you do this for 1 year, you will have an extra 15 days of time available to pursue your goals. Eight hours of sleep per night is the recommended amount.

8. Do not leave tasks unfinished. If a project or task is worth starting, it is worth finishing.
9. Write down important facts. This will help you remember what you might otherwise forget, and will save you time if for one reason or another you have to look these facts up again.
10. Do not attempt too much at one time or set unrealistic goals and time estimates. It is generally a good idea to concentrate on only one major activity at a time.
11. Too many interests can be a problem. The idea is to determine which interests are the most important and pursue them. In today's world of increasing specialization, it is impossible to be knowledgeable in every field.
12. Use the Yellow Pages. Call, do not drive around, when looking for things. If people will not help you over the phone, they must not want your business. This not only saves time, it saves money in the form of decreased fuel costs.
13. If you are going somewhere that you have not been before, call and get directions or consult a map or an online service such as MapQuest or MSN maps and directions before you leave. Again, this will save you both time and money.
14. Essential human activities, such as shaving, showers and baths, etc., take up a great deal of time. Any way that these activities can be shortened will lead to an increase in time availability.
15. The average American spends approximately 6 hours per day watching television. If you really want to get things done, do not turn on the television set!
16. Make duplicates of house and car keys and important documents. This not only saves you time in case of theft or loss, but also saves you the aggravation of being locked out of your car or house. The Boy Scout motto of always being prepared is very useful, and applies to every endeavor of life.
17. Keep things organized and get rid of clutter. Disorganization and clutter cause disorder in the mind, which decreases effectiveness. Being organized saves both time and money. Remember the old saying "a place for everything and everything in its place."
18. Remember Parkinson's Law - Work expands to fill the time allowed for its completion. To counter Parkinson's Law you can use incentives to finish work before a specified time.
19. Remember the Pareto Principle also known as the 80/20 law. The law states that for many phenomena 80% of consequences stem from 20% of the causes. What this essentially means is that a small percentage of causes yield the majority of the results. A few examples are listed below.
    - 20% of customers account for 80% of sales
    - 20% of the customers are responsible for 80% of the past due accounts
    - 20% of your products produce 80% of your profit
    - 20% of individuals in an organization perform 80% of the work
20. Remember the law of diminishing returns – This economic law states that if one input in the production of a commodity is increased while all other inputs are held fixed, a point will eventually be reached at which additions of the input yield progressively smaller, or diminishing, increases in output. For the individual this means that at a certain point spending additional time on a task only marginally improves the quality or quantity of the work. You receive diminishing returns from each amount of extra time spent on a task.
21. Perseverance and tenacity (persistent in maintaining, adhering to, or seeking something valued or desired) are two of the most powerful forces known to man. To persevere means to persist in a state, enterprise, or undertaking in spite of counter influences, opposition, or discouragement. Remember, perseverance pays!

As with all self-improvement programs, it is the desire or will to succeed that make any program work. In the long run, it is up to you to oversee the effectiveness of this and other self-improvement programs. Remember that success lies in accomplishments. After the day is over, just ask your self, what did I accomplish today? If you can honestly say that you accomplished a great deal, chances are you will feel good about yourself and your accomplishments. Being organized and knowing what you are doing and where you are going gives you a sense of security and pride. It not only helps you in your everyday endeavors, it also reduces worry and stress, both of which have been proven to be harmful to human health.

Conclusion - The Time is now

The goal of life is happiness. At all times you should seek happiness. One should not depend on others for their happiness. One should not depend on material things for happiness since material things come and go and to some, a lack of material things causes unhappiness. Rather, happiness should be a state of mind, a balance of life, an attitude that combines reflection and reason.

It is time to get started on the path towards a long and prosperous life. You have to make a choice whether you trust in Jesus, God, or Allah, or trust in reason and yourself. Humans control their own destiny. A successful happy life is determined by the choices you make and the skill you apply in executing these choices. Life is all about making the right decisions. If you make bad decisions, there is a high probability that you will have a miserable life. If you make good decisions, life can be a happy and rewarding experience.

When it was stated that socialism is a dismal failure, this is a fact. When it was stated that Marx was fundamentally wrong on every idea, this is a fact. When it was stated that capitalism is the most efficient economic system known to man, this is a fact. When it was stated that there are terrible costs associated with religion, this is a fact. When it was stated that starting a family without an education, a good income and savings you will most likely be poor, this is a fact. When it was stated that the choice between religion and science is based on the choice of faith versus reason, this is a fact. When it was stated that if you are obese or use tobacco you are going to have health problems and a shorter life, this is a fact. When it is stated that if you do drugs or commit a crime your life will be ruined, this is a fact. Now that you have the facts the rest is up to you. Each individual has to decide what is best for his or her own life. Part of that choice is whether you will live your life with your head in the sand, or you will face up to the facts and do something good for yourself and for humankind. Not everyone is going to have the same philosophy of life or worldview. The fundamental worldview that best fits reality based on our current knowledge is as follows:

1. The universe began as a singularity or quantum vacuum fluctuation as part of a natural process without the need of a creator or supernatural force in an event known as the big bang.
2. The universe, galaxies, solar systems, matter and life, including humans, evolved as a natural process.
3. Humans, through reason and the scientific process, have a fundamental understanding of existence, reality, and nature.

4. From a fundamental understanding of natural law, humans have created a system of ethics and the political and economic systems of democracy and capitalism, which are based on the concepts of freedom, liberty, and individual rights and are the most efficient and effective systems developed for human existence.

5. Through the acquisition of knowledge, humans have developed a reason for existence and an understanding of their place in the universe.

6. The requirements for living a happy and healthy, ethical and virtuous, and long and prosperous life have been determined, and it has been shown that it is up to the individual to make the right choices in life.

Even after completing this book you may still ask; why are we here? We are here to enjoy our existence. We are here to improve the pool of knowledge and the human condition. In this way, the question of whether or not there is life after death doesn't matter. Do the best you can for yourself, your fellow neighbor, your family, your wife and children, and your country now. We are here so that future generations that follow can enjoy the fruits of our labor. I have heard of people, and have myself told someone who has subsequently died, that if there is life after death please come back and let me know. No one has heard back from these people, so instead of worrying about heaven or hell, worry about your life on earth and what you can do to improve the planet and its people.

As mentioned in the introduction, this book contains a tremendous amount of information on what can be very complex topics. My hope is that it covers the topics in enough detail to give you a basic understanding of the way the world works and how you can use this knowledge to make your life better. If this book helps just one person lead a more prosperous and rewarding, healthier and longer life, it was worth the hundreds of hours of research and work it took to complete the book. Remember, life is but a mere second in time, make the most of it!

Glossary

Adaptive radiation - the division of a single species into many species specialized to diverse ways of life.

Agnostic - one who thinks it is impossible to know whether there is a god or a future life, or anything beyond material phenomena.

Amino acids – amino acids are organic compounds that are the building blocks of life. They follow the general formula H2 N-CHR-COOH, where R can be one of twenty or more different side chains. An amino acid is so named because it has a basic amine group, -NH2 and an acidic carboxyl group +COOH.

Animism - the doctrine of the reality of souls; Taylor's theory states that religion began in animism. People have two things belonging to them, life and a phantom. Animism can also be an aspect of nature worship, although not all nature worship is animistic. Sometimes the object is worshipped for the manna in it, its sacredness, or its potencies.

Antithesis - the second stage in a dialectic process

Appeasement - to buy off a potential aggressor by concessions usually at the sacrifice of principles

A priori - related to or derived by reasoning from self-evident propositions

Atheist - one who believes there is no god

Being - the quality or state of having existence; conscious existence; life; a living thing or person

Belief - an acceptance based on evidence of something as true

Bias - a particular tendency or inclination especially one that prevents unprejudiced consideration of a question

Biological Classification - binomial nomenclature is used which gives the name of the genus followed by the name of the species. An example of the classification system in biology is:

> Kingdom: Animalia (animals)
> Phylum: Chordata (chordates)
> Sub Phylum: Vertabrata (vertebrates)
> Class: Mammilia (mammals)
> Order: Primates
> Family: Hominidae (man and close relatives)
> Genus: Homo (modern man and precursors)
> Species: Sapiens (modern man)

Causality - the interrelation of cause and effect; the principle that nothing can exist or happen without a cause.

Christianity - the religion derived from the teachings of Jesus Christ based on the Bible as scripture and professed by Eastern Orthodox, Roman Catholic, and Protestant bodies

Comintern - Communist International - an organization formed by Trotsky that served as an international fellowship of Proletarians until its abolishment in 1943. The statutes of the Second Congress of the Comintern of 1929 sum up the primary function of this organization and the primary goal of the Soviet Union very well. It is the aim of the Communist International to fight by all available means, including armed struggle, for the overthrow of the International Bourgeoisie and for the creation of an International Soviet Republic as a transitional stage to the complete abolition of the state.

Deism - the faith that God exists and created the world but thereafter assumed no control over it or the lives of people. In philosophy, the belief that reason is sufficient to prove the existence of God, with the consequent rejection of revelation and authority.

Deity - the rank or essential nature of a god or a supreme being; a god or goddess

Determinism - the doctrine that everything is entirely determined by a sequence of causes, and that one's choice of action is not free and independent of his will.

Dialectic - development through the stages of thesis, antithesis, and synthesis, in accordance with the laws of dialectical materialism doctrine principles, policies, and concepts applicable to a subject which are derived from experience or theory, compiled and taught for guidance representing the best available thought that can be defended by reason.

Divine - god like, heavenly, supremely good; of, relating to, or proceeding directly from a deity

DNA - deoxyribonucleic acid - a complex organic compound found in all life on Earth. It is responsible for the storage of genetic information. It is composed of a double helix structure, which is made up of phosphates and sugars, and the four-nucleotide bases. It is named for the sugar deoxyribose, which it contains.

Dualism - in theology, the doctrine that man has two natures, physical and spiritual, and that there are two different principles in operation, those being good and evil. In philosophy, dualism is the doctrine that recognizes two radically independent elements as mind and matter underlying all known phenomena.

Eukaryote - an organism, which has its chromosomes, contained within a nucleus, and which is distinguished from the simpler prokaryotes by other cellular structures and certain differences in biochemical function. The eukaryotes include higher plants and animals, protozoa, fungi, and algae other than blue-green algae.

Empirical - capable of being verified or disproved by observation or experiment

Epicureanism - this school of philosophy taught that the supreme good in human life is happiness or pleasure achieved through reason.

Epistemology - the study or theory of the origin, nature, methods and limits of knowledge

Existentialism - a literary-philosophic cult of nihilism and pessimism, it holds that each man exists as an individual in a purposeless universe and that he must oppose his hostile environment through the exercise of his free will

Fact - an indubitable truth of actuality; a thing known to be true; what is true or existent in reality, the quality of being actual (actuality), something that has actual existence, an actual occurrence: event, a piece of information presented as having an objective reality

Faith - unquestioning belief; anything believed without proof by evidence; complete trust, confidence or reliance

Fallacy - any reasoning failing to satisfy the conditions of logical proof, or violating the laws of valid argument

Filial - of, pertaining to, or befitting a son or daughter: filial obedience.

First World Nations - capitalist economies including mixed and modified economies; characteristics include a pluralistic society with a multi-party government, high gross national product and per capita output (productivity), examples of First World Nations include: the United States, Canada, Great Britain, West Germany Japan, Taiwan, Singapore, and Hong Kong.

Genes - segments of genetic material, which determine the sequence of amino acids in specific polypeptides, such that there is a one-to-one relation between gene and polypeptide.

Genus - a group of organisms with common structural characteristics.

Gross National Product (GNP) - a statement of the distribution at market prices of the goods and services produced on national economy during a given year; distribution is shown in terms of consumer purchases, government purchases, gross private domestic investments, and exports of goods and services

God - the being perfect in power, wisdom, and goodness that men worship as creator and principal ruler of the universe

Gosplan - state planning committee of the Soviet Union ideology a systematic body of concepts about human life or culture, including the manner or content of characteristic thinking of an individual group or culture; a belief system

Hedonism - the pursuit and enjoyment of pleasure is life's main goal.

Holy - spiritually pure, godly, characterized by perfection, and transcendence

Humanism - the intellectual and cultural movement that stemmed from the study of classical Greek and Latin literature and culture during the Middle Ages and was one of the factors giving rise to the Renaissance; it is characterized by an emphasis on human interests rather than on the natural world or religion. A humanist credo by Robert Ingersoll: We are not endeavoring to chain the future, but to free the present. We are not forging fetters for our children, but we are breaking those our fathers made for us. We are the advocates of inquiry, of investigation and thought. This of itself is an admission that we are not perfectly satisfied with our conclusions. Philosophy has not the egotism of faith. While superstitions build walls and create obstructions, science opens all the highways of thought. We do not pretend to have circumnavigated everything, or to have solved all difficulties, but we do believe it is better to love men than to fear gods; that it is grander and nobler to think and investigate for yourself than to repeat a creed. We are satisfied that there can be but little liberty on earth while men worship a tyrant in heaven. We do not expect to accomplish everything in our day; but we want to do what good we can, and to render all the service possible in the holy cause of human progress. We know that doing away with gods and supernatural persons and powers is not an end it is a means to an end and that real end is the happiness of mankind.

Hypotheses - a hypothesis is a supposition; a proposition or principle, which is supposed or taken for, granted, in order to draw a conclusion or inference for proof of the point in question; something not proved, but assumed for the purpose of argument. The hypothesis is the starting point of any experiment. It is an idea, phrased as a general or tentative statement about a relation between two or more events that the scientist wishes to test in an experiment.

Idealism - any of various theories, which hold that the objects of perception are actually ideas of the perceiving mind and that, it is impossible to know whether reality exists apart from the mind (as opposed to materialism).

Information - the body of facts accumulated by mankind

Invertebrate - animals, which do not possess a backbone or spinal column

Irrationalism – an attitude or belief having a non-rational basis

Jesus Christ - the founder of the Christian religion

Knowledge - a clear and certain perception of something; the act, fact, or state of knowing; understanding. Learning is part of knowledge and is all that has been perceived or grasped by the mind.

Logical Positivism - a movement in science concerned with the unification of the sciences, especially by an analysis of the language of science and the consequent development of a vocabulary applicable to all sciences.

Light Year - the distance light to travels in one year, roughly 6 trillion miles; light travels at 3.27 miles per second; 1 parsec = 3.26 light years or 19.2 trillion miles. The closest star to earth is Alpha Centauri, which is 4.29 light years or 1.32 parsecs away.

Manna - the impersonal supernatural force to which certain primitive peoples attribute good fortune and magical powers

Materialism - in philosophy the doctrine that matter is the only reality and that everything in the world, including thought, will, and feeling, can be explained only in terms of matter

Metaphysics - the branch of philosophy that deals with first principles and seeks to explain the nature of being or reality (ontology); it is closely associated with a theory of knowledge (epistemology).

Monotheism - the doctrine or faith in the existence of only one God

Monolithic - undifferentiated, exhibiting mass uniformity naive showing a lack of informed judgment

Mortification - to punish (one's body) or control (one's physical desires or passions) by self-denial, for example fasting, abstaining from sex, etc. as a means of religious or ascetic discipline.

Muslim - an adherent of Islam

Mysticism – a doctrine of beliefs of mystics specifically the doctrine that it is possible to achieve communion with God through contemplation and love without the medium of human reason. Any doctrine that asserts the possibility of attaining knowledge of spiritual truths through intuition acquired by fixed meditation or a vague obscure thinking of belief.

Natural Law - in science, means the formulation of some uniform character, mode of behavior or uniform correlation of things or events; it is frequently used in describing uniform relationships among various phenomena. Any such uniformity may be called a natural law.

Naturalism - a theory denying that an event or object has a supernatural significance.

Nominalism - a middle ages doctrine that all universals or abstract terms are mere necessities of thought or conveniences of language and therefore exist as names only and have no realities corresponding to them

Nucleic Acids - any of a group of acids occurring in organic matter and consisting of a combination of phosphoric acid with a carbohydrate and a base. A complete hydrolysis of nucleic acid yields a mixture of breakdown products in the proportion of one mole of phosphate, one mole of a sugar, and one mole of a mixture of heterocylcic bases.

Ontology - area of metaphysics concerned with the nature of being

Pantheism - the doctrine or belief that God is not a personality, but that all laws, forces and manifestations of the self-existing universe are God, in other words that God is everything and everything is God. Some nature based religions follow this doctrine.

Peoples Democratic Republic - socialistic one-party rule

Perturbation - a deviation of an astronomical body from its computed orbit because of the attraction of another body or bodies.

Phylum - a high level category just beneath the kingdom and above the class, a group of related similar classes.

Polytheism - faith in or worship of many gods, or more than one god

Prayer - an approach to deity in word or thought. To pray is to request or plea to address god with adoration, confession, supplication, or thanksgiving

Prokaryotes - organisms having a simple cell lacking a nucleus, represented by bacteria and blue-green algae.

Protein - an organic molecule made up of a chain of amino acids. Proteins are variable in type, and have a wide range of functions in living organisms. Some are structural, in membranes for example; some have specialized functions, as do the proteins, which cause muscle contractions; and many act as enzymes, controlling the biochemical processes of the cell.

Proto - first, primary or lowest of a series

Proxy - an agent who acts as a substitute for another or the authority or power to act for another

Qualitative - relating to or involving quality, characteristics, or attributes as opposed to quantitative which relates to numerical quantities

Rational - based on or derived from reason

Rationalism - the principle or practice of accepting reason as the only authority in determining one's opinions or course of action. In philosophy, rationalism is the theory that the reason or intellect is the true source of knowledge, rather than the senses

Reason - to think coherently and logically; to draw inferences or conclusions from facts

Realism - (a) the doctrine that universals have objective reality; as opposed to nominalism (b) the doctrine that material objects exist in themselves, apart from the mind's consciousness of them; as opposed to idealism.

Reality - the quality or state of being real; corresponding to know facts supported by evidence; not illusory, fraudulent, or apparent, factual basis, truth, actuality, realness, substantiality, existence, substance, materiality, being, presence, actual existence, sensibility, corporeality, solidity, perceptibility, true being, absoluteness, tangibility, palpability

Regime - a political or social system

Religion - a system of beliefs and practices by which a group of people interprets and responds to what they feel is supernatural and sacred

Revolution - a fundamental change in political organization or a political system; this change is typically radical and complete; it generally involves either the overthrow or renunciation of one government or ruler which is then replaced with a totally new government or ruler

Righteous - characterized by uprightness or morality; a righteous observance of the law

RNA - ribonucleic acid - a complex organic molecule named for the sugar ribose, which it contains.

Schism - a split, division, or separation; discord or disharmony

Science - systemized knowledge derived from observation, study, and experimentation carried on in order to determine the nature or principles of what is being studied

Sincerity - freedom from deceit, hypocrisy, or duplicity; probity in intention or in communicating; earnestness.

Second World Nations - socialist economies; characteristics include monolithic government, dominated by a single party, state operation of agriculture, central planning of the economy, a gross national product and per capita output lower than that of the Western Industrialized Democracies, no ownership of private property. The Second World Nations include the former Soviet Union and the Eastern Bloc Nations of Rumania and Bulgaria.

Secularism - a system of doctrines and practices that rejects any form of religious faith and worship, and believes that religion and ecclesiastical affairs should not enter into the functions of the state and especially public education. Secularism affirms that this life is the only one of which we have any knowledge and that human effort should be wholly directed towards its improvement: it asserts that supernaturalism is based upon ignorance and assails it as the historic enemy of progress. Secularism affirms that progress is only possible on the basis of equal freedom of speech and publication; that liberty belongs of right to all; and that the free criticism of institutions and ideas is essential to a civilized State. Secularism, affirming that morality is social in origin and application aims at promoting the happiness and well being of mankind. Secularism demands the complete separation of the Church from the State and the abolition of all privileges granted to religious organizations. It seeks to spread education to promote the fraternity of all peoples as a means of advancing universal peace to further common cultural interests and to develop the freedom and the dignity of mankind.

Self-evident - evident without need of proof or discussion; that produces certainty or clear conviction upon mere presentation to the mind

Shambles - a state of great disorder and or confusion

Sluggard - a person who is habitually inactive or lazy

Species - a group of organisms that can all potentially interbreed to produce fertile offspring. The group is genetically isolated from other groups, and this genetic isolation allows distinctive features, characteristic of the species, to develop.

Spirit - animating or vital principle, the immaterial part of man, mental or moral nature or qualities disembodied soul, incorporeal being. A spirit is a shadow or phantom that people associate with future life after death.

Soul - the immaterial essence, animating principle, or actuating cause of an individual life; the spiritual principle embodied in human beings, all spiritual beings, or the universe; a persons total self; mans moral and emotional nature

Sovereign - enjoying autonomy and independence and freedom from external control

Subversion - an act designed to pervert of corrupt by undermining the morals, allegiance, and faith of a people

Supernatural - existing or occurring outside the normal experience or knowledge of man or caused by other than the known forces of nature

Surrogate - a person or state appointed to act in the place of another synthesis the dialectic combination of thesis and antithesis into a higher stage of truth

Theism - faith in God or gods who are the creator(s) and ruler(s) of the universe and are known by revelation

Theology - the knowledge of God or of divine things, theologians attempt to provide a total view of God, man, and the world.

Theory - a theory is the formulation of apparent relationships or underlying principles of certain observed phenomena, which is more thoroughly developed than a hypothesis and has been verified to some degree.

Theorem - is a proposition that is not self-evident but that can be proved from accepted premises and so is established as a law or principle.

Theosophy - any of various philosophies or religious systems that propose to establish direct contact with divine principle through contemplation, revelation, etc., and to gain thereby a spiritual insight superior to empirical knowledge

Thesis - the first and generally the least adequate stage of a dialectic process

Third World or Less Developed Countries - characteristics include one party or one man rule, limited agricultural and industrial output, low gross national product per capita production and per capita income, there are over 100 Second World Nations, the majority being in the Middle East, Africa, and South America

Totalitarianism - a political regime based on subordination of the individual to the state; characterized by strict and total control over all phases of society, such as communications and the economy; accompanied by an official ideology and a system of terroristic police control

Transcendent - to be prior to, beyond and above the universe or material existence

Trust - reliance on the integrity of a person. Trust implies instinctive unquestioning belief in and reliance upon something: to have trust in one's parents.

Vertebrates - the highest division of the animal kingdom so called from the presence in most cases of a backbone composed of numerous joints or vertebrae, which constitutes the center of the skeleton and at the same time supports and protects the central parts of the nervous system.

Virtue - moral excellence, goodness, or righteousness, including conformity of one's life and conduct to moral and ethical principles

Zionism - a movement formed for the establishment and advancement of the Jewish national state, currently Israel

186

References and Suggested Reading

Biology and Evolution

Life the Science of Biology, Sadava, Heller, Orians, Purves, Hillis, Copyright 2008
Sinauer Associates, Inc., Published by Sinauer Associates
Cosmic Dawn, Chaisson, Eric, Copyright 1986 Eric Chaisson, Published by W.W. Norton
Company
In Search of the Double Helix: Quantum Physics and Life, Gribbin John, Copyright 1985
John and Mary Gribbin, Published by Bantam Books
Molecular Biology of the Gene Volumes 1 & 2, Watson, James D., Hopkins, Nancy H.,
Roberts, Jeffrey W., Steitz, Joan Argetsinger, Weiner, Alan M., Copyright 1987 The
Benjamin/Cummings Publishing Co., Inc., Published by the Benjamin/Cummings
Publishing Co., Inc.
Origins: A Skeptics Guide to the Creation of Life on Earth, Shapiro, Robert, Copyright
1986 Robert Shapiro, Published by Bantam Books, Inc.
Life at the Edge, Gould, James L., Carol Grant, Copyright 1989 W. H. Freeman & Co.
Published by W. H. Freeman
Lifecloud: The Origin of Life in the Universe, Fred Hoyle Copyright 1978, Harper &
Row, Published by Harper & Row
Science News Volume 116/No.1 July 7, "Evolution the Bottom Line", Julie Ann Miller
The Emergence of Life: Darwinian Evolution From the Inside, Fox, Sidney, Copyright
1988 Sidney Fox, Published by Basic Books
The Origin of Life: A Warm Little Pond, Folsome, Clair Edwin, Copyright 1979 W.H.
Freeman & Co., Published by W. H. Freeman & Co.
The Origin of Species, Darwin, Charles, Copyright 1962 Macmillian Publishing
Company, Published by Macmillan Publishing Co. Based on the sixth edition of 1872.

Cosmology

A Brief History of Time, Hawkings, Stephen, Copyright 1989 Stephen Hawking,
Published by Bantam Books
Cosmology + 1, A Scientific American Book, Copyright 1977 W. H. Freeman & Co.,
Published by W. H. Freeman & Company
Einstein's Universe, Calder Nigel, Copyright 1979, Viking Press, Published by Viking
Press

In Search of the Big Bang, Gribbin, John, Copyright 1986 John and Mary Gribbin, Published by Bantam Books

Space-Time in the Modern Universe, P.C.W Davies, Copyright 1977 Cambridge University Press, Published by Cambridge University Press

The Early Universe: Reprints, Kolb, Edward W., Turner, Michael S., Copyright 1988 Addison-Wesley Publishing Co., Published by Addison-Wesley Publishing Co.

The Large-Scale Structure of the Universe, P.J.E. Peebles, Copyright 1980 Princeton University Press, Published by Princeton University Press

The Restless Universe, Shipman Copyright 1978, Hughton Mifflin Co., Published by Hughton Mifflin Co.

Economics

Capitalism: A Treatise on Economics, Reisman, George, Copyright 1990 George Reisman, Published by Jameson Books

Human Action: A Treatise on Economics, Von Mises, Ludwig, Copyright 1996 Bettina Bien Greaves, Published by Fox & Wilkes

The Wealth of Nations, Smith, Adam, Published by Penguin Books

Capitalism: The Unknown Ideal, Rand, Ayn, Copyright 1966 Ayn Rand, Published By Signet Books

The Economist – www.economist.com

Exercise and Fitness

Tae Kwon Do The Korean Martial Art, Chun, Richard, Copyright 1976 Richard Chun, Published by Harper & Row

Taegeuk: The New Forms of Tae Kwon Do, Gwon, Pu Gill, Copyright 1984, Ohara Publications, Published by Ohara Publications, Inc.

Paleontology, Archeology and Earth Sciences

Elements of Physical Geology, Zumberge-Nelson, Copyright 1976 John Wiley & Sons, Published by John Wiley & Sons

The Cambridge Encyclopedia of Archeology, Copyright 1980 Trewin Copplestone Books, Ltd. Published by Crown Publishers Inc. and Cambridge University Press.

The Cambridge Encyclopedia of Earth Sciences, Copyright 1981 Trewin Copplestone Books, Ltd. Published by Crown Publishers Inc. and Cambridge University Press.

Philosophy Psychology and History

Atheism: The Case Against God, Smith, George H., Copyright 1979 George H. Smith, Published by Prometheus Books

Religions of the World Vol. 1 & 2, Hardon, John A., Copyright 1963 The Missionary Society of Saint Paul the Apostles State of New York, Published by Image Books Div., Doubleday & Co., Inc.

The Encyclopedia of Military History, Dupuy, R. Ernest and Dupuy, Trevor, N., Copyright 1977 Trevor N. Dupuy, Published by Harper & Row

The History of Western Philosophy, Russell, Bertrand, Copyright 1972 Edith Russell, Published by Simon & Schuster

Why I Am Not a Christian, Russell, Bertrand, Copyright 1957 George Allen & Unwin Ltd., Published by Touchstone Books

Anarchism: Old and New, Runkle, Gerald, Copyright 1972 Gerald Runkle, Published by Dell Publishing, Inc.

The Great Political Theories, Vol. 1 & 2, Curtis, Michael, Copyright 1961 by Avon Books, Published by Avon Books

A History of Knowledge, Van Doren, Charles, Copyright 1991 Charles Van Doren, Published by Ballantine Books

Wit and Wisdom from Poor Richard's Almanac, Franklin, Benjamin, Published by Dover Publications

Confucius: Confucian Analects, The Great Learning, and the Doctrine of the Mean, translated by James Legge, Published by Dover Publications

How to Win Friends and Influence People, Carnegie, Dale, Copyright 1936 Dale Carnegie, Published by Pocket Books

Common Sense, Paine, Thomas

The Virtue of Selfishness: A New Concept of Egoism, Rand, Ayn, Copyright 1964, Published by Penguin Putman Books

The Varieties of Religious Experience, James, William, Copyright 1997 by Simon & Schuster, Published by Simon & Schuster

The Pursuit of the Millennium, Cohn, Norman, Copyright 1961 Norman Cohn, Published by Oxford University Press

Flow: The Psychology of Optimal Experience, Csikszentmihalyi, Mihaly, Copyright 1990 Mihaly Csikszentmihalyi, Published by Harper Collins

Wikipedia – www.wikipedia.org

BBC - www.bbc.co.uk

Quantum and Subatomic Physics

In Search of Schrodingers Cat: Quantum Physics and Reality, Gribbin, John, Copyright 1984 John and Mary Gribbin, Published by Bantam Books

Quantum Reality, Herbert, Nick, Copyright 1985 Nick Herbert, Published by Anchor-Doubleday Books

Particle Physics in the Cosmos, Carrigan, Richard A. Jr., Trower, Peter W., Copyright 1989 W.H. Freeman & Company, Published by W. H. Freeman & Company

Subatomic Physics, Frauenfelder, Hans, Henley, Ernest M., Copyright 1974 Prentice-Hall, Inc., Published by Prentice-Hall, Inc.

Superforce: The Search for a Grand Unified Theory, Davies, Paul, Copyright 1984 Glenister Gavin, Ltd., Published by Simon & Schuster, Inc.

The Feynman Lectures on Physics Vol. 3, Feynman, Richard, Leighton, Robert A., Sands, Mathew, Copyright 1965 California Institute of Technology, Published by Addison-Wesley Publishing Co.

Mathematics

A History of Mathematics, Boyer, Carl B., Copyright 1968 John Wiley & Sons, Published by Princeton University Press

Mathematics Today: Twelve Informal Essays, Steen, Lynn Arthur Copyright 1978 Conference Board of Mathematical Sciences, and Published by Vintage Books, Inc.

The Mathematical Tourist: Snapshots of Modern Math, Peterson, Ivars, Copyright 1988 Ivars Peterson, Published by W. H. Freeman Co.

Mathematics and the Physical World, Kline, Morris, Copyright 1959 Morris Kline, Published by Dover Books

Journey Through Genius, Dunham, William, Copyright 1990 by John Wiley & Sons, Inc., Published by Penguin Books

The Mathematical Universe, Dunham, William, Copyright 1994 by John Wiley & Sons, Inc., Published by John Wiley & Sons

MacTutor History of Mathematics - University of St. Andrews Scotland (http://www-history.mcs.st-andrews.ac.uk/history/index.html)

Relativity and Astrophysics

Foundations of Space-Time Theories: Relativistic Physics and Philosophy of Science, Friedman, Michael, Copyright 1983 Princeton University Press, Published by Princeton University Press

Gravitation, Wheeler, John, Misner, Charles, Thorne, Kip S., Copyright 1973 W. H. Freeman & Co., Published by W. H. Freeman & Co.

Space Time & Matter, Weyl, Herman, Copyright 1952 Dover Publications, Published by Dover Publications

The Evolution of Scientific Thought: From Newton to Einstein, d' Abro, A., Copyright 1950 A. d' Abro, Published by Dover Publications

Theoretical Principles in Astrophysics and Relativity, Copyright 1978 University of Chicago Press, Published by University of Chicago Press

The Principle of Relativity, Einstein, Albert, Copyright 1952 Dover Publications, Published by Dover Publications

Until The Sun Dies, Jastrow, Robert, Copyright 1977 Robert Jastrow, Published by Warner Books

Index

A

C

F

N

O

W

X

Y

Z

About the author:

Ralph Wing is the author of seven books including books on business, geopolitics and religion. Mr. Wing has a B.S. Degree in Political Science with an emphasis on Soviet Studies. Mr. Wing has as his mission, to seek the truth based on the best available evidence not on the emotions, faith, and preconceived notions of others, and to rid the world of primitive thought and actions through the power of knowledge.

www.ingramcontent.com/pod-product-compliance
Lightning Source LLC
LaVergne TN
LVHW061222060426
835509LV00012B/1393